Who Watches the Watchmen?

The Conflict Between National Security and Freedom of the Press

Gary Ross

National Intelligence University
Washington, DC
July 2011

Those who surrender true liberty to a false security defend nothing worth preserving, while those who abandon real security to an illusory liberty protect nothing worth safeguarding.

\- **Ronald K. L. Collins**,
Author and Law Professor

Gary Ross' book, *Who Watches the Watchmen?*, argues that the tension between maintaining national security secrets and the public's right to know cannot be "solved," but can be better understood and more intelligently managed.

Watchmen is the inaugural book in a new series titled, *The NI Press Series on Denial and Deception*. The series will present original research by faculty and students in the university's Denial and Deception Certificate Program, as well as writings sponsored by the Office of the Director of National Intelligence Foreign Denial and Deception Committee.

In August 2011, the National Defense Intelligence College was re-named the National Intelligence University. To reflect this change, the NDIC Press was re-named the National Intelligence Press. The goal of the NI Press is the same: to publish high quality, valuable, and timely books on topics of concern to the Intelligence Community and the U.S. government. Books published by the NI Press undergo peer review by senior officials in the U.S. government as well as outside experts.

How to order this book. Everyone may download a free electronic copy of this book from our website at *http://www.NI-U.edu*. U.S. government employees may request a complimentary copy of this book by contacting us at: press@NI-U.edu. The general public may purchase a copy from the Government Printing Office (GPO) at *http://bookstore.gpo.gov*.

Editor, NI Press
Center for Strategic Intelligence Research
National Intelligence University
Defense Intelligence Agency
Bolling Air Force Base
Washington, D.C. 20340-5100

ISBN	978-1-932946-29-1
GPO Sales Stock Number	008-020-01606-3
Library of Congress Control Number	2011930973

TABLE OF CONTENTS

TABLE OF CONTENTS (CONTINUED)

TABLE OF CONTENTS (CONTINUED)

TABLE OF CONTENTS (CONTINUED)

TABLE OF CONTENTS (CONTINUED)

TABLE OF CONTENTS (CONTINUED)

TABLE OF CONTENTS (CONTINUED)

List of Figures

COMMENTARY

Who Watches the Watchmen? could hardly be more timely as we debate the recent leaking of the largest trove of documents in American history. The "WikiLeaks" case drives home the need for what this book lays out: an approach to protecting classified information that goes beyond law enforcement. Gary Ross' application of Rational Choice Theory codifies, organizes, and extends what many of us have been trying to do instinctively when dealing with unauthorized disclosures. In Ross' discussions of "motivations" and "justifications," I see powerful echoes of what I personally experienced as Director of NSA and CIA. I only wish I had had access to this fully developed intellectual framework and the courses of action it suggests while still in government.

General Michael V. Hayden (U.S. Air Force, Retired)
Former Director, Central Intelligence Agency
Former Director, National Security Agency

COMMENTARY

In August 2000 the Hermes Society, a fellowship of dedicated government professionals committed to improving the Intelligence Community's effectiveness in countering foreign denial and deception activities, met to discuss the need for a rigorous studies program on denial and deception. As a result of this meeting and others that followed, the Denial and Deception Advanced Studies Program (DDASP) was conceived. The early vision of the program articulated by R. Kent Tiernan, currently the Foreign Denial and Deception Committee (FDDC) Vice Chairman, included three components: formal instruction, a research paper, and a certification phase.

The DDASP began in November 2002 at the Joint Military Intelligence College (JMIC), now the National Intelligence University (NIU). Twelve students graduated from the program in 2003. To date, the DDASP has seen more than 300 students graduate. The program has been able to flourish thanks to ongoing sponsorship by the FDDC, under the Office of the Director of National Intelligence (ODNI), and NIU.

The goal of the DDASP is to enhance the U.S. Intelligence Community's ability to identify, counter, and exploit foreign denial and deception (D&D) activities generally, and to create a cadre of certified counter-D&D specialists spread across the Intelligence Community's sixteen elements. Gary Ross is one such cadre member and the author of *Who Watches the Watchmen? The Conflict between National Security and Freedom of the Press.*

The DDASP teaches students to take into consideration the sources of foreign knowledge of U.S. intelligence capabilities, such as espionage and unauthorized disclosures in the media. The more an adversary understands how the Intelligence Community (IC) collects secrets the more effective and motivated it will be to engage in denial and deception.

Over the last nine years, graduates of the DDASP have produced a veritable archive of master's theses on many facets related to D&D. The NIU and FDDC intend to share these papers with the IC. Ross' book on unauthorized disclosures is the first such publication to be offered as part of this new series of topics relating to the many dimensions of D&D. Future publications will include such titles as *Russian Strategic Political Deceptions* and *The Hidden Threat to National Security: Human Smuggling Networks*.

In addition to student theses, the DDASP faculty and FDDC staff, in conjunction with NIU, select and make available other outstanding publications to various audiences to raise the level of foreign deception awareness among analysts throughout the IC. To date, the FDDC has published ten research papers written by DDASP students as part of its Analysis Capabilities Enhancement Summary (ACES) series, which seeks to encourage diverse and independent analyses throughout the IC.

Intelligence requires secrets. So says James B. Bruce in his article, "Laws and Leaks of Classified Intelligence: The Consequences of Permissive Neglect." Ross' work and those to follow are intended to educate the IC about the sources of foreign knowledge and the resulting advantage afforded to our adversaries.

America's intelligence advantage is critically dependent upon our ability to secretly collect secrets. Unauthorized disclosures degrade our ability to do so and thereby jeopardize our intelligence advantage. Gary Ross' book is a must read for those concerned about the implications to U.S. national security.

William A. Parquette
Foreign Denial and Deception Committee
National Intelligence Council

COMMENTARY

In his concurring opinion in the "Pentagon Papers" case,[1] Justice Black—always a First Amendment absolutist—expressed skepticism that claims of national security should ever overcome the First Amendment, especially the freedom of the press guaranteed therein. As he wrote:

> The guarding of military and diplomatic secrets at the expense of informed representative government provides no real security for our Republic. The Framers of the First Amendment, fully aware of both the need to defend a new nation and the abuses of the English and Colonial Governments, sought to give this new society strength and security by providing that freedom of speech, press, religion, and assembly should not be abridged.[2]

Yet, for every Justice Black, there is a Justice Jackson, who observed 22 years earlier in another First Amendment case that "the choice is not between order and liberty. It is between liberty with order and anarchy without either." Thus, Jackson warned, "if the Court does not temper its doctrinaire logic with a little practical wisdom, it will convert the constitutional Bill of Rights into a suicide pact."[3]

There is much to commend both viewpoints; popular government necessarily presupposes the ability of the people meaningfully to assess the full measure of their elected representatives' conduct, ability that in turn depends largely upon a free and independent press. And yet, one hardly needs to strain to understand how the publication of certain national defense information could gravely jeopardize the security of the United States—and the freedoms that make the nation worth securing in the first place. To be sure, I am not one of those who believe that balancing liberty and security is a zero-sum game, but it is well past time to concede that there is such a thing as information that the government should be able to protect from public disclosure, even by members of the news media acting with the purest of motives. And once we agree on that point, the question becomes how we sort out that information—and who does the sorting.[4]

The problem, as Gary Ross documents in Chapter 1 of this careful and thorough monograph, is that legislative attempts to broker some middle ground between these two principled guideposts have proven woefully ineffective—in both directions. The federal espionage statutes are antiquated in ways that undermine their practical utility and perhaps even their constitutionality.[5] And federal whistleblower laws, which might otherwise be the place to distinguish between the right and wrong kinds of disclosures, are instead a hodgepodge of confusing—and at times conflicting—mandates to government employees.[6] Thus, the law as it stands today serves neither the government's nor the media's best interests.

One possible response is to put the proverbial ball back in Congress' court, and to encourage the legislature to approach the various federal laws concerning unauthorized disclosures of national security information from a comprehensive perspective, tying together classification schemes with criminal laws for disclosing validly classified information, creating defenses to prosecution in cases where the disclosure can be justified either on the ground that the information was wrongfully classified or that the value of public disclosure outweighed the threat to national security, and so on. Thus, a number of prominent scholars from across the spectrum have felled forests in the past several decades attempting to suggest how such comprehensive legislative reform could—and should—be pursued.[7]

Ross is a realist, however, and his analysis should convince even the skeptical reader that meaningful and sufficiently thorough legislative reform is highly improbable. Moreover, even the most careful, sweeping, and systematic new legislation will not solve the problem at the heart of Ross' manuscript: how we account for the quite unrelated reasons why individual journalists might choose to disclose protected information, and how we assess the varying costs of disclosure across these different cases. Put another way, Ross' work demonstrates quite forcefully that there are two independent variables in these cases—the journalist's motives (which Ross exhaustively discusses in Chapter 2) and the government's harm (the subject of Chapter 3). Legislative reforms, no matter how clever, could hardly make one dependent upon the other, as Ross demonstrates in his walk-through of a not-so-hypothetical journalist's decision-making process in Chapter 4.

The solution Ross proposes is both intriguing and somewhat unorthodox. Although there has been an increasing amount of scholarship in recent years on the possibilities for self-control within the executive branch as an alternative to external oversight,[8] what Ross suggests in Chapter 5—what he calls "the proactive application of rational choice theory"—may in fact satisfy the two constituencies that count here by encouraging them, simply enough, to communicate with each other. Of course, none of this will stop a journalist who, for whatever reason, is dead-set on disclosing the protected information. If the goal is to *reduce* unauthorized disclosures, however, rather than eliminate them altogether, then it is hard to see any downside to the steps for which Ross so convincingly advocates. Indeed, on this topic in particular, it is no indictment of a proposal that it must necessarily be incomplete.

Nevertheless, I would be remiss if I did not mention the one other non-punitive way to convince journalists not to disseminate protected information: restore their confidence that only properly classified information is being protected. We live in an age of "unlawful secrets"—information that is either wrongly classified, or classified information about unlawful governmental programs. As a result, for all the good that it will do to assess the cost-benefit analysis of unauthorized disclosures from the perspective of the journalist as well as the government, it can only help if the well-documented upsurge in over-classification were also addressed from within. The *New York Times* and *Washington Post* waited over a year before publishing details on the government's warrantless wiretapping program.[9] Imagine how much longer they might have held off if that program was the only legally controversial Bush administration counterterrorism initiative that had been kept from the public. Indeed, I doubt I am exaggerating in suggesting that the government's credibility—or lack thereof—had as much to do with the upsurge in unauthorized disclosures in the latter years of the Bush administration as the collective media itself.

In the end, then, faith on the part of the media that protected information is being kept secret for the right reasons may be as powerful a weapon against unauthorized disclosures as even the most systematic application of cost-benefit analysis.

Stephen I. Vladeck
Professor of Law
Washington School of Law
American University

COMMENTARY

The unauthorized disclosure of classified information—leaks in plain parlance—is emerging as one of the more important security challenges of the post-9/11 era. Although the phenomenon of leaking, as Gary Ross reminds us in this comprehensive study, has been with us throughout our history, in the midst of the Global War on Terrorism it has become particularly acute.

Careless handling of information was to cost both the Confederacy and the Union untold lives during the Civil War. During World War I the dangers posed by leaks were one factor that prompted Congress to enact the Espionage Act of 1917, which stands today as our fundamental law governing secrets. On the eve of and during World War II, leaks were dearly paid for in treasure and blood. In the Cold War we responded to the experience of World War II—and to the new existential danger posed by nuclear weapons—by initiating unprecedentedly tight controls on information. It was only as the Cold War waned that we began to unwind from that crisis-driven approach and embrace maximum transparency, at least in our rhetoric if not always in reality. Then came September 11, 2001, and the default position of openness had to be flipped once again to its reverse. Yet, counter to what one might have expected, it is this era, when the imperative of secrecy is particularly important for success in the War on Terror, that leaking has intensified.

The problem of secrecy is double-edged and places key institutions and values of our democracy into collision. On the one hand, our country operates under a broad consensus that secrecy is antithetical to democratic rule and can encourage a variety of political deformations. The potential for excessive concealment has grown more acute as the American national security apparatus expanded massively in the decades since World War II, bringing with it a commensurately large extension of secrecy. With huge volumes of information pertaining to national defense walled off from the public, secrecy almost inevitably has become haphazard. Secrecy can facilitate renegade governmental activity, as we saw in the Watergate and the Iran-Contra affairs. It can also be a breeding ground for corruption.

Nevertheless, the obvious pitfalls are not the end of the story. A long list of abuses notwithstanding, secrecy, like openness, remains an essential prerequisite of self-governance. To be effective, even many of the most mundane aspects of democratic rule, from the development of policy alternatives to the selection of personnel, must often take place behind closed doors. To proceed always under the glare of the public would cripple deliberation and render government impotent. And when one turns to the most fundamental business of democratic governance, namely, self-preservation—carried out through the conduct of foreign policy and the waging of war—the imperative of secrecy becomes critical, often a matter of survival.

Even in times of peace, the formulation of foreign and defense policies is necessarily conducted in secret. However, this is not a time of peace; ever since September 11, 2001, the country has been at war. And we are not only at war; we are engaged in a particular kind of war—an intelligence war against a shadowy and determined adversary. The effectiveness of the tools of intelligence—from the recruitment of agents to the operation of satellite reconnaissance systems—remains overwhelmingly dependent on their clandestine nature. It is not an overstatement to say that secrecy today, as we engage in a struggle without a discernible end point, is one of the most critical tools of national defense.

Leaks of secret information to the press thus present a direct and serious challenge to our conduct of national security in an age of global terrorism. Here it is necessary to draw a crucial distinction. As any American government official or journalist will readily attest, leaking is part and parcel of our system of rule. Not a day goes by in Washington without government officials sharing inside information with journalists and lobbyists in off-the-record briefings and in private discussions over lunch. Some of the material changing hands in this fashion winds up getting published. A study by the Senate Select Committee on Intelligence counted 147 separate disclosures of classified information that made their way into the nation's eight leading newspapers in a 6-month period alone. As these startlingly high numbers indicate, leaks to the press are a well-established informal practice. They enable policymakers to carry out any one of a number of objectives: to get out a message to domestic and foreign audiences, to gauge public reaction in advance of some contemplated policy initiative, to curry favor with journalists, and to wage inter- or intra-bureaucratic warfare. For better or for worse, leaking has become part of the normal functioning of the U.S. government.

Yet, there are leaks of an entirely different and far more serious character: those which telegraph to our adversaries our methods and capabilities and compromise our ability to protect ourselves. Ironically, the years after September 11, 2001, when the imperative of national security secrecy has been particularly acute, have also been the years in which this kind of reckless leaking has proliferated. Among other things, major American newspapers have dropped into the public domain the means by which our intelligence agencies eavesdrop on al Qaeda terrorists and the methods by which we track the movements of their funds.

One of the virtues of Ross' study of leaking is the taxonomy it offers of both the causes and the effects of leaking. Having assembled a large catalog of leaks from the second half of the 20th century and the first decade of the 21st, he shows the great variety of motives that propel journalists to publish classified information. These range from, at one end of the spectrum, the promotion of informed public debate to, at the other end, advancing corporate interests in the competitive struggles of contemporary journalism. Ross also offers a taxonomy of the harm caused by leaks. Here, too, there is a wide range of outcomes. At one end of the spectrum there is the potential for loss of life and damage to sensitive intelligence sources and methods. At the other end of the spectrum, there are the modest—but still serious—consequences like a breakdown in intelligence sharing with allied powers.

Striking the right balance between security and liberty is a perpetual challenge in a democracy. With the two imperatives in constant tension, inquiry into the costs and consequences of disclosure of secrets is an essential task. Ross' study is a welcome and timely addition to the small body of literature examining this important subject.

Gabriel Schoenfeld
Senior Fellow
Hudson Institute
Author of *Necessary Secrets: National Security, the Media, and the Rule of Law* (W.W. Norton, May 2010)

COMMENTARY

There is probably no issue more vexing, more troublesome, and more irritating to intelligence agencies around the world than the legal and moral question of America's news media publishing and broadcasting classified information about intelligence matters. While U.S. news organizations are basically protected by the Constitution's provision for freedom of the press, and by the reluctance of the government to prosecute under a number of laws, their foreign counterparts have no such seeming immunity. Even in the United Kingdom, a nation whose concept of jurisprudence most closely parallels America's, the media are well aware that the Official Secrets Act is not to be ignored. Over the years, there have been times when foreign intelligence agencies have hesitated to share fully with their American counterparts for fear of leaks to the U.S. media.

Gary Ross has produced a scholarly work that looks fairly and comprehensively at the major aspects of this issue. While he proposes no legislative solution for this clash of principles, he offers some positive recommendations at the end that, to me, hold promise.

Ross describes an innovative but short-lived program at the National Security Agency to reach out to journalists writing about its activities. "SIGINT 101" explains what the NSA does and how it does it. The agency looked at published and broadcast stories, noted the harmful effects, and discussed how the stories could have been edited to remove the harm while retaining their purpose. However, NSA's program, which started in 2002, was discontinued two years later, apparently because of staffing changes in the agency's press office. Yet, this proactive effort had to have been effective in reducing the incidents of classified information being made public.

Ross also describes a parallel effort, initiated by a former CIA general counsel and former *Washington Post* reporter, to bring together major news organizations, intelligence agencies, and the Defense Department to engage in an ongoing dialogue. Representatives met at a private Washington club. One media participant credited the sessions with dissuading the Bush administration from proposing broader anti-leak legislation.

American journalists do not have the intent to harm the United States. They intend to tell a compelling story of something the government is doing in the public's name that may or may not be legal, that may not have received approval from legislative bodies tasked with authorizing certain actions, and that may run counter to government policies.

Furthermore, journalists do not obtain classified information by breaking and entering. Journalists obtain secrets because the classified information is given to them. A reporter's tradecraft, minus black bag jobs, wiretapping, and other techniques, is quite similar to an intelligence agent's: cultivating sources and asking informed questions.

A journalist who participated in SIGINT 101 would be more sensitive to the issue of harm and likely would take the extra steps needed to reduce harm. In my 40 years of journalistic experience—nearly 30 of them in Washington—I never met, nor heard of, a reporter who turned his back on a government agency willing to work with a news organization that had obtained classified information. For example, the *Washington Post*, no stranger to conflicts with the government over publishing secrets, deleted the identification of specific countries in its revelation that the CIA maintained secret detention facilities in Eastern Europe where suspected terrorists could be interrogated and held. The *Post* had responded to a government request in an attempt to limit what the administration viewed as damaging information—beyond the fact that the facilities' existence would be made public.

The government's challenge is to figure out how to reduce leaks. A number of government employees have lost their jobs for unauthorized disclosures and that punishment remains available to the government. It will not stop leaks, however. Ross quotes former Director of Central Intelligence Robert Gates: "The answer, if there is one, is the slower, more mundane and frustrating process of again instilling discipline through education and developing broad support."

Beyond losing their job, I can only assume that the prospect of criminal prosecution, however slight, may also deter some potential leakers. The fact that an FBI linguist was sentenced to 20 months in prison in May 2010 for charges related to leaks to a blogger should be sobering for others thinking of leaking. A former NSA official has also been indicted for activities associated with leaking secrets to a newspaper reporter. It is not known how the leaker was unmasked. However, a recently released FBI file shows that the agency used a wide variety of investigative tools, including polygraphs, to try to find a leaker in the mid-1980s. Reporters involved with published leaks have been subjected to wiretaps and other investigative methods over the years. The government is not completely incapable of identifying leakers, but prosecution is usually a political decision.

In the end, it is the media, in all their forms, that should be the focus of government agencies. Every intelligence and defense agency should have a "SIGINT 101" program. Journalists, by their nature, are interested in learning more; they would not resist hearing an agency's point of view and engaging in dialogue with the government. It is the vacuum of silence that the government should fill with proactive measures, as suggested by Ross.

One aspect of this dilemma that Ross might have addressed in greater detail is the historical development of media suspicion of government actions and support for leakers. It was not always thus. In World War II, reporters accompanying combat units wore uniforms and willingly subjected their stories to censors. Government employees heard constantly that "loose lips sink ships." There was a tendency to keep most secrets, even on the home front.

Nevertheless, that all changed for the media, in my view, during the Vietnam War. Reporters on the ground and in Washington came to realize that they were being lied to about the war, and very quickly trust was lost. The media were blamed by many in the government for "losing the war" by eroding public support. Publication of the leaked classified "Pentagon Papers" by the *New York Times* and the *Washington Post* revealed the government's willful deception of the American people about the war. It has been downhill ever since, and most of today's journalists have lived and worked in no other environment.

President George W. Bush's administration further fanned the media's mistrust of government information by falsely asserting, in an effort to build public support for invading Iraq after the attacks of 9/11, that Iraq was behind the attacks, that Iraq was developing weapons of mass destruction, and that Iraq's oil revenue would pay for the war. Yet, in the 2003 invasion of Iraq, reporters were embedded with combat units and kept operational secrets. Even though their communication with their home offices was not censored—satellite telephones assured that—there were no harmful leaks of classified information. (Note: TV correspondent Geraldo Rivera was removed from the battlefield for drawing the next day's plan of attack in the sand for his viewers, but I have never heard that the attack was compromised.) Embedded reporters responded to what SIGINT 101 sought to accomplish: reporters can keep secrets if they understand the big picture.

In addition to the major print and broadcast media, however, the government now must deal with blogs, electronic publications, and other channels for putting information "out there." For the last three years, an Internet site called WikiLeaks has invited anonymous individuals to share classified documents with the world. These posters are not likely candidates for SIGINT 101. Their contributions to WikiLeaks are made without any prior consultation with affected agencies, nothing like pre-publication meetings of, say, high-ranking CIA officials and a newspaper's editors.

Finally, I would like to take issue with one observation that Ross makes early in his book—that reporters who write major stories based on leaked classified information may be motivated by the possibility of winning the prestigious Pulitzer Prize, which is given annually for the best American news stories. Despite the deep satisfaction that comes with winning this career-enhancing prize, that is not the motivation behind an investigation that begins a year or two earlier. My former employer, the Copley News Service, in conjunction with the *San Diego Union-Tribune,* won a Pulitzer Prize in 2006 for stories that resulted in a corrupt Congressman going to prison. I know that exposing the politician as a crook, not winning the Pulitzer Prize, was the motivation. In short, it was what good journalism should be. The prize is just the cherry on top.

All in all, Gary Ross has pulled together in this splendid book all the raw material needed to spark a fresh discussion between the government and the media on how to function under our unique system of government in this ever-evolving information-rich environment.

Benjamin Shore
Retired Journalist and Editor
Washington Bureau
Copley News Service

FOREWORD

The "Democratic Dilemma"

From George Washington and the War for Independence to George Bush and the War on Terror, the conflict between the principle of maintaining a free press and the necessity for secrecy (the protection of intelligence sources and methods from unauthorized disclosure) has defied resolution. Retired CIA senior executive James Bruce, former Vice Chairman of the U.S. Intelligence Community's Foreign Denial and Deception Committee and Deputy National Intelligence Officer for Science and Technology, characterized this fundamental conflict as a *"democratic dilemma"*

> …that characterizes the relationship between secrecy and democracy. Unquestionably, democracies require openness to establish and sustain accountability. Anyone seriously interested in government accountability understands the democratic risks inherent in secrecy. Yet the greater openness that can facilitate U.S. democracy also serves its foreign adversaries.[10]

Attempts to reconcile this conflict between a journalist's motivations for publishing classified information and the perceived harm resulting from the loss of intelligence sources and methods is one of the primary themes explored in Gary Ross' book, *Who Watches the Watchmen? The Conflict between National Security and Freedom of the Press.*

Throughout *Who Watches the Watchmen?* Ross explores the history of this conflict. He explains that the topic of unauthorized disclosures has been a frequent subject for research in the government, academic, and legal communities. The issue has also been debated at Congressional hearings before the Senate Select Committee on Intelligence, the House Permanent Select Committee on Intelligence, the Senate Judiciary Committee and the Senate Armed Services Committee.

Beyond the government's recognition of a necessity to protect information in the interest of national security, the responsibility to maintain an enlightened citizenry in a democracy is documented and acknowledged in Ross' publication. The foundation for maintaining these democratic principles is found in the U.S. Bill of Rights, which contains the first ten amendments to the U.S. Constitution. Though not as prominent in the public consciousness as the Preamble to the U.S. Constitution, the Preamble to the Bill of Rights similarly captures the sentiments and aspirations of the Founding Fathers. The Preamble declares that the Bill of Rights was established "in order to prevent misconstruction or abuse of its [U.S. Constitution] powers . . . And as extending the ground of public confidence in the Government."

In Chapter One of *Who Watches the Watchmen?* Ross conducts an in-depth exploration of the history of the conflict between the principle of a free press and the necessity to protect intelligence sources and methods. Past government efforts to respond to the issue, primarily involving a legislative solution, are also examined. A potential framework for understanding a journalist's thought process when electing to publish classified information, Rational Choice Theory, is also presented. Chapter Two examines the motivations and justifications for members of the media to obtain and publish classified information. Historical examples are used to assist in identifying and analyzing individual motivations and justifications. Motivations for government employees to disclose classified information are also presented and analyzed, based on a book written by a former dean of the Columbia School of Journalism. Chapter Three identifies precise categories of harm attributed to unauthorized disclosures. Historic events are again used to differentiate and explore each category of harm.

Based on detailed information contained in Bob Woodward's 1987 book *Veil: The Secret Wars of the CIA, 1981-1987,* Chapter Four examines the process whereby members of the media rationally deliberated the publication of an actual unauthorized disclosure. This case study offers unique and valuable insights into a journalist's thought processes. Conclusions regarding Rational Choice Theory and its application to the democratic dilemma of unauthorized disclosures are presented in Chapter Five. Ross' book concludes by examining the legal foundations underlying the conflict, including the U.S. Constitution and the Bill of Rights, enacted and proposed legislation, Executive Orders, and case law.

Who Watches the Watchmen? The Conflict between National Security and Freedom of the Press offers an excellent examination of the ongoing conflict between a free press and the need to protect intelligence sources and methods. Its publication will promote an improved understanding of the "democratic dilemma" both for members of the U.S. Intelligence Community and for the public.

Warren E. Snyder, Ph.D.
Denial and Deception Advanced Studies Program
National Intelligence University

ACKNOWLEDGMENTS

My first Special-Agent-in-Charge once compared a successfully resolved criminal investigation to a wonderfully cooked jambalaya. In many ways, this book reminds me of that occasionally frustrating, yet ultimately rewarding, case. Though I may be the one serving the final dish, the flavor is a result of the ingredients brought together by the many individuals who assisted me throughout this process.

My sincere thanks to the members of the National Intelligence Council, Foreign Denial and Deception Committee, and the staff at the National Intelligence University for recognizing the significance of the issue and providing a forum to engage in this dialogue. Special thanks to William Parquette, Warren Snyder, George Mitroka, Cathryn Thurston, and William Spracher for their guidance and advocacy. I would also like to recognize journalists Siobhan Gorman of the *Wall Street Journal*, Pamela Hess of the Associated Press and Ben Shore, formerly of Copley News Service, for their willingness to lecture at the University, providing a voice to the media's viewpoint.

To Naval Criminal Investigative Service managers Steven Corbett and Barry Marushi, and to Office of the Director of National Intelligence managers Glenn Stampler and Raymond Wiggins: Thank you for supporting my efforts to complete both the Strategic Intelligence Master's Program and the research for this book. Barry, I'm grateful to you for giving me the opportunity to begin this process. Our time together was too short.

There are several friends and colleagues to whom I'm also indebted. To colleagues Dan Altman and Greg Lynch: Everyone should be fortunate enough to work with individuals "of your ilk" during their career. I think it's time to fire up the hookah. My gratitude to "devil's advocates" William Marotti and Kelly Logan for our many online discussions: They allowed me to hear what it was I was trying to say and shined the light of perspective (actually, the glow of my computer monitor) on my premise.

Above all, this book is dedicated to my lovely wife Tammy and our beautiful daughters Emma, Audrey, and Sophie. This book would never have been possible without their love and support (and patience).

And finally to the readers, for allowing me to offer up this bowl of jambalaya. My hope is that it will inspire additional dialogue among the government, the media, and the public.

Gershon (Gary) Ross
May 2011

AUTHOR'S PREFACE

*The only way we can know whether information is legitimately kept
secret is when it is revealed.*[11]

- WikiLeaks founder Julian Assange

On October 22, 2010, the Internet-based organization WikiLeaks released
what is being referred to as the largest unauthorized disclosure of classified
information in U.S. history. Over the vigorous objections of the U.S.
Department of Defense, WikiLeaks disclosed over 390,000 classified
reports concerning U.S. military operations in Iraq. Prior to posting the
documents on its website, WikiLeaks provided the material to several
media outlets, including the *New York Times*, the British newspaper *The
Guardian*, the German magazine *Der Spiegel,* and the Qatar-based news
organization *Al Jazeera*. These outlets each published independent articles
based on their analysis of the reports.

This was not the first time WikiLeaks defied the U.S. government by
disclosing classified information. In April 2010, WikiLeaks posted a video
on its website documenting an airstrike by two U.S. Apache helicopters in
Baghdad, Iraq. Three months later, WikiLeaks disclosed 77,000 additional
classified reports detailing U.S. military operations in Afghanistan.
In November 2010, WikiLeaks began releasing classified U.S. State
Department cables from a reported cache of more than 250,000 documents
it had obtained. Similar to the military reports, WikiLeaks provided media
outlets in England, Germany, Spain, and France with advance access to the
diplomatic cables.[12] In April 2011, WikiLeaks and multiple media outlets
also published information derived from over 700 classified "Detainee
Assessment Briefs" for individuals held at the U.S. military prison in
Guantanamo Bay, Cuba.[13]

Attempting to put the scope of the disclosures in context, the German
magazine *Der Spiegel* wrote:[14]

Never before in history has a superpower lost control of such vast amounts of such sensitive information – data that can help paint a picture of the foundation upon which US foreign policy is built. Never before has the trust America's partners have in the country been as badly shaken.

WikiLeaks' founder Julian Assange offered the following explanation for his decision to disclose the military reports involving U.S. operations in Afghanistan:[15]

These files are the most comprehensive description of a war to be published during the course of a war – in other words, at a time when they still have a chance of doing some good. They cover the small and the large. A single body of information, they eclipse all that has been previously said about Afghanistan. They will change our perspective on not only the war in Afghanistan, but on all modern wars.

This material shines light on the everyday brutality and squalor of war. The archive will change public opinion and it will change the opinion of people in positions of political and diplomatic influence. There is a mood to end the war in Afghanistan. This information won't do it alone, but it will shift political will in a significant manner.

During a subsequent interview, Assange discussed his rationale for releasing the classified diplomatic cables:[16]

If there are people in the State Department who say that there is some abuse going on, and there's not a proper mechanism for internal accountability and external accountability, they must have a conduit to get that out to the public; and we are that conduit.

When questioned whether he recognized the legitimacy of any state secrets, Assange responded:[17]

There is a legitimate role for secrecy, and there is a legitimate role for openness. Unfortunately, those who commit abuses against humanity or against the law find abusing legitimate secrecy to conceal their abuse all too easy. People of good conscience have always revealed abuses by ignoring abusive strictures. It is not WikiLeaks that decides to reveal something. It is a whistleblower or a dissident who decides to reveal it. Our job is to make sure that these individuals are protected, the public is informed and the historical record is not denied.

The *New York Times* reported that the compromised military reports offered no "earthshaking revelations," but did offer additional context and insight into what was already known by the American public.[18] For the Iraq-related documents, these insights reportedly included the deaths of Iraqi civilians during military operations, Iranian military support to Iraqi insurgents, and the reliance on public contractors to augment U.S. forces. The Afghan-related documents are reported to document expanded CIA paramilitary operations in the region, a relationship between Afghan insurgents and Pakistan's intelligence service, and CIA support to Afghanistan's intelligence agency. The Guantanamo Bay Detainee Assessment Briefs reportedly identify concerns that detainees were either being wrongfully held though they were not a threat, or wrongly released though they actually were.[19]

On the same day the *Times* published its first article containing information derived from the compromised State Department cables, it also published a "Note to Readers." The note explains the *Times'* motivation for disclosing classified information, as well as the deliberative process that preceded publication. The note read, in part:[20]

> The *Times* believes that the documents (United States embassy cables) serve an important public interest, illuminating the goals, successes, compromises and frustrations of American diplomacy in a way that other accounts cannot match.

> The *Times* has taken care to exclude, in its articles and in supplementary material, in print and online, information that would endanger confidential informants or compromise national security. The *Times*'s redactions were shared with other news organizations and communicated to WikiLeaks, in the hope that they would similarly edit the documents they planned to post online.

After its own redactions, the *Times* sent Obama administration officials the cables it planned to post and invited them to challenge publication of any information that, in the official view, would harm the national interest. After reviewing the cables, the officials – while making clear they condemn the publication of secret material – suggested additional redactions. The *Times* agreed to some, but not all.

The question of dealing with classified information is rarely easy, and never to be taken lightly. Editors try to balance the value of the material to public understanding against potential dangers to the national interest.

Of course, most of these documents will be made public regardless of what the *Times* decides. WikiLeaks has shared the entire archive of secret cables with at least four European publications, has promised country-specific documents to many other news outlets, and has said it plans to ultimately post its trove online. For the *Times* to ignore this material would be to deny its own readers the careful reporting and thoughtful analysis they expect when this kind of information becomes public.

The U.S. government strongly condemned the disclosures and related media reporting. Administration officials, including President Obama, characterized the compromise as potentially harmful to U.S. and coalition personnel and operations. In response to the disclosures involving military operations in Iraq, the Department of Defense issued the following statement:[21]

We deplore WikiLeaks for inducing individuals to break the law, leak classified documents and then cavalierly share that secret information with the world, including our enemies. We know terrorist organizations have been mining the leaked Afghan documents for information to use against us, and this Iraq leak is more than four times as large. By disclosing such sensitive information, WikiLeaks continues to put at risk the lives of our troops, their coalition partners and those Iraqis and Afghans working with us. The only responsible course of action for WikiLeaks at this point is to return the stolen material and expunge it from their Web sites as soon as possible.

We strongly condemn the unauthorized disclosure of classified information and will not comment on these leaked documents other than to note that "significant activities" reports are initial, raw observations by tactical units. They are essentially snapshots of events, both tragic and mundane, and do not tell the whole story. That said, the period covered by these reports has been well chronicled in news stories, books and films, and the release of these field reports does not bring new understanding to Iraq's past.

However, it does expose secret information that could make our troops even more vulnerable to attack in the future. Just as with the leaked Afghan documents, we know our enemies will mine this information, looking for insights into how we operate, cultivate sources and react in combat situations, even the capability of our equipment. This security breach could very well get our troops and those they are fighting with killed.

U.S. public opinion appears divided over the actions taken by both WikiLeaks and the media. In a survey conducted by the Pew Research Center, 47 percent of respondents believed the public interest was harmed by the disclosure of Afghan-related military reports.[22] Forty-two percent felt the disclosures served the public interest. The difference in public opinion over the compromise of U.S. State Department cables was more pronounced. Sixty percent of survey participants identified this disclosure as harmful while 31 percent believed the disclosures served the public interest. When questioned regarding the media's handling of the disclosures, 38 percent responded that news organizations had gone too far in reporting classified material. An almost identical 39 percent indicated that news organizations had struck a proper balance. Fourteen percent felt that the media had withheld too much classified material.

Beyond the U.S. government and public, allied governments also voiced their concern over the disclosures. U.K. Defence Secretary Liam Fox issued a statement which read, "We condemn any un-authorised release of classified material. This can put the lives of UK service personnel and those of our allies at risk and make the job of Armed Forces in all theatres of operation more difficult and more dangerous."[23] Afghan President Hamid Karzai described the WikiLeaks disclosures as "shocking and extremely irresponsible," adding that it placed the lives of Afghan informants working with allied forces at risk.[24]

Pakistani officials indicated that the allegations of cooperation between Pakistan's intelligence service and Afghan insurgents could harm relations with the United States.[25] The officials also questioned whether the United States could be trusted with sensitive information in the future. A senior official from Pakistan's intelligence service suggested that the agency might need to reexamine its cooperation with the United States if the CIA did not denounce the allegations.

Mexican President Felipe Calderon described the harm to U.S. relations from the disclosure of diplomatic cables as "severe."[26] Calderon also personally called for the removal of the U.S. ambassador to Mexico. The ambassador, who had been critical of the Calderon administration in several of the compromised cables, ultimately resigned his position and returned to the United States.[27]

U.S. adversaries have also commented on the disclosures. In a video released by Al Qaeda cleric and spokesperson Anwar Al-Awlaki, Assange's actions were praised and the U.S. response sharply criticized:

> [T]he war against the publication of truth [goes on], and, what is more, the U.S. is fighting to shut down websites like WikiLeaks, just because it reported facts about the American war in Iraq and about the conversations of American diplomats with their agents worldwide.

> The U.S. [accuses] anyone who censures its corruption of being a terrorist, and dumps a sack full of [other] readymade accusations over him in order to designate him as one of its Muslim and other opponents. [The U.S.] has leveled a similar accusation at the owner of WikiLeaks, in order to keep [his site] busy and neutralize its work in disseminating the domestic secrets of the musty American [White] House.[28]

Taliban spokesman Zabihullah Mujahid confirmed that the Taliban was reviewing the documents disclosed by WikiLeaks.[29] He explained, "We will investigate through our own secret service whether the people mentioned are really spies working for the U.S. If they are U.S. spies, then we know how to punish them." Mujahid added that the Taliban had become aware of the disclosures through media reporting.

Though Assange asserts that WikiLeaks followed a "harm minimization" process, it was widely reported that non-redacted documents disclosed by WikiLeaks identified hundreds of foreign nationals cooperating with U.S. forces. Representatives from five human rights organizations—Amnesty International, Campaign for Innocent Victims in Conflict (CIVIC), Open Society Institute (OSI), Afghanistan Independent Human Rights Commission, and the Kabul office of International Crisis Group (ICG)— contacted WikiLeaks to voice their concerns.[30] The representatives urged WikiLeaks to remove or redact the documents containing identifying information.

During an August 2010 interview, Assange discussed WikiLeaks' disclosure of the identities of individuals cooperating with U.S. forces:[31]

> We're faced with no easy choices. We are faced with economic constraints. We are faced with the reality that publication often brings justice and justice delayed is justice denied. We can't sit on material like this for 3 years, with one person to go through the whole lot line by line to redact. We have to take the best road that we can, and in this case that was listening to what the other press organizations were saying about the material.

> Now, it is regrettable that some number, and although the number is being inflated by some organizations, that some number of innocent people is named in that and they face some threat as a result. But that is the constraints that we are under. For other material that we are dealing with, we are now faced with this terrible conundrum. Do we go through it line by line? It will cost us approximately seven-hundred and fifty thousand dollars to do that, and there will be a delay in doing that.

> Where will the money come from? Because all those people who are so ready to pass blame and pretend that they are concerned about

the lives of Afghan civilians are not actually willing to step up to the plate to actually put the bat in to history. What do we do about that? It's not fair. It's a difficult thing. There are no easy choices for this organization.

Assange is reported to have given a different response during a private meeting with several journalists. In the book *WikiLeaks: Julian Assange's War on Secrecy,* a journalist from *The Guardian* documents a conversation with Assange concerning the identification of foreign nationals in the compromised documents. During the discussion, Assange reportedly remarked: "Well, they're informants. So, if they get killed, they've got it coming to them. They deserve it."[32] Assange has denied making this statement, adding that he intends to sue *The Guardian* for libel.[33]

In October 2010 a Pentagon spokesman commented on efforts to protect Iraqis identified in the compromised military reports:[34]

> There are 300 names of Iraqis in here that we think would be particularly endangered by their exposure. We have passed that information on to U.S. Forces Iraq. They are in the process right now of contacting those Iraqis to try to safeguard them.

The State Department also initiated a process to warn hundreds of human rights activists, foreign government officials, and businesspeople of the potential threat resulting from the disclosure of their identities. A "handful" of these individuals was reportedly relocated to safer locations, either within their home countries or abroad.[35] It was also reported that Afghan and Pakistani citizens had become more reluctant to speak with human rights investigators and that contact between human rights activists and diplomats had been negatively impacted.

In addition to the resignation of the U.S. ambassador to Mexico, the ambassador to Ecuador was also expelled from the country and the U.S. ambassador to Libya recalled to the United States.[36] The Ecuadorian government expelled the U.S. ambassador in response to a compromised cable reporting high-level corruption in the police force and possible knowledge by Ecuador's President.

Secretary of State Hillary Clinton denounced WikiLeaks' disclosure of the classified diplomatic cables.[37] Clinton stated that the compromise undermined efforts to work with other countries and tore "at the fabric of the proper function of responsible government." She added that individuals who dedicated their lives to protecting others faced serious repercussions, including imprisonment, torture, and death. Clinton was confident, though, that U.S. relationships with foreign governments would endure despite the more immediate harm.

Secretary of Defense Robert Gates also offered his perspective on the impact of the compromised State Department cables:[38]

> Now, I've heard the impact of these releases on our foreign policy described as a meltdown, as a game-changer, and so on. I think those descriptions are fairly significantly overwrought. The fact is, governments deal with the United States because it's in their interest, not because they like us, not because they trust us, and not because they believe we can keep secrets.

During a subsequent briefing before Congress, State Department officials reportedly assessed the disclosure of diplomatic cables to be "embarrassing" but "containable."[39] It was reported that one of the Congressional officials briefed believed the administration felt compelled to depict the harm as serious in order to support efforts to pursue criminal charges.

Multiple media outlets reported that the Defense Department established a 120-member task force to assess the impact of the disclosures. In August 2010 Secretary Gates presented preliminary findings for the Afghan-related military documents to the Senate Armed Services Committee. The initial conclusion was that no specific intelligence sources or methods were compromised but that the identification of cooperative Afghan nationals was likely to cause significant harm to national security.[40] Secretary Gates also informed the Committee that the military was working with coalition partners to assess the additional risk and consider mitigation options.

Beyond questions concerning the disclosures' perceived benefits or harm, the status of WikiLeaks as a media organization and Assange as a journalist has also been the subject of considerable debate. Assange identifies himself as "a publisher and editor-in-chief who organizes and directs other journalists."[41] Judith Miller, former *New York Times* reporter and Pulitzer Prize winner, remarked that Assange "may be a bad journalist, but he is a journalist."[42] *Washington Post* reporter and fellow Pulitzer Prize winner, Dana Priest, does not share Miller's opinion. At a 2011 American Bar Association event, Priest remarked, "I don't think of him as a journalist at all. I think of him as a source."[43] Executive editor of the *New York Times* Bill Keller wrote that the *Times* also regarded Assange as "a source, not as a partner or collaborator."[44] A statement released by the Society of Professional Journalists reported a lack of consensus among its members on whether WikiLeaks' actions could be considered "journalism."[45]

One other significant point of contention appears to be the ownership of the classified material. The U.S. government maintains its ownership of the material, asserting that WikiLeaks' only responsible course of action is to return the stolen documents and remove the information from its Web sites.[46] Assange contends that he is the owner of the information obtained by WikiLeaks. When *The Guardian* acquired a portion of the compromised diplomatic cables from a source other than WikiLeaks, Assange threatened to sue the newspaper.[47] Assange asserted that he had a financial interest in the information's disclosure and would take legal action if *The Guardian* failed to honor its prior agreement to coordinate publication.

In July 2010 U.S. Army Private First Class Bradley Manning was detained and charged under the Uniform Code of Military Justice for disclosing national defense information to an unauthorized person.[48] The information alleged to have been disclosed by Manning includes a video of U.S. military operations in Iraq and more than 50 classified State Department cables. Though not charged for disclosing the Iraq- and Afghanistan-related documents to WikiLeaks, Manning has been identified as a person of interest.[49] In March 2011, twenty-two additional charges were preferred against Manning, including the theft of public records, unauthorized transmittal of defense information, computer fraud, violation of Army regulations, and aiding the enemy. Though aiding the enemy may be considered a capital offense, military prosecutors indicated that they do not plan on pursuing the death penalty.[50] As of May 2011, Manning was being held in pre-trial confinement at Fort Leavenworth, Kansas.

Manning is reported to have been brought to the attention of law enforcement by Adrian Lamo, an individual with whom he had corresponded over the Internet. An online magazine published alleged chat-logs between Manning and Lamo.[51] In the logs, it appears Manning discusses how he was able to remove classified material from a military system and transfer the information to WikiLeaks:

(01:54:42 PM) **Manning:** i would come in with music on a CD-RW

(01:55:21 PM) **Manning:** labelled with something like "Lady Gaga"... erase the music... then write a compressed split file

(01:55:46 PM) **Manning:** no-one suspected a thing

(01:55:48 PM) **Manning:** =L kind of sad

(01:56:04 PM) **Lamo:** and odds are, they never will

(01:56:07 PM) **Manning:** i didnt even have to hide anything

(01:56:36 PM) **Lamo:** from a professional perspective, i'm curious how the server they were on was insecure

(01:57:19 PM) **Manning:** you had people working 14 hours a day... every single day... no weekends... no recreation...

(01:57:27 PM) **Manning:** people stopped caring after 3 weeks

(01:57:44 PM) **Lamo:** i mean, technically speaking

(01:57:51 PM) **Lamo:** or was it physical

(01:57:52 PM) **Manning:** >nod<

(01:58:16 PM) **Manning:** there was no physical security

(01:58:18 PM) **Lamo:** it was physical access, wasn't it

(01:58:20 PM) **Lamo:** hah

(01:58:33 PM) **Manning:** it was there, but not really

(01:58:51 PM) Manning: 5 digit cipher lock... but you could knock and the door...

(01:58:55 PM) Manning: *on

(01:59:15 PM) Manning: weapons, but everyone has weapons

(02:00:12 PM) Manning: everyone just sat at their workstations... watching music videos / car chases / buildings exploding... and writing more stuff to CD/DVD... the culture fed opportunities

(02:01:44 PM) Manning: hardest part is arguably internet access... uploading any sensitive data over the open internet is a bad idea... since networks are monitored for any insurgent/terrorist/militia/criminal types

(02:01:52 PM) Lamo: tor?

(02:02:13 PM) Manning: tor + ssl + sftp

(02:02:33 PM) Lamo: *nod*

(02:03:05 PM) Lamo: not quite how i might do it, but good

(02:03:22 PM) Manning: i even asked the NSA guy if he could find any suspicious activity coming out of local networks... he shrugged and said... "its not a priority"

(02:03:53 PM) Manning: went back to watching "Eagle's Eye"

(02:12:23 PM) Manning: so... it was a massive data spillage... facilitated by numerous factors... both physically, technically, and culturally

(02:13:02 PM) Manning: perfect example of how not to do INFOSEC

(02:14:21 PM) Manning: listened and lip-synced to Lady Gaga's Telephone while exfiltratrating possibly the largest data spillage in american history

(02:15:03 PM) Manning: pretty simple, and unglamorous

(02:16:37 PM) Manning: *exfiltrating

(02:17:56 PM) Manning: weak servers, weak logging, weak physical security, weak counter-intelligence, inattentive signal analysis... a perfect storm

(02:19:03 PM) Manning: >sigh<

(02:19:19 PM) Manning: sounds pretty bad huh?

(02:20:06 PM) Lamo: kinda

(02:20:25 PM) Manning: :L

(02:20:52 PM) Lamo: i mean, for the .mil

(02:21:08 PM) Manning: well, it SHOULD be better

(02:21:32 PM) Manning: its sad

(02:22:47 PM) Manning: i mean what if i were someone more malicious

(02:23:25 PM) Manning: i could've sold to russia or china, and made bank?

Five months after the initial charges were preferred against Manning, a bill was introduced in the Senate to amend Section 798 of the Espionage Act (Title 18, U.S. Code §§ 793-798). The proposed legislation is referred to as the "Securing Human Intelligence and Enforcing Lawful Dissemination (SHIELD) Act." The amendment identifies additional categories of information illegal to disclose without authorization. This includes the identity of a classified informant or source associated with the U.S. Intelligence Community and information concerning the human intelligence activities of the United States or a foreign government. A similar bill was introduced in the House of Representatives. Neither bill was enacted prior to the adjournment of the 111th Congress.

In December 2010 the House Judiciary Committee held a hearing entitled "WikiLeaks, the Espionage Act and the Constitution." The hearing examined the potential for imposing criminal sanctions, the relevance of the First Amendment to the U.S. Constitution, as well as the difficulties associated with defining the term "journalist." Witnesses included American University law professor Stephen Vladeck and author Gabriel Schoenfeld (both of whom provided Commentaries for this book). The Senate Homeland Security Committee also held a hearing in March 2011, "Information Sharing in the Era of Wikileaks: Balancing Security and Collaboration."

In the aftermath of WikiLeaks' disclosure of hundreds of thousands of classified U.S. documents, the *New York Times* has reportedly been examining whether the model could be replicated. One system being considered by the *Times*, an "EZ Pass lane for leakers," would provide government employees with the ability to anonymously submit large volumes of information to the newspaper electronically.[52] *Al Jazeera* is reported to have already established a "Transparency Unit," offering this capability.

Beyond the implications for the U.S. government and media, this incident has also reinvigorated a long-standing debate over the media's publication of classified information and government efforts to protect this information. Several difficult questions have been raised during the debate, such as:

- What entities constitute "the media" and what legal protections are afforded to them, particularly under the First Amendment to the U.S. Constitution?

- What role do media outlets play in promoting informed debate and exposing government misconduct?

- Can media outlets accurately assess the impact an unauthorized disclosure will have on national security?

- To what extent does the government overclassify some information while tolerating or even condoning the disclosure of other information?

- How does the motivation of advancing personal or corporate interests affect the decision to publish classified information?

- What impact do unauthorized disclosures have on alliances with foreign governments and allied intelligence services?

- What harm, including the loss of sources and methods, financial costs, and threat to life can be attributed to unauthorized disclosures?

- How effective is Congressional oversight of military and intelligence activities?

As the title of this book suggests, the issue of accountability extends beyond government self-oversight and external oversight by the media. The issue also encompasses accountability for the media and for organizations such as WikiLeaks. This topic was addressed at a conference attended by Assange and author Douglas Murray. During his presentation, Murray commented, "Governments are elected. You, Mr. Assange are not. Who guards the guardians?"[53]

The subject of oversight was also addressed during an interview with Assange on the CBS television news program "60 Minutes." During the interview, the correspondent remarked:[54]

> You [Julian Assange] see yourself as a check on the power of the United States and other big countries in the world and in the process of doing that you have now become powerful yourself. Who is the check on you?

Assange responded:

> It is our sources who choose to provide us with information, or not, depending on how they see our actions. It is our donors who choose to give us money, or not. This organization cannot survive for more than a few months without the ongoing support of the public.

The ability of sources and donors to provide adequate oversight for organizations such as WikiLeaks and the corresponding ability, or necessity, for oversight of the U.S. media are among the most complex issues related to the topic of unauthorized disclosures.

This book will examine each of the above issues. Historical events, including the WikiLeaks incident, will be explored in an effort to better understand the ongoing conflict between national security and freedom of the press. Ultimately, the topic of what approach, if any, the government should pursue to reduce the perceived harm from unauthorized disclosures will be addressed. Because this is a dynamic topic, with leaks occurring practically every day, an arbitrary cutoff date of May 1, 2011, has been established for inclusion of new information.

CHAPTER 1
Conflicting Principles

Whoever . . . publishes . . . classified information . . . concerning the communication intelligence activities of the United States . . . shall be fined under this title or imprisoned not more than ten years, or both.[55]

-18 USC § 798

Congress shall make no law . . . abridging the freedom . . . of the press . . .[56]

First Amendment to the U.S. Constitution

Since the founding of this nation, the U.S. press has been committed to promoting democracy through an informed citizenry. From the "lone pamphleteers" of 1776 to major metropolitan newspaper editors of 2011, each has recognized the significance of disseminating essential information to the public. This includes publishing information concerning government actions conducted on behalf of its citizens as well as exposing corrupt or illegal activity committed by its elected representatives. This free flow of information allows individuals to remain engaged with their government.

The Founding Fathers understood that an ability to participate in informed debate was crucial to the success of the newly formed republic. In 1822, James Madison famously wrote, "A popular government without popular information or the means of acquiring it, is but a prologue to a farce or a tragedy or perhaps both."[57] Madison established this principle as a cornerstone of U.S. jurisprudence in the Bill of Rights, which contains the first ten Amendments to the U.S. Constitution. Ratified in 1791, the First Amendment reads: "Congress shall make no law . . . abridging the freedom of speech, or of the press; or the right of the people peaceably to assemble . . ."[58] The prominence given to the concept of a free and independent press distinguishes the United States for its dedication to both a robust marketplace of ideas and a government accountable to the people.

Following the ratification of the First Amendment, however, the concept of a press free from government constraint has conflicted with the principle that information could be withheld from the public in the interest of national security. While there is seldom disagreement over the need to maintain both a strong national defense and an autonomous press, differences in opinion occur when the two are perceived to overlap. At no time is this conflict more evident than when media outlets elect to publish classified information—information identified by the government as necessary to withhold in the interest of national security. Concern over the impact of these "unauthorized disclosures"[59] can be traced back to the Revolutionary War.

In November 1775, eight months prior to the adoption of the Declaration of Independence, the Second Continental Congress passed a resolution concerning the necessity for secrecy. The resolution read, in part:

> [E]very member of this Congress considers himself under the ties of virtue, honor and love of his country not to divulge directly or indirectly any matter . . . which a majority of the Congress shall order to be kept secret and that if any member shall violate this agreement he shall be expelled from this Congress and deemed an enemy to the liberties of America and liable to be treated as such.[60]

Less than a year after formally declaring independence, a fledgling U.S. government faced its first scandal involving an unauthorized disclosure by the media.

In April 1777, the Second Continental Congress appointed Thomas Paine, the influential author of *Common Sense* and *The Rights of Man*, to a position with the Committee on Foreign Affairs. Upon taking office, Paine was administered an oath "to disclose no matter, the knowledge of which shall be acquired in consequence of his office, that he shall be directed to keep secret."[61] On January 2 and January 5, 1779, Paine published two articles in the *Pennsylvania Packet*, under the pseudonym "Common Sense." The articles disclosed that King Louis XVI of France had covertly provided military supplies to the Continental Army prior to the French government publicly acknowledging its alliance with the colonies.[62]

To avoid jeopardizing relations with France, the Continental Congress passed a resolution denying the allegation. Paine was called before

Congress, where he confirmed being both the source of the leak and the author of the articles. He ultimately resigned his position with the Foreign Affairs Committee.

The conflict between the principle of a free press and the necessity for national security continued to defy resolution following Paine's resignation. This conflict became manifest in Thomas Jefferson's attitude toward the press before and after being elected the nation's third President. Jefferson's writings prior to and immediately following the ratification of the U.S. Constitution and Bill of Rights describe an idealistic vision for an independent press:[63]

> Our liberty cannot be guarded but by the freedom of the press, nor that be limited without danger of losing it.

> No government ought to be without censors, and where the press is free, no one ever will.

> Printing presses shall be subject to no other restraint than liableness to legal prosecution for false facts printed and published.

And, perhaps most notably, he stated:

> Were it left to me to decide whether we should have a government without newspapers or newspapers without a government, I should not hesitate a moment to prefer the latter.

However, after his inauguration in 1801, Jefferson's faith in the press appears to have been severely tested. His statements reflect resentment toward the media for his perception of how they had evolved:[64]

> [I have seen] repeated instances of the publication of what has not been intended for the public eye, and the malignity with which political enemies torture every sentence from me into meanings imagined by their own wickedness only. . .

> These people [printers] think they have a right to everything, however secret or sacred.

> Indeed, the abuses of the freedom of the press here have been carried to a length never before known or borne by any civilized nation.

In 1807, in stark contrast to his earlier statement regarding his preference for newspapers above government, Jefferson lamented:

> The man who never looks into a newspaper is better informed than he who reads them, inasmuch as he who knows nothing is nearer to truth . . .

In his second inaugural address of March 4, 1805, Jefferson condemned the U.S. press for abusing the freedoms it was granted. Three of the address' fifteen paragraphs were devoted to this admonishment, including the following excerpt:

> During this course of administration, and in order to disturb it, the artillery of the press has been leveled against us, charged with whatsoever its licentiousness could devise or dare. These abuses of an institution so important to freedom and science are deeply to be regretted . . . but public duties more urgent press on the time of public servants, and the offenders have therefore been left to find their punishment in the public indignation.[65]

When considering Jefferson's sentiments, two important distinctions must be made: First, his dissatisfaction with the media appears to have focused primarily, though not exclusively, on the publication of falsehoods as opposed to classified information. Also, regardless of his degree of frustration, Jefferson maintained his belief in the underlying principle of an autonomous press. Jefferson concluded the portion of his inaugural address concerning the press as follows:

> [T]he press, confined to truth, needs no other legal restraint . . . If there be still improprieties . . . its supplement must be sought in the censorship of public opinion.[66]

Where You Stand Depends on Where You Sit

It is much to be wished that our printers were more discreet in many of their publications.[67]

- George Washington

Over the past 200 years, the clause "or of the press" has been the subject of considerable debate. Though secrecy may be considered both necessary and proper, it can still be perceived as inconsistent with the principles of self-government. Supreme Court Justice Potter Stewart referred to the "dilemma" which occurs when information is withheld from the public in a democracy.[68]

Achieving consensus on the proper balance between openness and secrecy has remained elusive. Debate over this dichotomy between the perceived need to both disclose and withhold information has persisted among academic and legal scholars, government officials, and the public. The intensity and longevity of this debate can be attributed to the deep convictions held by advocates on both sides of the issue. Both groups are convinced that their position is in the best interest of the American public.

A letter published by *New York Times* Executive Editor Bill Keller in 2006 illustrates this dilemma. In the letter, Keller responds to criticism surrounding the *Times'* publication of an article containing classified information. He acknowledges the government's intent to withhold certain information from the public while at the same time asserting the importance of an independent press:

> It's an unusual and powerful thing, this freedom that our founders gave to the press. Who are the editors of *The New York Times* . . . to disregard the wishes of the President and his appointees? And yet the people who invented this country saw an aggressive, independent press as a protective measure against the abuse of power in a democracy, and an essential ingredient for self-government. They rejected the idea that it is wise, or patriotic, to always take the President at his word, or to surrender to the government important decisions about what to publish.[69]

Former Director of National Intelligence Dennis Blair presents an alternative viewpoint. In a 2009 memorandum disseminated to the directors of the sixteen U.S. Intelligence Community agencies, Blair identifies the severe consequences posed by the unauthorized disclosure of classified information:[70]

> In accordance with my responsibility to protect sources and methods, I am committed to preventing unauthorized disclosures of classified information. I take this responsibility extremely seriously, recognizing that disclosures of classified information, including

"leaks" to the media can compromise sensitive sources and methods. These disclosures may allow our adversaries to learn about, deny, counteract, and deceive our intelligence collection methods, leading to the loss of critical capabilities, resources, and even lives. In recent years, unauthorized disclosures have severely diminished the capability of the Intelligence Community (IC) to perform its mission and support national security objectives. Furthermore, these disclosures greatly impact our relationships with our foreign partners, who become reluctant to share sensitive intelligence, fearing this information might appear in the media.[71]

Blair's assertions mirror the 2005 findings of the WMD Commission (Commission on the Intelligence Capabilities of the United States regarding Weapons of Mass Destruction). In its final report to the President, the Commission concluded that unauthorized disclosures by the media "significantly impaired U.S. capabilities against our hardest targets," caused "grave harm" to national security, and "collectively cost the American people hundreds of millions of dollars."[72]

Though these viewpoints may appear incompatible, the divide is not absolute. Former heads of the U.S. Intelligence Community have recognized and commended the press for their role in preserving and promoting democracy. In a 1986 speech presented to members of the Society of Professional Journalists, former Director of Central Intelligence (DCI) William Casey expressed his admiration for the press:

I cherish the first amendment and admire the diligence and ingenuity of the working press. I applaud your exposure of waste, inefficiency, and corruption. I salute and support your obligation to ferret out and publish the information the people need to be well informed about events around the world as well as the activities of their democratic government.[73]

Former DCI William Colby, a predecessor of Casey, acknowledged that the disclosure of classified information may be appropriate under certain circumstances:

There have been some "bad secrets" concerning intelligence; their exposure by our academic, journalist, and political critics certainly is an essential part of the workings of our Constitution. There have been some "non-secrets" which did not need to be secret; I have undertaken a program of bringing these into the open. But I think that responsible Americans realize that our country must protect "good secrets."[74]

Respected members of the media have also recognized that information may be classified based on legitimate national security concerns. Katharine Graham, former publisher and chairman of the board of the *Washington Post*, conceded that national security had been harmed and the lives of U.S. servicemen endangered by the publication of classified information:

> You may recall that in April 1983, some sixty people were killed in a bomb attack on the U.S. embassy in Beirut. At the time, there was coded radio traffic between Syria, where the operation was being run, and Iran, which was supporting it. Alas, one television network and a newspaper columnist reported that the U.S. government had intercepted the traffic. Shortly thereafter the traffic ceased. This undermined efforts to capture the terrorist leaders and eliminated a source of information about future attacks. Five months later, apparently the same terrorists struck again at the Marine barracks in Beirut; 241 servicemen were killed.[75]

Other prominent members of the media, including Walter Cronkite, Tom Brokaw, and Ted Koppel, understood the potential threat to national security posed by unauthorized disclosures. In a joint letter to the Senate Select Committee on Intelligence (SSCI) in 2006, Cronkite, Brokaw, and Koppel emphasized the obligation of their colleagues to seriously consider possible consequences before publishing classified information. They wrote:

> Leaks of classified information are a serious matter because some leaks can endanger national security. We recognize that the government has a legitimate interest in protecting our national security secrets, and the media have a responsibility to carefully consider the impact of its reporting . . . Investigating and prosecuting those who leak information that causes serious harm to national security is understandable.[76]

Polling data suggest public sentiment is closely divided over the perceived benefit or harm resulting from unauthorized disclosures. A 2007 survey conducted by the Pew Research Center illustrates this rift in public opinion. Fourty-four percent of respondents believed that unauthorized disclosures "hurt the public interest by revealing information that people should not have."[77] The percentage of those who believed that disclosures serve the public by "providing Americans with information they should have" was only a marginally less 42 percent. These findings were almost identical to the results of a Pew study conducted twenty years earlier. In the 1986 study, 43 percent of respondents believed that unauthorized disclosures served the public interest, while 42 percent held that the disclosures were harmful.[78]

A survey conducted in 2006 by the First Amendment Center identified a similar divide in public opinion.[79] Fifty-one percent of the survey's participants believed that "sensitive and classified government information" should only be published when exposing government wrong doing. Thirty-five percent responded that, regardless of its intended purpose, the media should not publish such information. Twelve percent believed newspapers should have the ability to publish information without restriction. Considering the above polling data, the one indisputable finding appears to be that the issue of unauthorized disclosures is disputable.

Questions regarding the role of the media in a democratic society are certainly not new. Concern over the ability to regulate the actions of those performing an oversight function can be traced back to Plato's *Republic*. Published in 360 B.C., the narrator, Socrates, describes a "Guardian Class" and its role in society. In a Latin translation of the dialogue, Socrates is asked, "Quis custodiet ipso custodes?" (Who will guard the guardians?)[80] Socrates' response, whether applied to government oversight of its citizens or media oversight of the government, does little to aid in resolving the dilemma of unauthorized disclosures:

> They will guard themselves against themselves. We must tell the guardians a noble lie. The noble lie will inform them that they are better than those they serve and it is therefore their responsibility to guard and protect those lesser than themselves.[81]

The Scope of Unauthorized Disclosures in the United States

I've been told that The New York Times has so much classified material, they don't know where to store it.[82]

- President Gerald Ford

In the 232 years following the publication of Paine's "Common Sense" articles, and the 206 years since Jefferson's second inaugural address, unauthorized disclosures by the U.S. media have persisted. Former Presidents, from Harry S. Truman through George W. Bush, have voiced their frustration over the practice.[83] In 2009, President Barack Obama joined his predecessors in expressing his displeasure.[84]

Quantifying precise figures for unauthorized disclosures in a historical context is difficult. Former Presidents have provided some insight, if only through hyperbole. In 1951, President Truman remarked "ninety-five percent of our secret information has been revealed in newspapers and slick magazines."[85] Twenty years later, President Nixon discussed administration efforts to respond to "massive leaks of vital diplomatic and military secrets."[86] In declassified minutes from a 1974 National Security Council meeting, President Ford noted: "I've been told that *The New York Times* has so much classified material, they don't know where to store it."[87] When asked in 1981 to identify the biggest disappointment of his presidency, President Reagan cited "the inability to control the leaks."[88] In 1985, President Reagan famously complained of being "up to my keister in leaks."[89]

Publicly available information concerning the actual number of unauthorized disclosures during a given period is rare. In 1988 former DCI Robert Gates wrote that there had been approximately five hundred documented disclosures between 1979 and 1988, 50 a year during a ten-year period.[90] In November 2000, an NSA official testified before the House Permanent Select Committee on Intelligence (HPSCI) that the NSA had identified 40 instances in 1998 where signals intelligence capabilities were disclosed for the first time in the media and an additional 34 instances in 1999.[91]

9

During testimony before the SSCI in June 2000, Attorney General Janet Reno stated that the Justice Department had been notified of an unauthorized disclosure approximately fifty times a year over "the last several years."[92] This is equivalent to the level identified by DCI Gates, approximately one unauthorized disclosure per week. Reno added that virtually all agencies within the Intelligence Community and the Defense Department had suffered "severe losses of sources, methods, and important liaison relationships" as the result of unauthorized disclosures.[93]

The most recent publicly available statistics were provided to the Senate Judiciary Committee by the Department of Justice in 2010.[94] The Justice Department reported receiving an average of thirty-seven notifications of unauthorized disclosures annually between 2005 and 2009. The relative consistency in the number of unauthorized disclosures over the past 30 years demonstrates their persistent nature, independent of which political party controls the White House or Congress.

Information regarding the number of criminal investigations initiated by the Justice Department in response to an unauthorized disclosure is also seldom released. In 1980, it was reported that the Federal Bureau of Investigation (FBI) had conducted 25 criminal investigations involving disclosures over the prior two years, approximately 12 per year.[95] A 1985 article revealed that there had been an average of 20-30 active unauthorized disclosure investigations between 1981 and 1985.[96] In response to a query from the SSCI, the Department of Justice reported that the FBI had completed 85 investigations predicated on an unauthorized disclosure between September 2001 and February 2008, approximately thirteen per year.[97]

Several factors may contribute to the persistent supply and demand for disclosures. Continued partisanship between political parties seeking to gain an advantage in a narrowly divided Congress, or a similarly divided public, is one possible factor. The increased quantity of information required to support U.S. interests worldwide and improvements in the quality of U.S. collection capabilities might be another. The abundance of print, broadcast, and electronic media outlets scrutinizing government activity is likely to play a role. A desire by the public to remain informed of government activity during a time of war may also help sustain this "leak economy." The consistent rate of disclosures over the past three decades, however, demonstrates that this economy is not entirely dependent on ongoing military hostilities.

History has also shown that unauthorized disclosures can sometimes take on an eerily repetitive quality. Other than a change in adversary and a 50-year improvement in technology, a striking similarity exists between a 1958 disclosure concerning the ability of military aircraft to monitor Soviet missile tests[98] and a 2007 article disclosing the monitoring of Chinese missile tests by satellite.[99]

History also appears to have repeated itself in 2005 when the *New York Times* published an article disclosing the existence of a National Security Agency (NSA) program to monitor specific domestic communications without a warrant. Thirty years earlier, in 1975, the *Times* exposed Operation SHAMROCK, a decades-long classified program that allowed the NSA and its predecessors to duplicate and analyze magnetic tapes of international telegrams.[100] Continuing the parallel, the 1975 article resulted in Congressional hearings to determine whether adequate oversight was performed. The hearings also examined the legality and propriety of the program.

Three recent unauthorized disclosures, each involving a classified counterterrorism program, have reinvigorated debate among members of the government, media, and public.

On November 2, 2005, the *Washington Post* published an article by Dana Priest reporting the existence of a system of covert CIA detention facilities in Eastern Europe.[101] On December 16, 2005, a *New York Times* article by James Risen and Eric Lichtblau disclosed that the President had authorized the NSA to monitor certain domestic communications without a warrant.[102] Lastly, on June 23, 2006, the *New York Times* published a second article by Risen and Lichtblau. The article revealed the existence of a classified CIA and Treasury Department program to analyze financial records from a foreign database named SWIFT (Society for Worldwide Interbank Financial Telecommunication).[103]

It was reported that the SWIFT database contained transactions involving U.S. citizens.

In recognition of the CIA detention facility and NSA surveillance articles, Priest, Risen, and Lichtblau were awarded Pulitzer Prizes for Journalistic Excellence. Alternatively, in response to the SWIFT database article, the House of Representatives passed a resolution condemning the media for their disclosure of classified information. These responses underscore the acute difference in opinion over the impact of unauthorized disclosures.

Considering the issue from an alternative perspective, the U.S. Intelligence Community has recognized the value of information published in the foreign media. In 2005, the Office of the Director of National Intelligence (ODNI) and CIA established the Open Source Center. The mission of the Open Source Center is to "advance the Intelligence Community's exploitation of openly available information."[104]

Other Intelligence Community agencies, including the Defense Intelligence Agency (DIA) and the FBI, have also reportedly tasked analysts to collect and assess information from publicly available sources.[105] This would include the analysis of foreign media to identify information concerning an adversary's capabilities and intentions. In 2008 Frances Townsend, former Deputy National Security Advisor for Combating Terrorism, commented that it had become routine for the President's Daily Brief to contain intelligence collected from open source material.[106]

Researching the Topic

Unauthorized disclosures remain a frequent subject for research in the government and academic/legal communities. The issue has been examined at academic symposia and in the law journals of prominent universities throughout the country, including Columbia, Stanford, and Harvard. Professional associations, including the American Society of Newspaper Editors, Brookings Institution, and the American Bar Association, have discussed the topic at national conferences and seminars.

The issue has been debated at Congressional hearings before the House Armed Services Committee (1980), the Senate Select Committee on

Intelligence (1978, 1998, 2000, and 2009), the House Permanent Select Committee on Intelligence (1979, 2005, and 2006), the Senate Judiciary Committee (2006 and 2010), and the Senate Homeland Security Committee (2011). Titles for these hearings include "The Effects of Unauthorized Disclosures of Classified Information," "Espionage Laws and Leaks," "Roles and Responsibilities of the Media with Respect to Unauthorized Disclosures of Classified Information," and "Leaks of Classified National Defense Information." Specific issues examined during these hearings include government efforts to safeguard classified information, the impact of unauthorized disclosures on national security, the role of the U.S. media, the applicability of criminal statutes, and the potential for enacting new legislation.

Research published in the previously cited law journals focus primarily on the applicability of existing legal statutes. These articles include "National Security Secrets vs. Free Speech," published in the *Stanford Law Review* in 1974; "Government Secrecy vs. Freedom of the Press," published in the *Harvard Law & Policy Review* in 2007, and one of the most often referenced articles in this debate, "The Espionage Statutes and Publication of Defense Information," published in the *Columbia Law Review* in 1973. As their titles suggest, these studies examine ambiguities in U.S. law related to free speech and national security.

In "Government Secrecy vs. Freedom of the Press," University of Chicago Law Professor Geoffrey Stone provides an apt description of the current "awkward, even incoherent, state of affairs."[107] Professor Stone contends that this dilemma is a consequence of apparent legal inconsistencies between the U.S. Constitution and its First Amendment:

> Although elected officials have broad authority to keep classified information secret, once that information gets into the hands of the press, the government has only very limited authority to prevent its further dissemination. This may seem an awkward, even incoherent, state of affairs. If the government can constitutionally prohibit public employees from disclosing classified information to the press in the first place, why can it not enjoin the press from publishing that information if a government employee unlawfully discloses it?

But one could just as easily flip the question. If the press has a First Amendment right to *publish* classified information unless publication will "surely result in direct, immediate, and irreparable damage to our Nation or its people," why should the government be allowed to prohibit its employees from *revealing* such information to the press merely because it poses a potential danger to the national security?

Federal judges, from the Circuit Court and Court of Appeals to the Supreme Court, have also published relevant opinions. A 1971 opinion, authored by Supreme Court Justice Potter Stewart, offers an eloquent summary of this controversial issue:

[T]he only effective restraint upon executive policy and power in the areas of national defense and international affairs may lie in an enlightened citizenry – in an informed and critical public opinion which alone can here protect the values of democratic government. For this reason, it is perhaps here that a press that is alert, aware, and free most vitally serves the basic purpose of the First Amendment. For without an informed and free press there cannot be an enlightened people.

Yet it is elementary that the successful conduct of international diplomacy and the maintenance of an effective national defense require both confidentiality and secrecy. Other nations can hardly deal with this Nation in an atmosphere of mutual trust unless they can be assured that their confidences will be kept. And within our own executive departments, the development of considered and intelligent international policies would be impossible if those charged with their formulation could not communicate with each other freely, frankly, and in confidence. In the area of basic national defense the frequent need for absolute secrecy is, of course, self-evident.[108]

The number of related articles published in newspapers, magazines and on the Internet is also remarkable. The positions expressed in these articles span the entire spectrum of the debate, from "Indict the *New York Times*" and "Stop the Leaks" to "A Leaky Bureaucracy is Good for Democracy" and "No More Secrecy Bills." The cover of the March 2006 edition of *Commentary* magazine asked the question, "Has the *New York Times* Violated the Espionage Act?" Though there may be several areas of disagreement, no one could contend that the issue of unauthorized disclosures has been overlooked.

Responding Through Law: The "Espionage Act"

It would be frivolous to assert . . . that the First Amendment, in the interest of securing news or otherwise, confers a license on either the reporter or his news sources to violate valid criminal laws. [N] either reporter nor source is immune from conviction for such conduct, whatever the impact on the flow of news.[109]

- Supreme Court Justice Byron White

In the First Amendment, the Founding Fathers gave the free press the protection it must have to fulfill its essential role in our democracy . . . The press was protected so that it could bare the secrets of government and inform the people.[110]

- Supreme Court Justice Hugo Black

Based on the harm attributed to unauthorized disclosures, the government has moved beyond debating the issue and has undertaken efforts to prevent the compromise of classified information. To date, the effort has largely focused on a legislative solution and criminal sanctions.

When a violation of federal law occurs involving the unauthorized disclosure of classified information, Intelligence Community agencies are required to notify the Department of Justice.[111] In consultation between the Department's National Security Division and the affected agency, primary consideration is given to initiating a criminal investigation. This decision is based on several factors, including the assessed harm to national security, the extent of official dissemination of the compromised information, and the willingness of the agency to support an investigation and potential prosecution. Administrative actions, such as the revocation of a security clearance or termination of employment, are only considered in cases "when a prosecution cannot be undertaken or is not successful."

The principal legal statutes related to unauthorized disclosures are Title 18 of the U.S. Code, Sections 793-798, more commonly referred to as the "Espionage Act." Proposed and enacted within two months of the United States' entrance into World War I in 1917, the Act criminalizes the disclosure of information "relating to the national defense."[112] Section 793 prohibits disclosures to "any person not entitled to receive it," while Section 794 specifically proscribes disclosures to "any foreign government."

Section 798, a 1950 amendment to the Act, contains several key distinctions from its predecessors. Section 798 criminalizes the disclosure of "classified information," specifically involving cryptographic or communications intelligence. Section 798 is the only section that expressly proscribes the *publication* of classified information. The American Society of Newspaper Editors is reported to have endorsed the passage of Section 798 in 1950.[113] Violations of Sections 793 and 798 are punishable by incarceration for up to ten years. A conviction under Section 794, specifically involving a foreign government, is punishable by incarceration for a term up to life. The death penalty may also be sought in certain cases, including a disclosure directly resulting in the death of a U.S. agent, or a disclosure of a "major element of defense strategy."

Separate legislation, enacted in 1933, 1954, and 1982, identifies additional categories of intelligence illegal to disclose without authorization. These include diplomatic codes, nuclear weapons intelligence, and the identities of covert U.S. agents. The statutes concerning diplomatic codes and covert agents were both predicated by the publication of classified information. In 1931 former intelligence officer Herbert Yardley published *Inside the Black Chamber*, detailing U.S. code breaking in the early 20th century. In 1978 former CIA case officer Philip Agee published the identities of CIA officers in the magazine *Covert Action Quarterly*.

Between 1946 and 2010, there were no less than 18 proposals to amend existing statutes related to unauthorized disclosures that were never enacted. A comprehensive analysis of the U.S. legal system, including the Constitution and Bill of Rights, proposed and enacted legislation, and case law is included in the Appendix.

In the United States, no member of the media has been indicted or convicted for the unauthorized publication of classified information. The government has considered the option on at least four occasions—in 1942, 1971, 1975, and 1986. In the 94 years following the passage of the Espionage Act, there have been only four criminal indictments specifically for the unauthorized disclosure of classified information to a member of the media.

The first, a 1973 indictment of RAND analysts Daniel Ellsberg and Anthony Russo, was dismissed due to prosecutorial misconduct.[114] Ellsberg had provided portions of a TOP SECRET Defense Department study concerning Vietnam to both the *New York Times* and *Washington Post*. The second indictment, in 1985, resulted in a successful conviction.[115] In this case, Navy analyst Samuel Morison was convicted under Sections 793 of the Espionage Act for providing classified satellite imagery to the magazine *Jane's Defence Weekly*. In August 2010, State Department contract analyst Stephen Jin-Woo Kim was indicted for disclosing the contents of a TOP SECRET intelligence report to a journalist.[116] Former CIA operations officer Jeffrey Sterling was indicted in December 2010 for disclosing classified information to a member of the media.[117] The information reportedly concerned a covert CIA operation involving Iran.

Each of the incidents identified above, as well as other relevant legal actions, will be discussed in greater detail in Chapters 2-4 and the Appendix. This includes four indictments for unauthorized disclosures to entities other than traditional media outlets, including a legal advocacy group, a political action committee, an Internet "blogger," and an Internet-based organization. One other indictment, for activity associated with an unauthorized disclosure though not specifically for the disclosure itself, will also be examined.

Of the approximately 1,500 unauthorized disclosures and 200 criminal investigations over the past three decades, an indictment rate of .3% (4 out of 1,500) and a conviction rate of .07% (1 out of 1,500) are clearly ineffective for an approach focused on criminal enforcement. Whether the four indictments or single conviction are considered appropriate, they have not created a significant deterrent for government employees to discontinue disclosing classified information to the media.

Seeking an Alternative to a Legislative Solution

Criminal prosecution is not the most effective way to address the leak problem.[118]

- Attorney General Janet Reno

Beyond the attention unauthorized disclosures have received in the academic, professional, and legal communities, at least ten government commissions, committees, and task forces have examined the issue over the past 50 years. Unauthorized disclosures by the media were the primary topic in three of the ten studies and part of the larger subject of government secrecy and security in the others. Titles for these reports include:

The Report to the Secretary of Defense by the Committee on Classified Information (The Coolidge Report), 1956

The Report of the Commission on Government Security (The Wright Commission), 1957

The Report of the Senate Select Committee on Intelligence by the Subcommittee on Secrecy and Disclosure, 1978

The Report of the Interdepartmental Group on Unauthorized Disclosures of Classified Information (The Willard Report), 1982

The Report to the Secretary of Defense by the Commission to Review DoD Security Policies and Practices (The Stilwell Commission), 1985

Report to the National Security Council on Unauthorized Media Leak Disclosures by the National Counterintelligence Policy Board, 1996

Report of the Commission on Protecting and Reducing Government Secrecy (The Moynihan Commission), 1997

Report of the National Commission on Terrorism (The Bremer Commission), 2000

Report to the Attorney General by the Interagency Task Force Concerning Protections against Unauthorized Disclosures of Classified Information, 2002

Report by the Commission on the Intelligence Capabilities of the United States Regarding Weapons of Mass Destruction (Silberman-Robb Commission), 2004

Several of the reports conclude that a legislative approach to reduce unauthorized disclosures is both inadequate and impractical. The reports acknowledge numerous limitations preventing the effectiveness of such a strategy.

The drafters of the 1956 Coolidge Report wrote: "No change in the statutes or Executive Orders has been suggested to us which would in our judgment contribute significantly to improving the situation."[119] Future Vice President Joseph Biden noted in his Preface to the 1978 Report of the Subcommittee on Secrecy and Disclosure: "[E]ven the most radical revision of the espionage statutes . . . may not resolve this dilemma."[120] The Committee's final report concluded that there had been a "major failure on the part of the Government to take action in leak cases." The Report added that "no present statute can be effectively enforced against leaks" and that it would be "a difficult task to draft a constitutional criminal statute which would solve the enforcement problems."

Members of the Willard Group reached a similar conclusion. The Group described the government approach, focused on criminal enforcement, as an "ineffectual system," "frustrating to all concerned," and "almost totally unsuccessful."[121] The report concluded that the threat of criminal prosecution had become "so illusory as to constitute no real deterrent to the prospective leaker." Former Director of Central Intelligence and Secretary of Defense Robert Gates concurred with this opinion. In 1988, while Deputy Director of Central Intelligence, Gates wrote: "I personally believe that new laws, even if they could be enacted, would not stop leaks."[122]

The 1996 report to the National Security Council noted that the lack of criminal prosecutions failed to create an adequate deterrent for the "seemingly risk-free enterprise" of disclosing classified information. Board members examined prior administrations' efforts to prevent unauthorized disclosures and found them to be largely unsuccessful. This ineffectiveness was attributed to several factors, including a lack of political will to deal firmly and consistently with the "leakers," as well as disagreements over the need for additional legislation. Former Attorney General Janet Reno similarly recognized the limitations of pursuing criminal sanctions. During testimony before the SSCI in 2000, Reno stated definitively that the Justice Department believed criminal prosecution was "not the most effective way to address the leak problem."

Almost five decades after the Coolidge Report, the Interagency Task Force Concerning Protections Against Unauthorized Disclosures examined the issue. In its 2002 report to Attorney General John Ashcroft, the Task Force reported that attempting to resolve the issue by amending existing statutes was likely not the proper approach:

> The extent to which such a provision (legislation specifically tailored to unauthorized disclosures of classified information) would yield any practical additional benefits to the government is unclear . . .[123]

Ashcroft expanded on this finding in his letter to Congress accompanying the Task Force report. He wrote that the government "must entertain new approaches to deter, identify, and punish those who engage in the practice of unauthorized disclosures of classified information."[124] Ashcroft added that legislation specifically focused on unauthorized disclosures "would be insufficient in my view to meet the problem . . ."

In an article published on September 5, 2001, less than a week before the terrorist attacks of September 11, 2001, former Secretary of Defense William Cohen expressed his doubts regarding the effectiveness of a legislative solution: "Legislation (to create a new criminal offense applying to any government official who intentionally discloses classified information to a person not authorized to receive it) would probably do little to prevent damaging leaks."[125]

The Difficulty Identifying Leakers: A Thousand Grains of Sand

Even if there had been consensus that an approach focused on criminal enforcement was practical, and the enactment of meaningful legislation possible, the most significant obstacle would still remain. This difficulty lies in the fundamental ability to identify the government employee responsible for disclosing classified information to the media.

After examining this issue, the 2002 Interagency Task Force concluded that identifying individuals responsible for disclosing classified information to the media was "difficult at best."[126] One of the Task Force working groups noted that, even in cases involving the compromise of highly sensitive information, it was typical for "literally hundreds, if not thousands of individuals" to have had access to the information. In the 1996 report to the National Security Council, "the challenge in identifying the leaker" was recognized as a primary factor contributing to the U.S. government's inability to control disclosures.[127]

The Willard Group documented a similar problem identifying the responsible government employee(s) in 1982. It acknowledged that "in most situations, hundreds or thousands of employees have had access to information (that is leaked) and there is no practical way to narrow the focus of the inquiry."[128] The 1978 Report of the Senate Select Committee on Intelligence noted that criminal investigations were often unsuccessful "because the leaked information has been disseminated broadly in such interagency classified materials . . . some of which have circulation in the thousands."[129] The last two statements are particularly noteworthy, considering that access to classified information through secure computer networks, such as SIPRNet (Secure Internet Protocol Router Network) and JWICS (Joint Worldwide Intelligence Communications System), was significantly less common in 1978 and 1982 than in 1996 or 2002.

Looking back to a period when the number of government employees, the volume of classified information, and the technical capability to share that information were even further reduced, the difficulty in identifying the "leaker" was still understood. In the 1956 Coolidge Report, the Committee reported:

> Due to the difficulties in identifying the sources of these leaks because of the large number of persons who have had access to the information in question, it is impossible to describe with certainty the individuals who are responsible and the reasons which motivated them.[130]

Recent policy changes within the Intelligence Community are likely to exacerbate this problem.

One of the principal findings of the 9/11 Commission (National Commission on Terrorist Attacks Upon the United States) was that a lack of information sharing contributed to the intelligence failures associated with the September 11, 2001, terrorist attacks. In response to this finding, new policies were implemented to increase collaboration and reduce stove-piping, the tendency to report information vertically within a closed channel rather than horizontally across related communities of interest.[131] In February 2008, Director of National Intelligence Michael McConnell published the "Information Sharing Strategy for the Intelligence Community." This strategy established a new standard for handling and disseminating classified information. Rather than considering an individual's "need to know" specific intelligence, the DNI revised the standard to a more proactive "responsibility to provide."[132]

Combined with improvements in technology and the additional requirement to collect intelligence during periods of international conflict, this new focus on a responsibility to provide has resulted in wider dissemination and increased access to classified information. These factors further complicate the already daunting task of successfully identifying and prosecuting government employees who disclose classified information to the media.

Ironically, another unauthorized disclosure may result in the pendulum swinging away from a standard of increased information sharing. In the wake of the 2010 disclosure of hundreds of thousands of classified documents by the Internet-based organization WikiLeaks, the Intelligence Community has begun to reexamine this policy. Director of National Intelligence James Clapper commented: "WikiLeaks and the continued hemorrhaging of leaks in the media don't do much to support the notion of integration and collaboration."[133] Clapper spoke of identifying a "sweet spot" between the need to share and the need to protect information. It remains to be seen whether such a "sweet spot" can be achieved, and the effect it will have on the flow of information to the media.

Beyond the primary difficulty of identifying a suspect, additional legal barriers exist. Former Assistant Attorney General for National Security

Kenneth Wainstein identified several of these obstacles to pursuing criminal prosecutions:

> Finding the leaker in the first place is hard ... Producing incriminating evidence is also difficult, since in most cases prosecutors are reluctant to subpoena the receivers of leaks – members of the press. Agencies from which the information was leaked are often not eager to prosecute, on the theory that open court proceedings might simply reveal more classified information. Plus, leak cases are often marked by zealous and novel legal defenses.[134]

Current Justice Department policy requires that all other methods for acquiring desired information be exhausted before the Department will consider issuing a subpoena to a journalist.[135] Subpoenaing a journalist also requires direct approval from the Attorney General. These difficulties were discussed in a 2010 Justice Department memorandum to the Senate Judiciary Committee.[136] The memorandum notes that, even in those infrequent cases when a member of the media is subpoenaed, there are often prolonged legal challenges and the journalist will likely elect to serve jail time rather than identify his or her source.

Both the 1978 SSCI Report and 1982 Willard Group Report recommend that an increased emphasis be placed on deterring unauthorized disclosures through the use of agencies' administrative authorities. Former Attorney General John Ashcroft similarly advocated an approach focused on administrative authorities. In a 2002 letter to Congress accompanying the findings of the Interagency Task Force on Unauthorized Disclosures, Ashcroft wrote:

> A comprehensive, coordinated, Government-wide, aggressive, properly resourced, and sustained effort to address administratively the problem of unauthorized disclosures is a necessity. Departments and agencies should use all appropriate investigative tools and techniques at their disposal to identify those who commit unauthorized disclosures of classified information. Immediate and consequential administrative investigations that are coordinated across agencies responsible for handling classified information would provide a large measure of deterrence.[137]

This sentiment was echoed in the Justice Department's 2010 memorandum to the Senate Judiciary Committee: "Because indictments in media leak cases are so difficult to obtain, administrative action may be more suitable and may provide a better deterrent to leaks of classified information."[138] These administrative sanctions would include the revocation of a security clearance or termination of employment. Title 5 of the U.S. Code, Section 7532, grants an agency head broad discretion to terminate an employee when such action is considered necessary "in the interests of national security."[139]

Emphasizing administrative authorities does offer several advantages over pursuing criminal prosecutions. These include avoiding legal issues over the applicability of the Espionage Act and the First Amendment, political issues related to a decision to prosecute, and concerns that classified information would be disclosed during a trial. Additional administrative authorities, such as the use of polygraph examinations and compelled interviews, would also appear to favor a strategy that relied more heavily on administrative sanctions.[140] Considering the scarcity of criminal indictments, even a modest increase in the number of administrative sanctions would represent an improvement.

Beyond any potential benefits, though, the single largest obstacle of identifying a suspect still remains. Unless there was a significant improvement in the ability to identify one government employee among thousands in a "need to know" environment, this approach is unlikely to have the desired effect. An individual undeterred by the remote possibility of a criminal indictment would be similarly unswayed by the perceived unlikelihood of administrative sanctions. Whether the recommendation to focus on administrative authorities was implemented, the rate of unauthorized disclosures does not appear to have diminished.

It is unlikely that the value the U.S. public places on information-sharing and collaboration within the government, or a free press outside the government, will diminish. Consequently, efforts to address the issue of unauthorized disclosures primarily through legal or administrative authorities will continue to be ineffective. In order to reduce the perceived harm from unauthorized disclosures, an alternative approach must be identified.

Over the past four decades, some unconventional approaches to respond to the threat of unauthorized disclosures have been employed. Unfortunately, some of these efforts included activities that exceeded legal authorities.

Statutory Abuses and Efforts to Prevent Unauthorized Disclosures

I don't give a damn how it is done, do whatever has to be done to stop these leaks and prevent further unauthorized disclosures.[141]

- President Richard Nixon

At the direction of the DCI, surveillance was conducted of Jack Anderson . . . to attempt to determine Anderson's sources for highly classified Agency information appearing in his syndicated columns.[142]

- CIA "Family Jewels" Memorandum

In June 2007, the Director of the Central Intelligence Agency, Michael Hayden, declassified a 1973 CIA report. The report documented activities conducted by the CIA that may have been "in conflict with the provisions of the National Security Act of 1947."[143] DCI James Schlesinger directed that the study be completed shortly after succeeding Richard Helms. The "Family Jewels" report documents three cases in which the CIA conducted surveillance of members of the U.S. media.[144]

At the direction of former DCI Helms, the CIA surveilled *Washington Post* reporter Michael Getler on three separate occasions in 1971 and 1972. This operation was code-named CELOTEX I. DCI Helms also directed the surveillance of columnist Jack Anderson under Operation CELOTEX II in 1972. Anderson's associates, Brit Hume, Leslie Whitten, and Joseph Spear, were also surveilled as part of CELOTEX II. The "Family Jewels" report also documents the 1972 surveillance of author Victor Marchetti as part of Operation BUTANE. In all three cases, the purpose for the surveillance was to uncover the journalists' government source.

In 1973 Daniel Ellsberg and Anthony Russo's indictments for the unauthorized disclosure of portions of a TOP SECRET government study, the "Pentagon Papers," was dismissed due to prosecutorial misconduct.

This misconduct included the wiretapping of Ellsberg's telephone and the burglary of his psychiatrist's office by a White House "Special Investigations Unit." This group, specifically created in response to the disclosure of the Pentagon Papers, would later gain infamy as the "Plumbers" implicated in the 1972 burglary of the Democratic National Committee headquarters at the Watergate Hotel.[145]

Rather than respond to unauthorized disclosures through legislation, or seek a solution outside the law, the government would be better served by improving its understanding of why members of the U.S. press elect to disclose classified information. Increased awareness of a journalist's rationale for publishing this information might provide the foundation for an approach to reduce its perceived harm.[146] Achieving an improved understanding of a journalist's decision-making process can be achieved through a field of study known as Rational Choice Theory.

Rational Choice Theory: An Alternative to a Legislative Approach

*Only a fundamental change in prevailing **attitudes** will alleviate the problem of unauthorized disclosures . . . Without a change in attitudes, no program to deal with unauthorized disclosures can possibly be effective.[147] (Emphasis added)*

- *Report of the Interdepartmental Group on Unauthorized Disclosures*

*The best approach is to work cooperatively with journalists to **persuade** them not to publish classified information that can damage national security.[148] (Emphasis added)*

- *Matthew Friedrich, Principal Deputy Assistant Attorney General*

*Until those who, without authority, reveal classified information are **deterred** . . . they will have no reason to stop their harmful actions.[149] (Emphasis added)*

- *Attorney General John Ashcroft*

Rational Choice Theory focuses on the internal decision-making process an individual performs prior to electing a course of action. Rational Choice Theory contends that individuals who choose to engage in a behavior often do so only after rationally assessing the perceived costs and benefits related to the behavior.

This process can be envisioned as a "psychological scale," allowing individuals to balance relevant factors in order to reach a conclusion.

COST   **BENEFIT**

FIGURE 1- PSYCHOLOGICAL SCALE
Source: Author

As a result of this rational weighing of options, Rational Choice Theory contends that an undesirable behavior can be discouraged by modifying an individual's evaluation of either the identified costs or benefits. By altering the individual's assessment, which previously resulted in the commission of an undesirable act, it would be possible to successfully reduce or eliminate the perceived harm associated with the behavior.

In the book *Choosing White-Collar Crime*,[150] Neal Shover and Andy Hochstetler explore the application of Rational Choice Theory to criminal behaviors involving non-violent, white collar offenses. The authors explain that Rational Choice Theory can also be applied to a wide range of behaviors, beyond white collar offenses:

> It [Rational Choice Theory] has been applied to a host of problems and processes, including managerial decisions, interpersonal exchange, consumer purchasing, and the dynamics of economic markets. Arguably, it is the dominant theoretical paradigm in political science.[151]

Among the behaviors that can be applied to Rational Choice Theory is the publication of classified information. In accordance with Rational Choice Theory, members of the media would only elect to perform this action after rationally assessing that the apparent benefits outweighed the perceived costs. If a journalist's cost-benefit analysis was altered to the point in which the alternative conclusion, not to publish classified information, was reached, the frequency of unauthorized disclosures and, consequently, their potential harm would decline.

Relying on criminal or administrative sanctions to deter individuals from disclosing classified information has proven to be an ineffective approach. Applying the principles of Rational Choice Theory by proactively engaging members of the media to examine their decision-making process offers an alternative that can ultimately prove more effective.

Before a conclusion can be reached regarding the feasibility or desirability of an approach incorporating Rational Choice Theory, the individual elements that comprise a journalist's cost-benefit analysis must be understood. This book identifies and examines the motivations and justifications considered by members of the media prior to disclosing classified information, as well as the categories of harm these motivations and justifications are weighed against. Chapter Two examines the motivations and justifications for members of the media to obtain and publish classified information. Historical examples are used to assist in identifying and analyzing specific motivations and justifications. Motivations for a government employee to disclose classified information are also discussed.

Chapter Three identifies precise categories of harm attributed to unauthorized disclosures. Historic events are again used to distinguish each category of harm. Chapter Four presents a case study to examine the actual process whereby members of the media deliberated the publication of classified information involving a clandestine operation code-named IVY BELLS. This case study provides unique and valuable insight into a journalist's thought processes. Conclusions regarding Rational Choice Theory and its application to the issue of unauthorized disclosures are discussed in Chapter Five.

CHAPTER 2

Journalist Motivations and Justifications

I have never seen any trace of a threat to the national security from the Publication. Indeed, I have never seen it even suggested that there was such an actual threat. It quickly becomes apparent to any person who has considerable experience with classified material that there is massive overclassification and that the principal concern of the classifiers is not with national security, but rather with governmental embarrassment of one sort or another.[152]

- Former Solicitor General Erwin Griswold discussing the Pentagon Papers

For advocates of the expansive rights of a free press, unauthorized disclosures are viewed not only as justified, but as essential, for preserving democracy. They contend that any potential harm to national security is outweighed by the benefits of an independent press. Jerry Berman, former chief legislative counsel for the American Civil Liberties Union, wrote:

> Although I would not question the fact that some leaks may endanger national security, I would argue that they are necessary in this country, because in a democratic society the national security interest must be balanced against the public's right to know.[153]

As evidenced by the quotes of former DCIs William Casey and William Colby in Chapter 1, recognition of the benefits of a robust press extend beyond the news media. In 2007 former CIA Director Michael Hayden joined his predecessors in recognizing the media for the vital function they perform:

> I have a very deep respect for journalists and for their profession. Many of them—especially in the years since 9/11—have given their lives in the act of keeping our citizens informed. They are smart, dedicated, and courageous men and women. I count many of them as colleagues. We each have an important role to play in the defense of the Republic.[154]

The degree of support for the press may vary, though, as well as the belief in the propriety of publishing appropriately classified information.

In accordance with the principles of Rational Choice Theory, individuals who recognize the legitimacy of publishing classified information have concluded that the benefits can outweigh potential costs. In these circumstances, they would be motivated to publish classified information to achieve these benefits.

Journalist Motivations for Disclosing Classified Information

There are two general categories of motivations: altruistic and non-altruistic. The term "motivation" in this case is defined as "a desire which gives purpose and direction to behavior."[155] The primary focus for altruistic motivations is the welfare of others, while non-altruistic motivations are concerned with benefits to the individual.

Two altruistic motivations for members of the media to disclose classified information can be identified. As their name implies, their focus is on promoting societal rather than individual interests. Though closely related, they are distinct and will be examined separately.

Altruistic Motivation – Promoting Informed Debate

Enlightened choice by an informed citizenry is the basic ideal upon which an open society is premised, and a free press is thus indispensable to a free society.[156]

- *Justice Potter Stewart*

Being a democracy, the government cannot cloak its operations in secrecy. Adequate information as to its activities must be given to its citizens or the foundations of its democracy will be eaten away.[157]

- *Coolidge Report*

The motivation cited most frequently by proponents of the media's right to publish classified information is the desire to increase public knowledge and promote informed debate. The press embraces its role as a "Fourth Estate," publishing information regarding actions taken by the government on the public's behalf. In these cases, the publication of classified information is viewed as enhancing the American public's knowledge. The public can then use this information to debate the propriety and desirability of government actions.[158]

As described in the preamble to the Society of Professional Journalists' (SPJ) Code of Ethics, "Public enlightenment is the forerunner of justice and the foundation of democracy."[159] The body of the SPJ Code identifies four basic principles, the first of which is "Seek Truth and Report It." By placing such a high value on the dissemination of truth, the SPJ effectively increases the perceived benefit of publishing classified information. This, in turn, impacts the journalist's internal cost-benefit analysis, increasing the likelihood that he or she will conclude that these benefits outweigh any identified costs.

The Newspaper Association of America and the National Newspaper Association also recognize the significance of the media's role in informing the public. Prior to May 2006 Congressional hearings concerning unauthorized disclosures, the associations submitted a joint letter to the House Permanent Select Committee on Intelligence. The letter reads, in part: "The immediate effect of publication may arguably be harmful or beneficial. But the overall effect of public disclosures concerning the affairs of government is to enhance the people's ability to understand what the government is doing and to hold the government accountable."[160]

Members of the news media, as well as other advocates of the propriety of publishing classified information, identify several historical examples in which the value of an enlightened citizenry was perceived to overcome the potential harm to national security. The incident cited most frequently is the Pentagon Papers case.

Pentagon Papers

In June 1971, the Nixon administration obtained court orders enjoining both the *New York Times* and *Washington Post* from publishing articles containing information from a TOP SECRET study of the Vietnam War. Both papers had published articles containing classified information prior to the injunction. The *Times* and *Post* appealed the orders and the

Supreme Court ultimately agreed to hear the case. Arguing before the court, attorneys for both newspapers asserted that the public's right to be informed of decisions and actions taken by the government outweighed potential national security concerns.

In this case, the controversial government actions included the expansion of air strikes and ground operations in Laos, Cambodia, and North Vietnam and the alleged politicization of the timing of military operations. The *Times* specifically identified the motivation of informing the public in the opening paragraph of its first published article. The paragraph referred to the commitment of the Eisenhower, Kennedy, Johnson, and Nixon administrations to a non-communist South Vietnam "to a much greater extent than their public statements acknowledged at the time."[161]

On June 30, 1971, in a 6-to-3 decision, the Court ruled that the government had not overcome the heavy presumption against prior restraint and that the *Times* and *Post* could resume publication. In a rare occurrence, all nine justices published either a concurring or dissenting opinion. Three frequently cited excerpts, all from concurring opinions, specifically discuss the media's motivation to maintain an enlightened citizenry.[162]

In his concurring opinion, Justice William Douglas wrote: "Secrecy in government is fundamentally anti-democratic . . . Open debate and discussion of public issues are vital to our national health. On public questions, there should be uninhibited, robust, and wide-open debate." Justice Hugo Black wrote: "The press was protected so that it could bare the secrets of government and inform the people." He added, "The guarding of military and diplomatic secrets at the expense of informed representative government provides no real security for our Republic."

Justice Potter Stewart also recognized the benefits of an unrestrained press and an informed citizenry. Justice Stewart wrote: "The only effective restraint upon executive policy and power in the areas of national defense and international affairs may lie in an enlightened citizenry—in an informed and critical public opinion which alone can here protect the values of democratic government . . . For, without an informed and free press, there cannot be an enlightened people." Twenty-six years after the Supreme Court ruling, Katharine Graham, former chairman of the board of the *Washington Post*, published her memoirs. Graham had ultimately made the decision to publish the Pentagon Papers articles in the *Post*. In her memoirs, Graham explained her rationale for disclosing information from the classified government study: "[T]he material in the Pentagon Papers was just the kind of information the public needed in order to form its opinions and make its choices more wisely."[163] Graham believed that the publication was not a breach of national security, but the "obligation of a responsible newspaper."

Members of the media also routinely cite the failed CIA-supported coup in Cuba in 1961, the "Bay of Pigs" incident, as an example in which the nation was harmed by information being inappropriately withheld from the public. They conclude that preventing informed debate is contrary to the interests of the American public, and actually represents a greater threat to national security than the disclosure of classified information.

Bay of Pigs

In April 1961, the *New York Times* informed the Kennedy administration that it intended to publish an article regarding the CIA's training of anti-Castro guerrillas in Florida and Guatemala.[164] In response to an appeal from the administration, which focused on the potential harm to national security, the *Times* withheld much of the information and published a condensed article on April 7, 1961. One week later, the guerrilla forces landed in Cuba and were defeated. The defeat embarrassed the United States and solidified Castro's hold on Cuba. President Kennedy publicly condemned the media for "indiscriminate and premature reporting."[165] Privately, though, Kennedy is reported to have told the *New York Times* managing editor, "Maybe if you had printed more about the operation, you would have saved us from a colossal mistake."[166]

Forty-five years later, when defending their decisions to publish information related to the SWIFT financial database, editors from both the *New York Times* and *Los Angeles Times* referenced the Bay of Pigs incident. In an article published in the *Los Angeles Times*, Editor Dean Baquet wrote that the press had "an obligation to cover the government" and "offer information about its activities so citizens can make their own decisions."[167] Rather than citing an example in which the public benefited from the disclosure of information by the media, Baquet referenced the Bay of Pigs incident. Baquet wrote that Kennedy regretted persuading the press to withhold information on the invasion and might have terminated the operation had it been exposed.

In a similar editorial, *New York Times* Senior Editor Bill Keller also wrote of his paper's withholding of information related to the Bay of Pigs invasion. Keller added that the *Times'* "biggest failures have generally been when we failed to dig deep enough or to report fully enough."[168] Keller concluded that if the *Times* had not played down its advanced knowledge of the Bay of Pigs invasion, it might have "prevented a fiasco."[169]

Altruistic Motivation – Exposing Government Misconduct

There is a tradition of ferreting out governmental wrongdoing – waste, corruption, inefficiency – by disclosures to the press, which function as the guardians of the public in many, many cases.[170]

- Senator Arlen Specter

In addition to promoting informed debate, advocates of the legitimacy of disclosing classified information characterize the disclosures as an essential tool for exposing government abuse or illegal activity. Though federal whistleblower protections do not apply to disclosures of classified information to the media, many consider the press to be a legitimate forum for government employees to report misconduct, regardless of classification.

Reporting on the activities of the U.S. government has been a hallmark of the American media as far back as the country's first newspapers, such as Benjamin Franklin's *Pennsylvania Gazette*. The tradition of the media uncovering political (and corporate) corruption continued with the investigative reporting of the "muckrakers" of the late nineteenth and early twentieth centuries. These journalists published historically significant articles documenting illicit activity, including public corruption, abusive treatment in mental institutions, and objectionable conditions in the garment and meat-packing industries. On several occasions, the exposure of improprieties led to the enactment of legislation to address identified concerns.

In the early and mid-twentieth century, the U.S. media continued publishing information to keep the public informed of government activities. Throughout both World War I and World War II, media outlets were the primary means for the public to follow the progress of the war. War correspondents, such as Ernie Pyle and Edward R. Murrow, provided information to supplement information released by military press offices. Though the correspondents represented a source outside the military, journalists working in combat zones voluntarily agreed to government constraints, including allowing the military to review and censor their reporting. This trust between the government and media changed drastically in the latter half of the twentieth century.

The change can be traced to the late 1960's and early 1970's and the Vietnam War. Unprecedented political and public opposition to the war led to a desire for information outside official government channels. For many, Daniel Ellsberg's disclosure of the "Pentagon Papers" in 1971 signifies a turning point in the public's confidence and trust in government. Revelations from the Pentagon Papers included contradictions between public statements made by government officials and actual facts, as well as a confirmation of the politicization of both military operations and intelligence.

The disclosure of the Pentagon Papers validated an increasingly held belief that a robust oversight mechanism outside the government was necessary. It was during this period that the term "credibility gap" became widely used to describe the skepticism felt toward government officials. White House Chief of Staff H.R. Haldeman specifically discussed the impact of the Pentagon Papers' disclosure on the relationship between the government and the public:

> But out of the gobbledygook, comes a very clear thing: you can't trust the government; you can't believe what they say; and you can't rely on their judgment; and the – the implicit infallibility of presidents, which has been an accepted thing in America, is badly hurt by this, because it shows that people do things the President wants to do even though it's wrong, and the President can be wrong. [171]

If the existence of a credibility gap was validated by the Pentagon Papers, the Nixon administration's response to the disclosure only widened the chasm.

As noted above, after the initial disclosures in the *New York Times* and *Washington Post*, the administration attempted to enjoin the newspapers from publishing additional articles. The *Times* and *Post* appealed the government injunction and the Supreme Court ultimately ruled that the government had not met the high standard necessary to invoke prior restraint against the media. After losing its case in the Supreme Court, the administration indicted Ellsberg and Anthony Russo for disclosing classified information to the media. The government's waning credibility was further damaged when charges against Ellsberg and Russo were dismissed due to prosecutorial misconduct. This misconduct included the wiretapping of Ellsberg's telephone and the burglary of his psychiatrist's office by a White House "Special Investigations Unit," more infamously known as the "Plumbers."[172]

Beyond the Vietnam War and the Pentagon Papers, there are several additional examples in which unauthorized disclosures by the media are believed to have played an essential role in informing the public of government misconduct. These include:

The Family Jewels

On December 22, 1974, the front page of the *New York Times* read, "Huge CIA Operation Reported in U.S. against Antiwar Forces, Other Dissidents in Nixon Years."[173] The accompanying article detailed several incidents of CIA misconduct. Beyond the previously discussed surveillance of American journalists, the article identified additional abuses, including domestic CIA operations targeting anti-war organizations. The article's assertions were based on information contained in a classified 1973 CIA study known as the "Family Jewels."

The *New York Times'* disclosure of portions of this study is reported to have directly contributed to the establishment of three government commissions to examine Intelligence Community activities.[174] In 1975, President Ford established the President's Commission on CIA Activities within the United States, also known as the "Rockefeller Commission." The Senate and House of Representatives each established their own committees: the United States Senate Select Committee to Study Governmental Operations with Respect to Intelligence Activities (Church Committee) and the House Select Committee on Intelligence (Pike Committee). In addition to abuses committed by the CIA, the committees also identified misconduct by the National Security Agency, including the monitoring of international telegrams and communications of U.S. citizens involved in the anti-war movement.[175]

As a direct result of the committees' findings, several changes to the Intelligence Community were implemented, including enhanced Congressional and executive oversight. In 1978 the Federal Intelligence Surveillance Act (FISA) was enacted, and the Federal Intelligence Surveillance Court (FISC) was established to oversee requests for surveillance of suspected foreign agents inside the United States. Permanent committees for intelligence oversight were also established in the House (HPSCI) and Senate (SSCI). Based on findings concerning CIA involvement in plots to assassinate foreign leaders, including Fidel Castro, President Ford issued Executive Order 11905.[176] The Executive Order specifically prohibits government-sanctioned assassinations.

In 2007, Central Intelligence Agency Director Michael Hayden declassified greater portions of the Family Jewels report. The National Security Archive released these newly declassified portions in June 2007.[177]

Colonel Alpirez

In March 1995, the *New York Times* published an article identifying Guatemalan Colonel Julio Alpirez as a paid CIA informant.[178] The article alleged that, while working with the CIA, Alpirez was involved in the deaths of Michael Devine, a U.S. citizen living in Guatemala, and Efrain Bamaca, the spouse of a U.S. citizen. CIA officials were reportedly aware of the allegations but concealed their knowledge of Alpirez's involvement. The *Times* article cited a letter from Congressman Robert Torricelli of New Jersey to President Clinton.

After the allegations concerning Alpirez were published, the CIA's inspector general conducted an internal investigation. In response to the 700-page IG report, DCI John Deutch enacted several procedural changes within the agency.[179] These included the establishment of new standards for recruiting foreign sources and selecting managers for overseas offices. Deutch also made a commitment to report all human rights abuses by paid informants and to sever relations with these informants, if necessary. Deutch added that the CIA would ensure that Congress and relevant ambassadors were kept more informed of overseas CIA activity. In addition to the CIA's internal investigation, the Departments of Justice and State, and the President's Intelligence Oversight Board, conducted independent investigations.

The CIA IG report identified 26 officials culpable for maintaining the relationship with Alpirez and for withholding information.[180] At least two CIA officials, the chief of station in Guatemala and the chief of Latin America operations, were dismissed. Congressman Torricelli, identified as the source for the *New York Times* article, was not punished due to "ambiguity" in Congressional procedural rules.[181] Rules in the House of Representatives were subsequently modified to include a secrecy oath both for Congressmen and staffers. Torricelli was later elected to the U.S. Senate.

State Department employee Richard Nuccio, identified as having provided the original information to Torricelli, lost his security clearance and resigned. A State Department investigation determined he had prepared classified documents on his home computer and may have disclosed classified information to members of the media.[182] After his resignation, Nuccio was hired by Torricelli as his senior foreign policy advisor.

In 1997, two years after the original article concerning Alpirez was published, the *New York Times* reported that the CIA had severed ties with approximately 100 foreign agents. The agents, almost half from Latin America, were reportedly terminated because their value as informants was outweighed by their human rights abuses.[183]

Beyond the altruistic motivations identified by members of the media—informing the citizenry and exposing misconduct—several non-altruistic motivations can also impact a journalist's decision whether to publish classified information. These motivations, acknowledged by the media less frequently, if at all, include: (1) advancing corporate interests; (2) advancing personal interests; and (3) advancing foreign interests.

When defending the decision to publish classified information, members of the media, including Katharine Graham, Bill Keller, Dean Baquet, Dana Priest, and Eric Lichtblau, have each referred to the desire to inform the public and/or the responsibility to expose government misconduct. The desire to advance corporate interests (increase circulation and profits), personal interests (advance a career or personal agenda), or foreign interests (co-opted by a foreign government) were not cited. Though not identified in this context, members of the media, as well as U.S. and foreign government officials, have discussed these motivations.

Non-Altruistic Motivation – Advancing Corporate Interests

News organizations are highly competitive and sometimes their drive to be first to disclose major news can outweigh concern for disclosing sensitive secrets.[184]

- Jack Nelson, former Los Angeles Times Washington bureau chief

Members of the media recognize that a media outlet must be profitable to survive. Journalists' salaries must be paid, and the owners of television networks and newspapers, whether private or public, expect to earn a profit. Because the American public has several options for obtaining information, these outlets must compete to increase or maintain their market share. As the number of media outlets expands with the advent of new sources and media, such as cable television and the Internet, competition has only become more intense.

Former *Baltimore Sun* and *Boston Globe* reporter Lyle Denniston provided one of the most candid portrayals of this profit motive. At a 1984 panel sponsored by Columbia University, Denniston described a journalist's responsibility as it relates to the publication of classified information:

As a journalist, I have only one responsibility and that is to get a story and print it. It isn't a question of justification in terms of the law; it's a question of justifying it in terms of the commercial sale of information

39

to interested customers. That's my only business. The only thing I do in life is to sell information, hopefully for a profit.[185]

One method for a news organization to increase public interest is to be the first, or only source, to provide information to the public, to "scoop" the competition. Beyond Denniston, other members of the media have discussed the competitive nature of the news industry and the desire to be the first to "break the story." In 1986 former *Washington Post* CEO Katharine Graham wrote: "The electronic media in the United States live or die by their ratings, the number of viewers they attract," adding, "As a result, each network wants to be the first with the most on any big story. It's hard to stay cool in the face of this pressure."[186] *New York Times* journalist Eric Lichtblau echoed this sentiment two decades later. During a radio interview regarding his articles on the SWIFT database and NSA Terrorist Surveillance Program, Lichtblau stated, "Journalism for better or worse is a very competitive business and there's a high premium on having something exclusively."[187]

Government officials also recognize the impact of this motivation among members of the media. During debate on a House Resolution condemning the *New York Times* for publishing an article related to the SWIFT database, Congressman Michael Oxley expressed his belief that the editors of the *Times* are "more concerned about their sagging circulation rates and about damaging the Bush administration than they are about disrupting terrorist financing."[188] Recognition of this profit motive extends beyond U.S. borders.

In 1992 Stanislav Lunev, former intelligence officer for Russia's military intelligence organization, Glavnoye Razvedovatel'noye Upravlenie (GRU), defected to the United States. Prior to his defection, Lunev collected intelligence in the United States under non-official cover. After defecting, Lunev published his biography, *Through the Eyes of the Enemy*. In it, Lunev discusses this non-altruistic motivation, writing: "In my view, Americans tend to care more about scooping their competition than about national security, which made my job easier."[189]

One example in which the desire to advance corporate interests was identified as a contributing factor in the publication of classified information is the aforementioned Pentagon Papers case. Though it may not have been the primary motivation for the *New York Times* or the *Washington Post*, it appears to have played a role in their decision-making process.

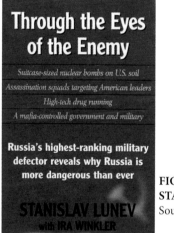

FIGURE 2 – *THROUGH THE EYES OF THE ENEMY* – STANISLAV LUNEV [190]
Source: Regnery Publishing. Used with permission.

Pentagon Papers

When the *New York Times* began publishing articles containing excerpts from the "Pentagon Papers," *Washington Post* Executive Editor Ben Bradlee did not applaud the *Times'* ability to increase public knowledge or expose government misconduct. In his memoirs, Bradlee wrote, "[W]e found ourselves in the humiliating position of having to rewrite the competition."[191] In her memoirs, Katharine Graham, former CEO of the Post wrote that Bradlee "anguished over being scooped."[192] When the Nixon administration obtained an injunction to prevent the Times from publishing additional articles, rather than denouncing the government's attempt to suppress the free flow of information Bradlee wrote, "At least the *New York Times* had been silenced, never mind how."

When detailing the *Washington Post's* acquisition of portions of the Pentagon Papers and the decision to publish its own articles, Bradlee discussed the benefits, not only for the public, but also for the Washington Post Corporation. Bradlee wrote, "I knew exactly how important it was to publish, if we were to have any chance of pulling the *Post* up – once and for all – into the front ranks." After the Supreme Court ruled that the government could not impose prior restraint to prevent publication, Graham wrote that publishing the Pentagon Paper articles "went a long way toward advancing the interests of the *Post*."

The motivation of advancing corporate interests was apparently not confined to the *Washington Post*. Supreme Court Chief Justice Warren Burger recognized that the *New York Times* also shared this motivation. In his concurring opinion, Burger discussed how the motivation of advancing corporate interests might have surpassed the motivation to enlighten the citizenry. Burger points out that the *Times* elected to copyright material it had published from the Pentagon Papers and had also considered enjoining the use of the material by other publishers.[193] These actions would have diminished the public's ability to obtain this information.

The aversion to being "scooped" and the connotation of its harm to corporate interests is often discussed in relation to the disclosure of classified information. During a 2006 interview, Ben Bradlee discussed NBC's decision to broadcast a news report related to the classified operation IVY BELLS while his paper was still considering government objections. Rather than blaming NBC for acting irresponsibly, Bradlee referred to "an excess of caution on our part, which cost us the story."[194] Robert Kaiser, former managing editor of the *Post*, also identified how delaying publication to consider government concerns ultimately harmed the newspaper:

> We equivocated for weeks. Finally, NBC News scooped us on our own story, then we published our version. As the editor supervising preparation of the story, I was humiliated; I also learned a good lesson.[195]

There are additional historical examples in which a media outlet was "scooped" after taking the time to consider government objections. Rather than faulting the other media outlet for acting irresponsibly, members of the media have expressed regret for withholding the information. Discussing the *Los Angeles Times*' decision to publish its article related to the SWIFT database, after previously withholding publication, Editor Dean Baquet stated: "I wish I'd gotten my story up before the *New York Times* did."[196] After the *Los Angeles Times* published a 1975 article regarding the classified operation AZORIAN, Seymour Hersh, who had agreed to withhold publication a year earlier, stated, "I hit my head and said 'Dumbbell.'"[197]

After it was determined that a 2004 CBS broadcast that raised questions about President Bush's service in the Air National Guard had relied on forged documents, the network established an independent panel to examine the incident. The panel faulted CBS executives for their "myopic zeal" to be the first to broadcast the information.[198]

Non-Altruistic Motivation – Advancing Personal Interests

The authority and responsibility to determine what information to protect in the national interest is given to the President; it is not for private individuals to decide to disclose information in their own self interest.[199]

- Rep. Peter Hoekstra (R-NY)

Beyond any benefit to a corporation, such as the *New York Times* or the *Washington Post*, the potential for personal advancement can similarly impact the decision to disclose classified information. This personal benefit can come in many forms, from an increased salary or promotion, to more prominent placement of articles in a newspaper or magazine, to professional and public recognition. Unauthorized disclosures can also advance personal interests through the promotion of an individual's political ideology or other agenda.

Both the journalism community and the public recognize the prestige associated with being awarded a Pulitzer Prize. In addition to the $10,000 cash award, recipients are often referred to as "Pulitzer Prize- winning author/journalist . . ." Acknowledgment for excellence in any field also normally corresponds directly to career advancement.

Journalists recently awarded a Pulitzer Prize for articles that disclosed classified information include *Washington Post* journalist Dana Priest and *New York Times* journalists James Risen and Eric Lichtblau. Priest was awarded the Pulitzer Prize for Beat Reporting in 2006 for her article concerning overseas CIA detention facilities. Risen and Lichtblau were awarded Pulitzer Prizes for National Reporting, also in 2006, for their article related to the NSA Terrorist Surveillance Program. Though the authors of the *New York Times*' Pentagon Papers articles did not receive an individual award, the *New York Times* was awarded a Pulitzer Prize for Public Service in 1972.

FIGURE 3 – DOONESBURY, DECEMBER 22, 1986
Source: DOONESBURY@1986, G.B. Trudeau. Reprinted with permission of UNIVERSAL UCLICK.

Members of the media have cited the awards as an affirmation of the propriety of disclosing classified information. Speaking about the 2006 prizes, Bill Keller stated: "The Pulitzer judges have put a premium . . . on journalism that demonstrated the press standing up to power, often with substantial consequences," adding "Prizes don't always say anything terribly important about the state of our business, but this year's Pulitzers do, and what they say is: The country has never needed us more than it does today."[200] In a joint column, ABC correspondent Cokie Roberts and her husband, former *New York Times* reporter Steve Roberts, wrote that the 2006 Pulitzer Prizes "recognize the sort of journalism—courageous, costly and comprehensive—that only papers can provide."[201]

In addition to the prospective career benefits of a Pulitzer Prize, the disclosure of classified information has also been used in a more direct manner to promote a journalist's personal interests. This includes the publication of classified information in a book rather than in a newspaper. If the assumption is made that it takes longer to publish a book than a newspaper article, then the decision must have been made by the author to withhold information from the public until the book could be published.

This decision to withhold classified information for inclusion in a book has been a source of controversy on at least two occasions.

Veil

In 1987, *Washington Post* reporter Bob Woodward published the book *Veil: The Secret Wars of the CIA 1981-1987*. The book contained information obtained from interviews with former DCI William Casey. This information reportedly could have had an impact on the prior year's Tower Commission, which investigated the sale of arms to Iran and the diversion of funds to support Contra rebels in Nicaragua.[202] Rather than publishing the information in the *Washington Post* prior to or during hearings, Woodward withheld the information until after the Commission had published its final report.

As described by journalist Tim Hackler, "In this case, the 'public's right to know' seems to have been superseded by Woodward's right to high royalty payments."[203] *New York Times* columnist Flora Lewis wrote: "There is a risk of undermining the important constitutional guarantee on which we all rely if the judgment on when to publish and how is seen to turn on sheer commercial impact."[204]

State of War

Similar questions regarding the timing of publication and withholding of information were raised in 2006 when reporter James Risen's book *State of War* was published. It was less than a month before the book's publication that the *Times* published Risen and Lichtblau's article regarding the NSA Terrorist Surveillance Program. In a separate article, published by the *Times*' Public Editor, it was reported that the *Times* had been aware that *State of War* was scheduled to be published in the near future.[205] The article speculates that the decision to disclose classified information the *Times* had previously withheld may have been affected by the motivation of advancing corporate interests: "the paper was quite aware that it faced the possibility of being scooped by its own reporter's book in about four weeks." In a published statement, *New York Times* Executive Editor Bill Keller denied that the decision to publish the article was related to the publication of Risen's book.[206]

After Risen was reportedly subpoenaed to testify before a grand jury about information appearing in the book, the *Times* published another article. This article emphasized that the paper had not published the information appearing in the chapter in question.[207] What was unclear was whether the *Times* had been aware of the information and chose not to publish, or if Risen had withheld the information from the newspaper.

The authors of *Choosing White-Collar Crime* specifically discuss the motivation of advancing personal interests in reference to Rational Choice Theory. They describe how additional variables, such as the pressure to succeed, can impact the ability to rationally weigh costs and benefits. This may be particularly relevant in the intensely competitive news business:

> Performance pressure . . . (has) been linked repeatedly to increased likelihood that criminal choices will be made. Performance pressure is anxiety or fear induced in individuals or organizational units by the perceived need to maintain or improve performance standards. This can be the need to increase profit margins . . . but in all cases it stems from belief that performance has not measured up in the eyes of peers of superiors. Performance pressure is communicated in countless ways, and it can cause employees to be less concerned with legalities.[208]

Collateral Murder

Personal interests can be advanced, not only through professional recognition or financial gain but also by promoting a personal agenda. In April 2010, the Internet-based organization WikiLeaks posted a video on its website documenting an airstrike by two U.S. Apache helicopters in Baghdad, Iraq. Of the 11 reported casualties, two were employees of the news agency Reuters. One of the Reuters employees had been carrying a camera with a telephoto lens, mistaken for a weapon by an Apache crewman. Two children seated inside a van were also injured during the attack.

WikiLeaks founder Julian Assange edited the original 39-minute video to a 17-minute video he titled "Collateral Murder."[209] Both videos were posted on the WikiLeaks website, though Assange confirmed that 90 percent of the viewers accessed only the edited video. The 17-minute video makes no mention of prior gunfire in the area and focuses attention on the Reuters reporters and not on the Iraqis, who were later confirmed to have been armed with an AK-47 and a rocket-propelled grenade launcher. Assange confirmed editing the original video and adding the title for "maximum possible political impact." Assange added that he believed the attack was equivalent to murder. During a subsequent interview, Assange identified his desire for WikiLeaks disclosures to change the opinions of policymakers and the public, and to end the war in Afghanistan.[210]

Whether the motivations of advancing corporate or personal interests are discussed less often than their more altruistic counterparts, journalists would certainly not volunteer information concerning the third non-altruistic motivation, advancing foreign interests.

Non-Altruistic Motivation – Advancing Foreign Interests

It is no secret that foreign intelligence agencies use reporters as agents. During the Cold War, KGB agents routinely used reporters' credentials as cover for their activities.[211]

- Rep. Benjamin Gilman, Chairman, House International Relations Committee

During testimony before the House International Relations Committee in 2000, an FBI official verified that the Bureau was aware of foreign intelligence officers assuming notional positions as journalists.[212] Prior to his defection to the United States in 1992, former Russian GRU intelligence officer Stanislav Lunev worked in the United States under journalistic cover. Lunev worked as a correspondent for the Russian news organization TASS. In a 2000 article Lunev wrote that, in addition to posing as journalists, Russian intelligence officers actively recruited members of the American media due to their access to political, military, and intelligence officials.[213] Lunev confirmed that he had personally recruited American journalists to collect information and described the number of American journalists working on Russia's behalf as "very big." Lunev believed that Russia had successfully penetrated all major press outlets in the United States.

A second Russian intelligence officer, KGB Colonel Vitaly Yurchenko, also discussed Russia's recruitment of a member of the American media. After defecting to the United States in August 1985, Yurchenko identified NSA analyst Ronald Pelton and former CIA case officer Edward Lee Howard as Soviet spies. Pelton was convicted of espionage and Howard defected to the Soviet Union prior to being arrested. In addition to Pelton and Howard, Yurchenko reportedly informed the CIA that *Washington Post* Moscow Bureau Chief Dusko Doder had accepted money from a KGB officer.[214]

After the FBI was unable to corroborate Yurchenko's information regarding Doder, FBI Director William Webster discussed the issue with *Washington Post* Executive Editor Ben Bradlee. Doder was scheduled to return to Washington to cover the Intelligence Community for the *Post*. When confronted, Doder denied the allegations and agreed to submit to a polygraph examination. In his autobiography, Ben Bradlee wrote that the examination was never conducted because Ed Williams, an attorney for the *Post*, opposed the idea.[215] Before the matter was resolved, Doder resigned from the *Post* and accepted an assignment in China with the *U.S. News and World Report*. In November 1985, three months after defecting, Yurchenko redefected to the Soviet Union.

Journalist Justifications for Disclosing Classified Information

In addition to the five identified motivations, advocates of the media's ability to publish classified information cite several justifications for this action. The term "justification" is defined as a fact or circumstance that shows an action to be reasonable or necessary.[216] Beyond Rational Choice Theory's balance of risk and reward, an individual must conclude that his/her action will be considered reasonable or necessary by peers and the general public (as well as internally). This ability to justify an action, once completed, must be considered along with the motivations that initially directed the behavior. If an individual cannot conclude that a combination of perceived motivations and justifications outweigh the identified costs, he/she will discontinue the activity.

The five identified justifications for a member of the media to publish classified information include: (1) government overclassification; (2)

the hypocrisy of the government condoning politically advantageous disclosures; (3) the inability or unwillingness of Congress to provide adequate oversight; (4) the perceived legal authority under the First Amendment; and (5) the ability to handle classified information in a responsible manner.

Justification – Government Overclassification

A very first principle . . . would be an insistence upon avoiding secrecy for its own sake. For when everything is classified, then nothing is classified, and the system becomes one to be disregarded by the cynical or the careless, and to be manipulated by those intent on self-protection or self-promotion . . . [S]ecrecy can best be preserved only when credibility is truly maintained.[217]

- Justice Potter Stewart

I have revealed no secrets because I have told nothing that was, or I conceive, ought to be a secret.[218]

- Thomas Paine

The U.S. government classifies a vast amount of information. A study completed by the National Archives concluded that 8.7 million classification decisions were made in 2001.[219] According to a 2002 report by the Information Security Oversight Office (ISOO), the 8.7 million classification decisions were the highest recorded level for classification actions and a 44 percent increase over the prior year.[220] In 2005, after the commencement of military operations in Afghanistan and Iraq, the number of classification decisions climbed from 8.7 million to 14 million.[221] A 2006 ISOO report indicated that the level had risen once more, to over 20 million classification decisions.[222]

Continued globalization will increase the number of world events impacting U.S. interests. This will require the U.S. Intelligence Community to collect and analyze greater amounts of information. As technology improves, IC collection capabilities will similarly progress. Taken together, globalization and enhanced collection capabilities will likely result in a continued increase in the quantity of classified intelligence maintained by the government.

In terms of personnel, a 2010 *Washington Post* article reported that over 850,000 civilian employees, military personnel, and government contractors held a TOP SECRET security clearance.[223] The article also reported that there were more than 1,000 government organizations and almost 2,000 private companies in the United States conducting work on intelligence, counterterrorism, and homeland security programs.

One of the most frequently cited justifications for the media's publication of classified information is the perception that the U.S. government classifies information unnecessarily. This overclassification results in information being improperly withheld from the U.S. public. Examining the issue of overclassification in 1979, a Government Accountability Office (GAO) study concluded that 24 percent of documents classified by the Department of Defense contained instances of overclassification.[224] As a consequence of the increased volume of classified information and the number of individuals authorized to make classification decisions, there is a legitimate concern that the level of improperly classified information will also have increased. If the percentage of overclassifications reported in the Defense Department in 1979 were extrapolated to the 20 million classification decisions made in 2006, it would equate to approximately five million instances of overclassification.

Recognition of the issue of overclassification extends throughout all levels of government as well as the private sector. Former DCI William Colby acknowledged that there were both "bad secrets" and "non-secrets" in addition to appropriately classified intelligence.[225] Former DCI William Casey agreed that too much information was classified.[226]

Moving from the Executive Branch to the Legislative, several Congressmen have discussed the issue of overclassification. In June 2000, while chairman of the SSCI, Senator Richard Shelby stated: "There's too much classified, and a lot of it is classified for the wrong reasons, to probably withhold things from the public that should never have been withheld."[227] Six months later, while condemning President Clinton's veto of his proposed amendment to amend the Espionage Act, Senator Shelby conceded, "Critics also cite—correctly—the Government's tendency to overclassify information, especially embarrassing information, the disclosure of which would not damage national security..."[228]

During 2006 Senate hearings concerning unauthorized disclosures, Senator Patrick Leahy (nicknamed "Leaky Leahy" for his own alleged involvement in the disclosure of classified information) commented: "We know some . . . intelligence information was classified simply to cover up mistakes made by this administration. In fact, many, many, many times things were classified to cover up mistakes by the administration."[229]

The Defense Department recognized the danger of overclassification as far back as the 1956 Coolidge Report:

> [O]verclassification has reached serious proportions. The result is not only that the system fails to supply to the public information which its proper operation would supply, but the system has become so overloaded that proper protection of information which should be protected has suffered. The press regards the stamp of classification with feelings which vary from indifference to active contempt.[230]

In addition to government officials, several prominent members of the media have discussed overclassification as a justification for the publication of classified information. During a 1988 interview for the *American Intelligence Journal, Washington Post* reporter Bob Woodward remarked that he believed overclassification was "totally out of control."[231] In his 1995 autobiography, former *Washington Post* Executive Editor Ben Bradlee wrote, "Officials—more often than not, in my experience—use the claim of national security as a smoke screen to cover up their own embarrassment."[232]

As the result of studies conducted by ISOO documenting increased levels of classified information in the executive branch, President Obama established the National Declassification Center in January 2010. The mission of the Center is to develop greater efficiencies and to expedite the declassification process.[233] In October 2010, President Obama also signed into law P.L. 111-258, the "Reducing Over-Classification Act."[234] The law is intended to discourage overclassification by, among other things, requiring inspectors general to annually assess classification activities within executive branch agencies, and mandating regular training on proper classification procedures. J. William Leonard, director of ISOO, summarized the issue fittingly. Leonard remarked he had seen information classified that he had also seen published in third grade textbooks.[235]

Justification – Continued Toleration for Politically Advantageous Disclosures

[T]he most damaging revelations of intelligence sources and methods are generated primarily by Executive Branch officials pushing a particular policy . . . Preventing damage to intelligence sources and methods from media leaks will not be possible until the highest level of the Administration ceases to disclose classified information on a classified basis for political purposes.[236]

- Senator Jay Rockefeller

As opposed to withholding information that should not be classified, critics also identify the hypocrisy of government officials publicly decrying unauthorized disclosures as harmful, while simultaneously condoning or even encouraging politically advantageous disclosures. Allegations of this double standard do not appear to be a partisan issue. Both Democrat and Republican administrations have been accused of placing political considerations above national security concerns.

The practice of disclosing classified information to the media to influence policy, and its associated harm, was recognized by the 1978 SSCI Subcommittee on Secrecy and Disclosure. In a report to the full Committee, the Subcommittee noted:

[T]his type of security leak (the disclosure of classified information to a journalist) has become part of a flourishing informal and quasi-legal system . . . There are two major drawbacks to the sub rosa practice of providing selected intelligence information to the news media and other sources. First, the public does not necessarily receive a balanced view from the leaked information because the process is informal. Second, and more importantly, information whose secrecy is vital to our national security is sometimes disclosed.[237]

In the 1996, Report to the National Security Council on unauthorized disclosures, "selective leaking" was identified as one of the primary reasons why efforts to prevent disclosures were not successful. The report cited the following excerpt from the 1987 Tower Commission Iran-Contra report: "[S] elective leaking has evolved to the point that it is a principal means of waging bureaucratic warfare and a primary tool in the process of policy formulation and development in Washington."[238]

In response to the 2006 *New York Times* disclosure related to the SWIFT database, the House of Representatives passed a resolution condemning the unauthorized disclosure of classified information. During deliberation, Representative Louise Slaughter, chairman of the House Rules Committee, stated that the Bush administration had "always been willing to leak even the most sensitive information if it thought it would benefit from it politically."[239] She added: "But if a leak contradicts their agenda, suddenly they call it treason. They suffer from a case of selective outrage." The Bush administration was also perceived to have condoned the disclosure of classified information to garner public support prior to the 2003 invasion of Iraq. Opponents accused the Bush administration of "cherry-picking" intelligence reports and assessments that supported their position.

Pre-War Intelligence on Iraq

Five months prior to the March 2003 invasion of Iraq, Senator Bob Graham, chairman of the SSCI, accused the Bush administration of "selectively disclosing classified information that corresponds more closely to its political agenda than to national security concerns."[240] In a letter to the Director of National Intelligence regarding the Bush administration's use of intelligence, Senator Jay Rockefeller also decried the abuse of intelligence for political purposes.[241] Rockefeller specifically cited disclosures of classified information concerning Iraq's acquisition of aluminum tubes, intelligence regarding Iraq's attempts to purchase uranium, and the Iraqi government's alleged connections with Al Qaeda.

Critics of the politicization of prewar intelligence also cite the February 5, 2003, briefing by General Colin Powell to the United Nations Security Council. During the UN briefing, Powell disclosed communications, imagery, and human intelligence.[242]

The debate over the Bush administration's politicization of intelligence became even more divisive when Robert Novak published a column in

FIGURE 4 – FEBRUARY 5, 2003, PRESENTATION TO THE UN [243]
Source: Department of State.

July 2003 identifying Valerie Plame as a covert CIA officer.[244] A special prosecutor was appointed to investigate the disclosure, which ultimately led to the indictment of Vice President Dick Cheney's Chief of Staff, Scooter Libby. Libby was indicted for perjury, obstruction of justice, and making false statements (Assistant Secretary of State Richard Armitage was identified as the individual who had initially disclosed Plame's identity).

During court proceedings, Libby testified that he had received approval from the President, through Vice President Cheney, to disclose portions of a classified National Intelligence Estimate (NIE) to defend the administration's use of pre-war intelligence.[245] During the same period Libby had reportedly received authority to disclose this information to the media, National Security Advisor Stephen Hadley and other administration officials were in the process of debating whether to declassify the information.[246]

Special Prosecutor Patrick Fitzgerald concluded that the intent of authorizing the disclosure of NIE material was to respond to criticism by Plame's husband, former Ambassador Joe Wilson.[247] Though not convicted for the disclosure of Plame's identity, Libby was convicted for obstruction of justice. Before leaving office, President George W. Bush granted Libby clemency.

Democratic administrations have also been accused of condoning the selective disclosure of classified information. In 1980 the Carter administration faced accusations regarding the politically motivated disclosure of intelligence concerning the development of Stealth technology.

Stealth

Three months prior to the November 1980 Presidential election, an ABC broadcast and articles published in the *Washington Post* and *Aviation Weekly* disclosed classified information regarding a program to develop military aircraft that could evade enemy radar.[248] On August 22, 1980, in response to the disclosures, Secretary of Defense Harold Brown held a press conference confirming the existence of the "Stealth" program. The reason given for acknowledging the program was to create a firewall to prevent future disclosures.[249]

President Carter's opponent in the upcoming election, Ronald Reagan, accused the Carter administration of deliberately leaking the information to make Carter appear stronger on defense issues. Prior events, including the cancellation of the B-1 bomber program and the failed attempt to rescue American hostages in Iran, may have led to a perception that President Carter had been weak on defense issues. It was reported that Secretary Brown's press conference regarding the Stealth program was scheduled to precede the release of the government report concerning the failed hostage rescue attempt.[250]

General Richard Ellis, commander of Strategic Air Command, stated that the disclosures regarding the Stealth program gave the Soviets years of advance warning, increasing their ability to create countermeasures and reduce the effectiveness of Stealth technology.[251] Ellis had requested that the administration disavow the information. The Carter administration concluded that leaks of the program were inevitable, as a consequence of the thousands of workers involved in the program.

Between August and October 1980, the House Armed Services Committee held hearings regarding the impact of the disclosures. The committee had been briefed on the program two days prior to the media disclosures, but had reportedly received less information than had been disclosed by the press.[252] During the hearings, Benjamin Schemmer, editor of *Armed Forces Journal*, testified regarding an article he had published.[253] Schemmer claimed that he had been contacted by the Pentagon and given approval to publish an article he had previously withheld at the administration's request. He also testified that William Perry, Under Secretary of Defense and future Secretary of Defense, had provided additional information for the final article. Schemmer told the committee that he believed the information regarding Stealth technology was disclosed for political reasons.

A former Chief of Naval Operations, Admiral Elmo Zumwalt, testified that President Carter had deliberately disclosed information on the Stealth program so that its existence could be officially announced and the administration could take credit for it.[254] Admiral Zumwalt identified David Aaron, Deputy Assistant to the President for National Security Affairs, as the media's source of information. Aaron denied disclosing classified information, but refused to testify before the committee based on a dispute over executive privilege. The final Congressional report, released in February 1981, concluded that official confirmation of the program had caused "serious damage . . . to the security of the United States and our ability to deter or to contain a potential Soviet threat."[255]

As long as the appearance persists that senior government officials are willing to disclose classified information for political gain, attempts to persuade the media to reduce other "non-sanctioned" disclosures will be difficult.

Justification – Inadequacy of Congressional Oversight

Congressional oversight of the Executive branch is anemic. [I]f we fail to conduct serious oversight, then we are inviting the problem.[256]

- *Rep. Jane Harman (D-CA)*

Closely tied to a journalist's motivation of maintaining an informed citizenry is the belief that the press is the entity most capable of providing oversight of government activity. Congressional oversight is often portrayed as inadequate, either due to a lack of will or a lack of ability, particularly when a single political party controls both the White House and Congress.

In this case Congress is depicted simply as a "rubber-stamp" rather than a true oversight body. Alternatively, if the opposition party controls a narrowly divided Congress, the ability to perform oversight is perceived to be impaired by political partisanship.

Members of both the media and the Intelligence Community have expressed concern over the effectiveness of Congressional oversight. *Washington Post* reporter Dana Priest described Congressional oversight as "dysfunctional"[257] and *New York Times* reporter James Risen depicted Republican oversight of the Bush administration as "docile."[258] Senator Lee Hamilton, former Chairman of the HPSCI and Vice Chairman of the 9/11 Commission, concluded that Congressional oversight was broken due to partisanship, a lack of far-sightedness, and the infrequency of oversight meetings.[259] In 1986 Senator Patrick Leahy, former Vice Chairman of the SSCI, made the remarkable assertion that members of both the HPSCI and SSCI often learned of IC activities through unauthorized disclosures in the media.[260]

In 2006, the minority (Democratic) staff for the House Committee on Government Reform prepared a report regarding Congressional oversight during the Bush administration. Fifteen instances were identified in which proper oversight was believed not to have occurred.[261] Of these fifteen identified instances, four were specifically related to Intelligence Community activities. During opening remarks for a 2006 Senate Judiciary Committee hearing, Committee Chairman Arlen Specter stated that one purpose of the hearing was to examine "growing concern that the Congress of the United States has not exercised its constitutional responsibilities on oversight."[262]

Intertwined with the perceived lack of intelligence oversight is the alleged inadequacy of current federal whistleblower statutes. The 1998 Intelligence Community Whistleblower Protection Act (ICWPA) specifically addresses procedures for reporting fraud, abuse, or illegal activity involving classified programs through appropriate channels. Similar to the concerns raised over Congressional oversight, media and government officials have expressed their apprehension over the effectiveness of the whistleblower process. In 2006 *New York Times* reporter Eric Lichtblau offered his perspective on this issue:

There are whistleblowers who will tell you that they have done just that (gone to the Intelligence Committee in the House or the Senate) and have found that they've been retaliated against or could not find a venue, even in Congress. So whether or not that process works is debatable.[263]

During 2006 HPSCI hearings regarding the publication of classified information, HPSCI chairman, Rep. Peter Hoekstra remarked, "We need to make sure the whistleblower process is working so people don't feel their only alternative is going to the press."[264]

Former NSA senior executive Thomas Drake, indicted in 2010 for activities related to the disclosure of classified information to the media, is reported to have attempted to pursue internal whistleblower processes prior to his alleged disclosures to the media.[265] According to media reporting, Drake was a source for a 2001 complaint filed with the Defense Department inspector general's office. The complaint alleged mismanagement of a program named Trailblazer, intended to analyze digital data collected by NSA. Drake was a proponent of an earlier program, Thin Thread, which Trailblazer had replaced. In addition to the inspector general, Drake reportedly notified his superiors and members of Congress before allegedly providing classified information to the media.

The *Baltimore Sun* published articles concerning Trailblazer in 2006 and 2007. At the time the articles were published, NSA's inspector general is reported to have already concluded that Trailblazer had been mismanaged. The NSA Director, General Michael Hayden, also reportedly acknowledged that Trailblazer was ineffective and had run millions of dollars over its intended budget.

Additional details regarding federal whistleblower statutes and the indictment of Thomas Drake are included in the Appendix.

Justification – Legal Protection for the Press under the First Amendment

We have a first amendment right to publish things, even irresponsibly.[266]

- Bob Woodward

Members of the media contend that the Founding Fathers specifically provided protections under the First Amendment to the U.S. Constitution for the press to collect and publish classified information. They reference this justification frequently when discussing the issue of unauthorized disclosures, asserting that this protection is based on a recognition of the benefits to the American public.

Journalists Dana Priest from the *Washington Post* and Eric Lichtblau from the *New York Times*, each awarded a Pulitzer Prize for articles containing classified information, have acknowledged the critical role of the First Amendment in American journalism. At a 2006 American Bar Association Conference, Priest remarked: "Most of the protections in the Bill of Rights are for individuals, but the free press clause protects an institution, the publishing business."[267] In response to a question concerning journalists acquiring classified information, Lichtblau stated: "Most lawyers will tell you that it is not a crime for any news organization in this country to disseminate information that could arguably be considered classified. That's why we have the First Amendment . . ."[268]

Support for Priest's and Lichtblau's position can be found within the Judicial Branch. In a 1974 speech, Justice Potter Stewart remarked that the primary purpose of the First Amendment was to create "a fourth institution outside the government as an additional check on the three official branches."[269] Several judges have held that national security concerns cannot easily, or perhaps ever, override First Amendment protections. Though Fourth Circuit Court of Appeals Judge Harvie Wilkinson upheld the conviction of Samuel Morison for disclosing classified information to the media, he wrote: "The First Amendment interest in informed popular debate does not simply vanish at the invocation of the words 'national security.' National security is public security, not government security from informed criticism."[270] In a concurring opinion in the Pentagon Papers case, Justice Hugo Black wrote:

> "The term 'security' is a broad, vague generality whose contours should not be invoked to abrogate the fundamental law embodied in the First Amendment. The guarding of military and diplomatic secrets at the expense of informed representative government provides no real security for our Republic."[271]

One other significant legal issue concerns the applicability of the 1917 Espionage Act to members of the media. Individuals who recognize the collective benefits of unauthorized disclosures contend that the provisions of the Act do not, and were never intended to, apply to journalists and are overridden by First Amendment protections. Though the Espionage Act originally included a provision which would have made it unlawful to publish certain information during a time of war, the provision was ultimately rejected.[272] Jack Nelson, former *Los Angeles Times* Washington bureau chief, wrote: "The legislative history of the Espionage Act clearly shows that Congress' original intent was to punish spies, not those who disclose information to inform the public."[273] *New York Times* reporter James Risen justified the legality of unauthorized disclosures, including his own, by observing, "I think the First Amendment came first, before the Espionage Act."[274]

Whether intentional or not, Risen's comment appears to be a reference to the historic Supreme Court case Marbury v. Madison, 5 U.S. 137 (1803). In Marbury v. Madison, the Supreme Court ruled that if a law enacted by Congress conflicts with the Constitution, the law would be invalid. At least one federal judge appears to share Risen's sentiments regarding the applicability of the Espionage Act to members of the press. In the 1988 Fourth Circuit ruling denying Samuel Morison's appeal of his conviction, Judge Harvie Wilkinson wrote: "[P]ress organizations . . . probably could not be prosecuted under the espionage statute."[275] Capturing the essence of this justification, Judge Wilkinson added: "Criminal restraints on the disclosure of information threaten the ability of the press to scrutinize and report on government activity."[276]

The contention that the media should be considered a legitimate entity to provide oversight, particularly for Intelligence Community programs, requires one additional justification. In order to respond to allegations that unauthorized disclosures harm national security, advocates of the propriety of these disclosures assert that members of the media have the ability to handle classified information responsibly.

Justification – The Ability of the Media to Handle Classified Information Responsibly

I have been gratified by the readiness of many of you (members of the Society of Professional Journalists) to carefully consider on occasion withholding publication of information which could jeopardize national interests or to present a story in a way that meets the public need yet minimized potential damage to intelligence sources.[277]

- DCI William Casey

When the media obtains especially sensitive information, we are willing to tell the authorities what we have learned and what we plan to report. (The media) want to do nothing that would endanger human life or national security. We are willing to cooperate with the authorities in withholding information that could have those consequences.[278]

- Katharine Graham

The justification cited most frequently by advocates of the media's right to publish classified information is that journalists are capable of balancing the responsibility to inform the public with the necessity to protect national security. When discussing this justification, the media often refer to their willingness to speak with government officials prior to publication and seriously consider any concerns they might have. As described by the Newspaper Association of America and the National Newspaper Association, this dialogue helps protects against the publication of information that could truly harm national security.[279]

Both the journalists who compose articles containing classified information and the senior editors who authorize their publication have identified the desire to make informed decisions. In a joint letter to the HPSCI, Tom Brokaw, Walter Cronkite, and Ted Koppel wrote that deliberations regarding the publication of classified information almost always involve discussions with government officials.[280] Editors from the *Wall Street Journal, New York Times*, and *Los Angeles Times* have each discussed their willingness to inform government officials when considering the publication of classified information.

In a joint 2006 article entitled "When Do We Publish a Secret," Bill Keller, executive editor of the *New York Times*, and Dean Baquet, editor of the *Los Angeles Times*, wrote"

> No article on a classified program gets published until the responsible officials have been given a fair opportunity to comment. And if they want to argue that publication represents a danger to national security, we put things on hold and give them a respectful hearing. Often, we agree to participate in off-the-record conversations with officials, so they can make their case without fear of spilling more secrets onto our front pages.[281]

Four years later, in 2010, the *New York Times* published another article discussing its decision-making process.[282] The article followed the publication of an article by the *Times* detailing the contents of thousands of classified military reports provided by the Internet-based organization WikiLeaks:

> Deciding whether to publish secret information is always difficult, and after weighing the risks and public interest, we sometimes chose not to publish. But there are times when the information is of significant public interest, and this is one of those times. The documents illuminate the extraordinary difficulty of what the United States and its allies have undertaken in a way that other accounts have not.
>
> Most of the incident reports are marked "secret," a relatively low level of classification. The *Times* has taken care not to publish information that would harm national security interests. The *Times* and the other news organizations agreed at the outset that we would not disclose— either in our articles or any of our online supplementary material— anything that was likely to put lives at risk or jeopardize military or antiterrorist operations. We have, for example, withheld any names of operatives in the field and informants cited in the reports. We have avoided anything that might compromise American or allied intelligence-gathering methods such as communications intercepts. We have not linked to the archives of raw material. At the request of

the White House, the *Times* also urged Wikileaks to withhold any harmful material from its Web site.

In addition to DCI Casey, quoted at the beginning of this section, at least four other Directors of Central Intelligence have commended mainstream media outlets for their willingness to consider government objections. In 1979 former DCI William Colby testified before the HPSCI that he had "successfully convinced members of the press that they should not publish some things out of a sense of patriotism and decency and judgment."[283] In 1988 former DCI Robert Gates wrote, "There have been a number of instances in which the press has withheld stories or written them in a way that preserved the confidentiality of intelligence sources."[284]

Eight years later, in 1996, it was reported that former DCI John Deutch spoke with newspaper editors on at least two occasions to request that classified information not be published.[285] Deutch stated, "Each time the editor in less than 20 seconds said okay." In 2006 former DCI James Woolsey reportedly approached senior members of the media on two occasions "because a particular fact that one of their reporters had been asking about, if revealed, would have seriously put at risk a source or a method."[286] Woolsey added, "In each case, they said the story doesn't depend on this fact, and thanks for letting us know, and they ran the story without the fact."

Members of the media also identify several instances in which information regarding the existence of a classified program or operation was withheld until disclosed by an alternative source. These sources have included foreign governments, foreign media outlets, or even U.S. officials. Once the information was disclosed, members of the media concluded that the necessity to protect national security no longer overrode the responsibility to inform the public. One difficulty media organizations face when discussing this justification is only being able to reference information that was ultimately disclosed. Ironically, some of the best examples of the media agreeing to withhold classified information cannot be cited without the media acting irresponsibly. This is similar to government frustration over the inability to identify the extent of harm caused by a disclosure without the requirement to disclose additional classified information.

Members of the media have spoken on numerous occasions about their ability to make responsible decisions regarding the publication of classified information. In his memoirs, former *Washington Post* editor Ben Bradlee wrote, "In my time as editor, I have kept many stories out of the paper because I felt that national security would be harmed by publication."[287] In 1988, *Washington Post* reporter Bob Woodward confirmed that he was frequently talked out of running stories."[288] In the joint 2006 *New York Times* article, Bill Keller and Dean Baquet wrote, "Each of us has, on a number of occasions, withheld information because we were convinced that publishing it would put lives at risk."[289]

Beyond these generalities, several specific instances have been identified in which classified information obtained by the media was withheld from publication. Several examples of media restraint during both the Cold War and the wars in Iraq and Afghanistan have been discussed publicly. Examples in which the media identified the responsible use of classified information during the Cold War include:

U-2

The *Washington Post* is reported to have been aware of U-2 surveillance missions over the Soviet Union at least a year prior to Francis Gary Powers being shot down in May 1960.[290] The decision was made to withhold publication in the interests of national security, including the recognition of a need to collect intelligence regarding Soviet missile capabilities. The *New York Times* also reportedly had knowledge of the U-2 missions in Soviet air space.[291]

Even after Powers was shot down, the media continued to show restraint in publication. During research for a book on the U-2 program in 1962, two authors discovered that the United States had also been flying U-2 missions over Cuba.[292] In response to a request from Attorney General Robert Kennedy, this information was withheld. One of the authors later stated that he believed he had made the correct decision, particularly after a U-2 identified the presence of Soviet missiles and missile bases in Cuba later that year, leading to the Cuban missile crisis.

FIGURE 5 – OCTOBER 14, 1962, U2 IMAGES OF SOVIET MISSILES IN CUBA [293]
Source: Central Intelligence Agency.

IVY BELLS

In 1985 *Washington Post* reporter Bob Woodward reportedly obtained classified information concerning IVY BELLS, a clandestine operation to intercept Soviet communications transmitted across undersea cables.[294] The operation involved U.S. submarines entering Soviet territorial waters to attach and service the IVY BELLS device, which was secured to Soviet communication cables. After discussions with government officials, the *Post* agreed not to disclose the operation's existence. During a 2006 interview, Ben Bradlee stated, "there is no damned way we were going to run this if it was still operating. So, we didn't run it."[295]

One year later, Bob Woodward learned that the IVY BELLS device had been removed by the Soviets. It was subsequently determined that a former

NSA employee, Ronald Pelton, had disclosed the program's existence to the KGB. After Pelton's espionage was discovered, Bradlee notified the government of his intent to publish an article containing the previously withheld information, stating, "Once it was certain that the Russians knew everything about IVY BELLS, there was no issue of national security."[296] He added, "[I]f the Soviets knew all about IVY BELLS, why shouldn't the American public know about it?"

In response to continued government concerns, Bradlee and *Post* CEO Katharine Graham discussed the article's contents with government officials on approximately twenty occasions, including conversations with DCI William Casey and President Ronald Reagan.[297] Drafts of the article were provided for review during these discussions. Ultimately, NBC broadcast its own version of the story while the Post was still considering government concerns. This incident will be examined in detail in Chapter 4.

Project *AZORIAN*

During a 1975 CIA operation to recover a sunken Soviet submarine, several media outlets obtained information regarding the project's existence. One section of the submarine was reported to have been successfully recovered and attempts to salvage the remaining portion were planned.[298] DCI William Colby personally met with several journalists, including *New York Times* reporter Seymour Hersh. Hersh agreed to Colby's request to withhold the information while operations were ongoing.[299] Though *Los Angeles Times* reporter Jack Nelson did not agree with Colby's rationale, the editor for the *Los Angeles Times* also agreed not to publish the information.[300]

In addition to the *New York Times* and *Los Angeles Times*, Colby is reported to have convinced *Time*, *Newsweek*, the *Washington Post*, the *Washington Star*, and all three major television networks to withhold the story.[301] (Author's note: Similar to IVY BELLS, the existence of the operation was eventually disclosed, in this instance by columnist Jack Anderson. As part of an arrangement with the other outlets, DCI Colby contacted them when it became apparent the program would be exposed.)[302]

Media restraint during the Cold War was not limited solely to classified programs involving the Soviet Union. In at least two instances, the media reportedly withheld classified information related to terrorist acts.

Hostage Crises

In November 1979, Iranian militants seized the American Embassy in Tehran. For over a year, 53 Americans were held hostage. At least five U.S. news organizations, including the *New York Times, Newsweek, Time,* NBC, and CBS learned that six Americans had not been taken hostage and had sought refuge in the Canadian Embassy.[303] All five organizations agreed to withhold disclosure of the information until the other hostages were released. Six years later, when Lebanese terrorists hijacked TWA Flight 847, media outlets learned that one of the hostages was an NSA employee.[304] Again, the information was withheld from publication. Even in the Pentagon Papers case, the incident most commonly cited as confirming the media's right to publish without government interference, members of the media identified steps taken in an effort to handle classified information responsibly.

Pentagon Papers

While examining portions of a TOP SECRET study provided by Daniel Ellsberg, the *Washington Post* discovered that two CIA agents stationed in Saigon were identified. In a 2006 interview, Ben Bradlee stated: "[W]hen we noticed that, everybody said, 'Well, God, we're not going to name CIA agents.' So we said, 'No,' and took that out."[305] In her memoirs, Katharine Graham, former CEO of the *Post*, also discussed the consideration given to government objections. Graham wrote: "[W]e had independently, and in an effort to act responsibly, decided we wouldn't publish those items that had been specified in the Solicitor General's secret brief as being those most threatening to the national interest."[306] Graham added: "[W]e would not publish information based on intercepted communications, signal intelligence, and cryptography in general, adhering to this policy as we had in the past." Graham also wrote that Ellsberg had withheld portions of the Pentagon Papers from the *Post* and that the newspaper did not have access to much of the material the government appeared to have been most concerned about.

In addition to Cold War examples, several contemporary examples of media restraint have been identified, particularly related to current antiterrorism efforts and the wars in Iraq and Afghanistan. In addition to the examples provided below, media outlets have suggested that there are several other unreported cases in which classified information was obtained but never disclosed. Cases cited by the media as evidence that issues of national security were handled responsibly include:

CIA Detention Facilities

Dana Priest, author of the 2006 *Washington Post* article concerning the existence of overseas CIA detention facilities, discussed the *Post*'s pre-publication process at a 2006 American Bar Association conference. Priest stated that all elements of the article were provided to the CIA prior to publication and that issues regarding the content of the article were discussed with senior government officials, including President Bush.[307] As a result of concerns regarding the negative repercussions of identifying the countries hosting CIA facilities, *Washington Post* Executive Editor Len Downie agreed not to disclose the countries' identities. Downie stated that the purpose of the article was accomplished without having to name the countries.[308]

Downie also indicated that, during research for the article, Priest obtained information regarding additional classified counterterrorism programs that were never disclosed. Downie stated: "Right from the outset it was clear to us that details . . . would not be important to readers," and would be "injurious to Americans potentially or could damage these programs potentially."[309]

Terrorist Surveillance Program

In 2006 Bill Keller, executive editor for the *New York Times*, revealed that the *Times* had withheld publication of its article concerning the NSA Terrorist Surveillance Program for more than a year. During that period, the *Times* discussed national security concerns with government officials. Keller stated that, when the decision was made to publish the article,[310] "We satisfied ourselves that we could write about this program . . . in a way that would not expose any intelligence-gathering methods or capabilities that are not already on the public record."[311] Keller added that technical details of the program were also withheld.

SWIFT Banking

Less than a week after his SWIFT database article was published in the *New York Times*, Eric Lichtblau discussed how the decision to disclose classified information was reached. In response to accusations of being unpatriotic and treasonous, Lichtblau stated, "We wrestled with this (the decision to publish the story) for many weeks and listened to the government's arguments."[312] Lichtblau added that the government argued that the disclosure would weaken the program's effectiveness and harm the relationship with the SWIFT organization but that "the paper and the top editors felt that this was an important issue in the current public policy debate about the war on terrorism and that the reasons for not publishing were outweighed by the public interest."

Bill Keller concurred with Lichtblau's statements. Keller described that paper's deliberative process as follows:

Our decision to publish the story of the administration's penetration of the international banking system followed weeks of discussion between administration officials and the *Times*, not only the reporters who wrote the story but senior editors, including me. We listened patiently and attentively. We discussed the matter extensively within the paper. We spoke to others—national security experts not serving in the Administration—for their counsel . . . We believe the *Times* . . . served the public interest by accurately reporting on these programs so that the public can have an informed view of them.[313]

The assertion that the article did not disclose information that had not been previously discussed publicly was one of the most oft-cited justifications for publication of the SWIFT article. Lichtblau and Keller each asserted that terrorists were already well aware that their finances were being tracked, based at least partially on information disclosed by U.S. government officials.[314]

U.S. Troops in Afghanistan

In the week following the terrorist attacks of September 11, 2001, the Knight Ridder Washington Bureau obtained information that U.S. special operations forces had entered Afghanistan to locate Osama bin Laden. In response to a request from the Pentagon, the decision was made not to publish the information.[315] Knight-Ridder's Washington Bureau chief agreed with the Pentagon's contention that disclosing the information could increase the risk to the troops, remarking "based on what we knew, we believed that making (the operation) public could have substantially increased the risk to the Americans involved and could even have been seen as contributing to a loss of life."

Though Knight-Ridder chose not to disclose the information it had obtained, *USA Today* reached a different conclusion, publishing a front-page article on September 28, 2001. *USA Today* also believed it was acting responsibly and in the public's best interest. The author of the article justified the disclosure by contending that the information was already widely known within Afghanistan. The article stated, "Their (U.S. operatives) arrival here two weeks ago and subsequent movement into Afghanistan have been reported by English and Urdu language newspapers here, and would not come as a surprise to bin Laden or Afghanistan's ruling Taliban."[316]

In at least two identified instances, beyond simply electing not to publish classified information, a media outlet proactively contacted government officials to discuss what had been disclosed to them. In the first case, in 1981, the *Washington Post* obtained a manuscript written in Russian with mathematical computations and diagrams. Rather than attempt to translate or publish the information, *Post* Executive Editor Ben Bradlee provided the manuscript to the CIA.[317] Bradlee was informed thirteen years later that the document contained information regarding the design and function of a new Soviet Intermediate-Range Ballistic Missile (IRBM). In 1994 a CIA Soviet weapons expert reportedly stated that the manuscript "gave us the best insights we had . . . on their (Soviet) IRBM engineering capabilities,[318] on their propellant capabilities." The Deputy Director of Central Intelligence, Bobby Ray Inman, reportedly described the document as "unique material . . . judged to be valuable."[319]

The second incident, also involving Bradlee and the *Washington Post*, occurred in 1988. A source, described by Bradlee as a disgruntled low-level Navy analyst, provided reporter Bob Woodward with information regarding three classified U.S. operations to penetrate Soviet systems used to control their nuclear forces. Woodward later learned that the source had an East German girlfriend. After meeting the source, Bradlee stated, "We quickly agreed that there was no useful social purpose in publishing the story, and recognized a responsibility to alert the government to a potential disaster."[320] Though Woodward and Bradlee refused to testify against the source, they provided the information to DCI William Webster.

Government Employees and Their Motivations: The "Supply Side"

Members of the media represent only one half of the previously identified "leak economy." This economy cannot endure simply because journalists, the "demand side" of the equation, recognize a need to disclose classified information. In order to thrive, a "supply side" is also required. The "supply side" of the relationship consists of government employees with security clearances willing to disclose classified information to members of the media. Just as members of the media are motivated to publish classified information under certain circumstances, government employees have distinct rationales for their actions. Though the primary focus for this book is an analysis of the journalist's decision-making process, an examination of the "supply side" of this process will assist in illustrating the complexities of this issue.

Government agencies are aware that unauthorized disclosures would not occur without government employees willing to provide classified information to members of the media. Beyond the threat of criminal prosecution or administrative sanctions, government agencies attempt to deter these disclosures through training and education programs. The intent of these programs is to diminish the rationale for disclosing classified information and to dissuade the employees from engaging in this undesirable behavior.

In the book *LEAKING: Who Does It? Who Benefits? At What Cost?* Elie Abel offers an academic and professional perspective on the topic of government employees who disclose classified information. Abel, a former *New York Times, Los Angeles Times* and CBS reporter, also a Stanford professor and former Dean of the Columbia School of Journalism, examines who these government employees are, the types of information they disclose, and why they elect to provide classified information to the media.

According to Abel, the categories of information disclosed to the media most often involve foreign policy and defense issues. He recognizes that Intelligence Community activities, particularly those involving the CIA and NSA, are also the subject of unauthorized disclosures, but to a lesser extent. Because of the perceived focus on political issues, Abel believes that the primary government sources are senior political appointees, policymakers, and senior executives from Executive Branch agencies. He shares the sentiment of President John F. Kennedy, who remarked that "the Ship of State is the only ship that leaks at the top."[321] Abel also identifies members of Congress and their staffs as significant sources of classified information for the media.

Abel contends that mid-level bureaucrats and civil servants are normally not involved in unauthorized disclosures. He writes that these individuals do not have access to information the media would have the greatest motivation to publish, the kind that "makes a front-page splash."[322] Without offering additional detail, Abel asserts that low- and mid-level civil servants are also less likely to be the source of an unauthorized disclosure because "the risk of exposure outweighs the possible gain." In order for this assertion to be valid, the civil servant's perception of the likelihood of discovery would either have to be higher than research indicates or his/her perception of the possible benefit would need to be slight.

Abel implies that another reason why senior officials are more often the source of unauthorized disclosures is that they either have an existing relationship with journalists or are more likely to engage or be approached by members of the media. Abel adds that it is government officials who instigate contact with the media in the majority of cases. He believes that unauthorized disclosures are seldom the product of a reporter's probing, though he recognizes that some unauthorized disclosures are also "the products of hard work by enterprising newsmen and newswomen."

Before identifying the motivations for government employees to disclose classified information, Abel makes one additional distinction. He differentiates between classified information provided to the media that is sanctioned by an administration official, and information the administration does not condone. He refers to sanctioned disclosures as "plants" and non-approved disclosures as "leaks." Abel does not identify which he considers more prevalent.

Abel recognizes six distinct motivations for a government employee to disclose classified information to members of the media. These categories are based on a book written by former White House staffer and Presidential advisor Stephen Hess. Though presented individually, the six motivations can be grouped into three general categories: disclosures meant to benefit an individual or a policy the individual supports, disclosures meant to harm an adversary or a policy the individual opposes, or an altruistic disclosure meant to bring attention to a perceived wrong.

Included in the category of disclosures meant to benefit an individual or policy are:

THE EGO LEAK: An unauthorized disclosure meant to "satisfy the leaker's sense of his own importance." Abel indicates that the intent of the disclosure is to gain a feeling of worth that the government employee may not receive in the workplace. Because the individual has an impression that he/she is not appropriately recognized for his/her accomplishments, he/she seeks validation from another source, a member of the media.

THE POLICY LEAK: An unauthorized disclosure intended to increase the probability that a desired policy will be enacted. The expectation is that additional support will be garnered from the disclosure, both from the public and within the administration.

THE GOODWILL LEAK: The primary purpose for this type of disclosure is to "earn credit with a reporter, to be cashed in at a later date." In this case, the government employee believes the journalist would be more likely to publish a future disclosure intended to satisfy a separate motivation.

THE TRIAL BALLOON LEAK: The objective for this category is to test how a potential policy will be received by others, including both lawmakers and the public. The risk of being associated with an unfavorable policy can be decreased if its reception is gauged before an official position is taken.

The second category, unauthorized disclosures motivated by a desire to harm an adversary or a policy the government employee opposes, includes:

THE ANIMUS LEAK: The intent of the disclosure is to embarrass or otherwise injure another person or political faction. The disclosure is meant as a hostile attack directed toward an opponent to weaken his/her position.

THE POLICY LEAK: Abel recognizes that a disclosure to the media can be used not only to promote a desired policy but also to increase attention to negative aspects of a specific proposal or political agenda. Abel distinguishes between disclosures meant to injure an individual, the "Animus" leak, and disclosures that target a policy.

The final category identified by Abel includes unauthorized disclosures meant to correct a perceived wrong, which includes:

THE WHISTLEBLOWER LEAK: These disclosures are characterized by Abel as an altruistic last resort for "frustrated civil servants who feel they cannot correct a perceived wrong through regular channels."[323] He does not make a distinction between those government employees who attempt to obtain a remedy through an officially sanctioned process and those who elect to eschew the process entirely by going directly to the media.

Beyond the six motivations to disclose classified information acknowledged by Abel, there are at least two additional reasons why an unauthorized disclosure might occur—ignorance and accident. Government employees not accustomed to handling classified information, or those improperly trained, can disclose classified information without realizing or understanding the consequences of their actions. Government employees aware of their obligation to protect classified information can also unintentionally disclose information. These accidental disclosures can result from a momentary lapse in judgment or from persistence on the part of a journalist intent on acquiring classified information. Though the disclosures resulting from ignorance or accident may not have been the product of a premeditated act, the outcome is the same.

Other than acknowledging Hess' belief that the "Ego Leak" is the most common, Abel does not offer an opinion on the relative frequency of the six identified motivations. He does recognize that the motivations are not mutually exclusive. When providing an example of an "Ego Leak," Abel indicates that the government source had not only been passed over for promotion but also disagreed personally with a policy decision.

Near the end of his book, Abel presents the results from a study conducted by the Institute of Politics at Harvard's Kennedy School of Government. Though the results of the study do not directly correlate with the six identified motivations, some parallels can be drawn.

In the study, 42 percent of respondents, identified as "former federal officials in policymaking positions," acknowledged disclosing classified information to the media. Rationales for disclosing classified information were ranked as follows:

90% –   To counter false or misleading information

75% –   To gain attention for a policy option or issue

64% –   To consolidate support from the public of a constituency outside of government

53% –   To force action on an issue

32% –   To send a message to another part of the government

31.5% – To stop action on an issue

30% –   To test reactions to a policy consideration

30% –   To protect their own position

29% – In response to a reporter's skill and persistence in eliciting information

The majority of these categories relate to what Abel refers to as a Policy Leak. Four of Abel's categories, Ego, Goodwill, Animus, and Whistleblower, do not appear to be represented. Though Abel does not discuss this apparent discrepancy, one possible explanation may be the reliance on the poll's respondents to self-identify their motivations. Just as members of the media rarely discuss some motivations, the study's respondents may have under-reported or non-report motivations, such as Ego, Goodwill, or Animus.

In reference to the legalities surrounding unauthorized disclosures, Abel offers his opinion that it is not illegal for government officials to provide classified information to the media, or for members of the media to accept and publish this information. He does identify an exception in cases involving the disclosure or publication of information related to communications intelligence: "the government's capacity to eavesdrop on the communications of foreign governments" and "intelligence gathered by those methods."[324] This would appear to be a reference to prohibitions specified under Section 798 of the Espionage Act.

In Leaking, Abel cites several reasons why unauthorized disclosures will continue for the foreseeable future. He refers to several of the justifications previously identified in this chapter, including government overclassification and the perceived hypocrisy of tolerating advantageous disclosures. Abel also recognizes that members of the media perpetuate the cycle based on motivations other than promoting an informed citizenry or exposing government misconduct.

Abel acknowledges the impact of a journalist's motivation to advance personal or corporate interests. He refers to the media's risk of sacrificing independent judgment "pursuing its self-interest in leaks, which serves to advance the career aspirations of reporters and the prestige of their organizations." Abel adds: "A reporter profits by appearing to be more enterprising and better-informed than his colleagues or competitors. That way lies professional recognition, salary increases, and the path to advancement."[325]

Abel ultimately agrees with one of the primary conclusions of this book, that it is unrealistic to believe that unauthorized disclosures can be reduced through new legislation or harsh administrative sanctions. He believes that a legal remedy cannot be instituted without "doing violence to the fabric of American freedoms." Abel concludes that any attempt to reduce the perceived harm caused by unauthorized disclosures must come through voluntary reforms.

Conclusion

This chapter examined the multiple motivations and justifications comprising the "benefit" side of the journalist's cost-benefit analysis related to the publication of classified information. Before a conclusion can be reached regarding the applicability of an approach incorporating Rational Choice Theory, the "cost" side of the equation must also be examined. Understanding the media's perception of the harm caused by these disclosures is as essential a component as recognizing their motivations and justifications. Chapter 3 identifies and examines the specific categories of harm associated with unauthorized disclosures of classified information by the media.

CHAPTER 3

The Cost of Disclosing
Classified Information: Identifying Harm

There is no doubt and ample evidence that unauthorized disclosures of classified information cause enormous and irreparable harm to the Nation's diplomatic, military, and intelligence capabilities.[326]

- Attorney General John Ashcroft

Newspapers recognize that the government has a duty to preserve national security and that some leaks may cause damage.[327]

- Newspaper Association of America and National Newspaper Association

Government officials, particularly those affiliated with the Intelligence Community (IC), believe that incidents of unauthorized disclosures must be reduced due to their harm to national security. While these officials recognize that unauthorized disclosures may produce a more informed citizenry, they believe the overall public interest in preserving national security will outweigh any potential benefits in almost all instances. Individuals intent on reducing disclosures do not consider this conflict to be between a government interest in maintaining secrecy and a public interest in acquiring knowledge of government activity. They contend that maintaining legitimate secrets is as much a public interest as a government interest. As noted by University of Chicago Law Professor Gerhard Casper in 1986:

[G]overnment interests are also the interests of the American people. They have a need for secrecy in some circumstances as compelling as their need for information. Representative government to some extent substitutes deliberation by representatives for deliberation by the people. The Founders understood that unrestrained freedom of information may impose prohibitive social costs.[328]

Numerous examples have been identified in which Intelligence Community capabilities have been damaged or lost as the result of an unauthorized disclosure by the media. This harm, in turn, decreases the ability of the IC to perform its mission and support U.S. interests. The recognition of harm is not limited solely to government officials. Members of the media renowned for their disclosure of classified information also realize the potential for harm. Jack Nelson, former Washington bureau chief for the *Los Angeles Times*, wrote in 2002, "There are instances where the media is irresponsible in using classified information that might endanger national security."[329] As seen by the quote at the beginning of this chapter, both the Newspaper Association of America and National Newspaper Association recognize that disclosures may harm national security.[330]

Former Directors of the Central Intelligence Agency, from James Schlesinger (1973) to Michael Hayden (2008), have also addressed the issue. In 1988 former DCI Robert Gates provided an overview of the breadth of harm attributed to unauthorized disclosures by the media:

> In recent years, U.S. foreign policy has been undercut, and the ability of American intelligence to help protect the security of the nation against our adversaries has been weakened by unauthorized disclosures of classified information. Deliberate leaks of intelligence information have jeopardized American lives, hampered U.S. effectiveness in combating terrorism . . . and have required the expenditure of billions of dollars in order to revamp or replace sophisticated technical collection systems that have been compromised. Unauthorized disclosures have damaged U.S. relationships with other intelligence services and have dissuaded potential agents from accepting the risks of working on behalf of the United States.[331]

Though he vetoed the 2001 Intelligence Authorization Act because of a provision to expand coverage of the Espionage Act, President Bill Clinton acknowledged that unauthorized disclosures could be "extraordinarily harmful to United States national security interests":

> I have been particularly concerned about their potential effects on the sometimes irreplaceable intelligence sources and methods on

which we rely to acquire accurate and timely information I need in order to make the most appropriate decisions on matters of national security. Unauthorized disclosures damage our intelligence relationships abroad, compromise intelligence gathering, jeopardize lives, and increase the threat of terrorism . . . Those who disclose classified information inappropriately thus commit a gross breach of the public trust and may recklessly put our national security at risk.[332]

In upholding the conviction of Samuel Morison for providing classified satellite imagery to the media, Circuit Court Judge Harvie Wilkinson also detailed several potential categories of harm:

When the identities of our intelligence agents are known, they may be killed. When our electronic surveillance capabilities are revealed, countermeasures can be taken to circumvent them. When other nations fear that confidences exchanged at the bargaining table will only become embarrassments in the press, our diplomats are left helpless. When terrorists are advised of our intelligence, they can avoid apprehension and escape retribution.[333]

Beyond the recognition of potential harm, concern over the impact of unauthorized disclosures has sometimes led to a more visceral response. In 1971 President Gerald Ford exclaimed that he was "damned sick and tired of a ship that has such leaky seams" and that his administration was "being drowned by premature and obvious leaks."[334] DCI John Deutch remarked in 1996, "There's something sick about the kind of people (that leak details of ongoing CIA operations)." [335] At the 1999 dedication ceremony for the CIA's George Bush Center for Intelligence, former President George H.W. Bush expressed "contempt and anger for those who betray the trust by exposing the names of our sources." He added that these government employees are "the most insidious of traitors."[336]

Categories of Harm

Unauthorized disclosures by the media are perceived to impact seriously the ability of IC agencies to provide senior officials with intelligence to support national security objectives. In addition to the recognized harm to the United States, classified information disclosed by the media is also viewed as benefiting U.S. rivals. Adversaries provided access to intelligence concerning U.S. capabilities and intentions can exploit this information to further their own objectives.

Six distinct categories of harm caused by unauthorized disclosures can be identified. They include: (1) damage to sources and methods; (2) potential loss of life; (3) impact to foreign policy; (4) effect on international alliances; (5) financial costs; and (6) the decrease in public knowledge resulting from disclosures of incomplete or inaccurate information. Critics of unauthorized disclosures maintain that, in almost all cases, these consequences outweigh any justification the media may have for publishing classified information.[337] In order to more fully understand these categories of harm, each will be examined individually.

Damage to Sources and Methods

In recent years, publication of classified information by the media has destroyed or seriously damaged intelligence sources of the highest value. Every method we have of acquiring intelligence . . . has been damaged by the publication of unauthorized disclosures.[338]

- DCI William Casey

Unauthorized disclosures of classified information threaten the survivability of the sources and methods that we depend on. We have lost opportunity, if not capability, because of irresponsible leaks and we have made it easier for our enemies.[339]

- DCI Porter Goss

When an unauthorized disclosure in the media occurs, the impact extends beyond the specific information compromised. Disclosures increase an adversary's knowledge of U.S. collection capabilities and potentially allow an adversary to identify the manner in which the information was originally collected, such as a human source, satellite, or covert listening device. Adversaries can then employ countermeasures to decrease U.S. knowledge of their actual capabilities and intentions.

In July 2009, Director of National Intelligence Dennis Blair noted that unauthorized disclosures "allow our adversaries to learn about, deny, counteract, and deceive our intelligence collection methods, leading to the loss of critical capabilities . . ."[340] The 2005 WMD Commission Report focused particular attention on the harm that disclosures have caused to intelligence sources and methods. The Commission concluded that "unauthorized disclosures of U.S. sources and methods have significantly impaired the effectiveness of our collection systems."[341] The Commission also reported that U.S. adversaries had "learned much about what we can see and hear, and have predictably taken steps to thwart our efforts."

Members of the media have also recognized the potential impact of unauthorized disclosures on intelligence sources and methods. Speaking at a 2007 American Society of Newspaper Editors (ASNE) conference, *Washington Post* Executive Editor Len Downie acknowledged that classified information disclosed by the media "increases knowledge of those who could harm national security."[342] Former *Washington Post* CEO Katharine Graham publicly discussed the damage caused by the loss of an intelligence source prior to the bombing of the Marine Corps barracks in Beirut in 1983.[343]

Several examples of harm to U.S. Intelligence Community sources and methods have been identified over the past half century. Instances in which sensitive sources and methods were compromised during the Cold War include:

Soviet ICBM Testing

On January 31, 1958, an article in the *New York Times* disclosed that the United States had the ability to monitor countdowns for Soviet missile launches.[344] This ability allowed the U.S. to deploy aircraft to observe and collect data from the splashdown sites. After the article was published, the Soviets reduced the length of these countdowns from eight hours to four hours. The shorter countdown did not provide the lead-time necessary for U.S. aircraft to reach their landing areas. President Dwight Eisenhower was reportedly "livid" about the disclosure.[345] To regain a portion of the lost collection capability, the United States had to rebuild and staff an airfield in Alaska.

Operation BROADSIDE

During the 1960s and 1970s, a clandestine listening post inside the U.S. embassy in Moscow intercepted calls made from the limousines of Soviet Politburo members. Intelligence obtained from these intercepts was classified with the code name GAMMA GUPPY.[346] On September 16, 1971, columnist Jack Anderson published an article in the *Washington Post* disclosing the capabilities of the program. Beyond making a veiled reference to the operation or implying a capability, Anderson entitled his article "CIA Eavesdrops on Kremlin Chiefs."[347] After the disclosure, the Soviets began encrypting these communications.

Project AZORIAN

In 1974 a company owned by Howard Hughes constructed a salvage vessel for the CIA. The ship, Glomar Explorer, was specifically built to attempt a recovery of a sunken Soviet submarine in the Pacific Ocean. Though accounts vary, it was reported that at least one section of the submarine was successfully recovered, along with several nuclear torpedoes.[348] Before an attempt could be made to salvage the remainder of the submarine, media outlets obtained information concerning the operation's existence.

On February 8, 1975, the *Los Angeles Times* and the *New York Times* published articles related to the attempted salvage. The *Los Angeles Times* article was titled "U.S. Reported after Russ Sub."[349] The story did not identify Project AZORIAN by name and incorrectly reported that the sunken submarine was located in the Atlantic Ocean and not the Pacific. Though DCI William Colby successfully convinced several news organizations, including the *Los Angeles Times*, to withhold additional reporting, columnist Jack Anderson ultimately disclosed a detailed account of the project's existence during a radio broadcast on March 18, 1975.[350] Other news organizations, such as the *New York Times*, subsequently published their own articles.[351] After the disclosure, and before an attempt could be made to recover the remaining portion of the submarine, the Soviet Union sent signal vessels to patrol the salvage site.

DCI Colby stated, "There was not a chance we could send the Glomar out again on an intelligence project without risking the lives of the crew and inciting a major international incident . . . The Glomar project stopped because it was exposed."[352] Colby believed the recovery of the submarine would have been the "biggest single intelligence coup in history."[353] Beyond attempts to continue salvaging the Soviet submarine, *Time* magazine later reported, "The Glomar Explorer sits idle . . . Had its cover not been blown, the ship would have been used for recovering other seabed prizes like missile re-entry vehicles and underwater listening devices. Instead, the Government has put the vessel up for sale."[354]

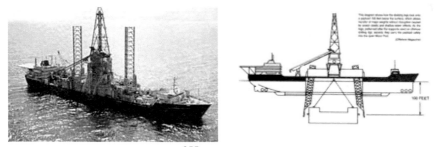

FIGURE 6 – GLOMAR EXPLORER [355]
Source: U.S. Government photo provided by National Security Archive.

Beneficiaries of unauthorized disclosures are not confined to traditional Cold War adversaries, such as the Soviet Union. Critics also recognize the negative impact to ongoing counterterrorism efforts. In 2007 CIA Director Michael Hayden observed that the ongoing disclosure of Intelligence Community sources and methods could be "just as damaging as revelations of troop or ship movements were in the past." [356] During his confirmation hearing, Hayden criticized the media for aiding terrorists in avoiding capture by disclosing information that improved their understanding of U.S. methodologies.[357] Former DCI Porter Goss agreed that "terrorists gain an edge when they keep their secrets and we don't keep ours."[358]

A 2002 CIA memo appears to corroborate these observations. The memorandum concludes that information made available by the U.S. media had decreased the effectiveness of U.S. efforts to identify and capture members of Al Qaeda:

Information obtained from captured detainees has revealed that al-Qa'ida operatives are extremely security conscious and have altered their practices in response to what they have learned from the press about our capabilities.[359]

A translated Al Qaeda training manual also confirms the group's recognition that significant intelligence concerning U.S. capabilities and intentions can be collected through the exploitation of the U.S. media:

[W]ithout resorting to illegal means, it is possible to gather at least 80% of information about the enemy. The percentage varies depending on the government's policy on freedom of the press and publication. It is possible to gather information through newspapers, magazines, books, periodicals, official publications, and enemy broadcasts.[360]

Since the inception of the War on Terror and wars in Iraq and Afghanistan, there have been numerous reported instances of unauthorized disclosures by the media. Disclosures identified as having harmed Intelligence Community sources and methods include:

FIGURE 7 – UNAUTHORIZED DISCLOSURE SATIRE [361]
Source: Roger Harvell. Used with permission.

OBELISK

On September 7, 2007, ABC News revealed that the U.S. government had obtained a video of Osama bin Laden four days before its public release by Al Qaeda.[362] The disclosure reportedly resulted in an order from Al Qaeda's internal security division to discontinue use of its Internet communications network, known as "Obelisk."[363] Obelisk, which had previously been penetrated, was described as a network of sites used for operational activities, such as internal communications, expense reporting, and the distribution of propaganda.

An Associated Press article reported, "Sources that took years to develop are now ineffective" and "[A] rare window into the world of al-Qaeda has now been sealed shut."[364] Focusing on the disclosure of the video to the media, and not the media's subsequent publication of the information, the *New York Sun* described the loss of access to Obelisk as an "intelligence blunder."[365]

SWIFT Banking

On June 23, 2006, the *New York Times* published an article revealing the existence of a classified program for analyzing international financial records from the Brussels-based SWIFT database.[366] The article stated that the program was implemented legally, that Congress had received multiple briefings, and that several safeguards were established to prevent abuse, including the use of an outside auditing firm. The article identified several of the program's successes, including contributions to the capture of "Hambali," the mastermind behind the 2002 bombings in Bali, Indonesia. Hambali was the operations chief of Jemaah Islamiyah, an Asian terrorist group and Al Qaeda affiliate. The article also reported that information from SWIFT was used to identify Uzair Paracha, a Brooklyn man convicted for agreeing to launder funds for Al Qaeda. Both President Bush and Vice President Cheney described the disclosure as "disgraceful."[367]

On June 28, 2006, the U.S. House of Representatives passed a resolution condemning the program's disclosure.[368] The resolution read in part: "The Administration, Members of Congress, and the bipartisan chairmen of the 9/11 Commission requested that media organizations not disclose details of the Terrorist Finance Tracking Program so that terrorists would not shift their financing to channels in the international financial system that are less easily observed by intelligence agencies." The resolution also stated, "Unauthorized disclosures of sensitive intelligence information inflict significant damage to United States activities in the global war on terrorism by assisting terrorists in developing countermeasures to evade United States intelligence capabilities." During Congressional debate over the resolution, it was also reported that a recovered Al Qaeda memo explicitly stated that the group's efforts had been harmed by the tightening of financial outlets.[369]

Beyond the reported impact of unauthorized disclosures on past and present conflicts, critics also identify instances in which the media may have compromised sources and methods critical to defending against potential future adversaries, such as Iran. These disclosures include:

Operation MERLIN

In the book *State of War*, author James Risen detailed a CIA operation codenamed MERLIN, which allegedly involved attempts to provide counterfeit blueprints to Iran for a trigger to a nuclear device that contained subtle flaws.[370] Risen wrote that President Clinton approved the operation and that the Bush administration had endorsed the plan. In addition to disclosing the existence and objectives of Operation MERLIN, Risen also revealed that the NSA allegedly had the capability to intercept communications from the Iranian mission in Vienna and decipher the codes of Iran's intelligence ministry.[371] The *New York Times*, which had previously published Risen's article concerning the NSA Terrorist Surveillance Program, did not publish information related to Operation MERLIN prior to the publication of *State of War*. The *Times* did not confirm whether it was aware of the information, but chose not to publish, or if Risen had withheld the information.

In April 2010, the *Washington Post* reported that a federal grand jury had subpoenaed Risen to testify concerning his sources for classified information contained in *State of War*.[372] The article reiterated that the *New*

York Times had not published the information appearing in Risen's book related to attempts to infiltrate Iran's nuclear program. A judge ultimately quashed the subpoena and Risen did not testify. Risen had previously been subpoenaed in 2008, but the grand jury had expired prior to the issue being resolved.[373]

In December 2010, former CIA Operations Officer Jeffrey Sterling was indicted for disclosing classified information to a member of the media.[374] Although the indictment does not specify whether Sterling's disclosure is related to *State of War*, multiple media outlets have reported the connection. As of May 2011, Sterling's trial was pending in U.S. District Court for the Eastern District of Virginia.

National Intelligence Estimate – Iran

In December 2007 the Bush administration declassified findings from a National Intelligence Estimate (NIE) related to Iran. The NIE concluded that Iran had halted its nuclear weapons program in 2003.[375] Beyond the declassified finding, though, several unauthorized disclosures concerning the intelligence underlying the NIE conclusions were also disclosed. The *Washington Post* reported that the CIA had obtained a laptop computer from an Iranian who had contacted a German intelligence officer in Turkey.[376] The laptop reportedly contained information related to Iran's nuclear program. The article also reported that the NSA had intercepted a conversation between Iranian officials in 2007, including one military officer whose name had appeared on the laptop computer.

A separate article published in the *New York Times* reported that notes from Iranian officials involved in its weapons development program had been obtained by the United States in 2006.[377] The *Times* article also discussed the 2007 NSA intercept and laptop computer obtained by the CIA. The *Times* article added that the Iranian who had provided the laptop computer was an engineer.

In 1996 Secretary of Defense William Perry summarized the harm to sources and methods resulting from disclosures. In a memorandum aimed at strengthening controls over classified information, Perry stated that intelligence sources and methods were becoming less effective as the result of the disclosure of information from classified intelligence reports. Perry requested that the Department of Defense and CIA review distribution procedures to "significantly reduce the access to information revealing intelligence sources and methods."[378]

" THIS ONE IS FOR NOT LEAKING ANY MILITARY SECRETS."

FIGURE 8 – UNAUTHORIZED DISCLOSURE SATIRE [379]

Source: Harley Schwadron and *www.CartoonStock.com*. Used with permission.

If implemented, this tightening would have had the secondary effect of limiting legitimate access to intelligence by intelligence professionals and policymakers. This failure to share information was specifically cited as contributing to the intelligence failures identified by the WMD Commission nine years later. Ultimately, unauthorized disclosures of sources and methods may not only increase our adversaries' knowledge of U.S. capabilities but also decrease critical information sharing within the U.S. Intelligence Community.

Potential Loss of Life

> *I can say as a matter of first principal that the unauthorized disclosure of classified information has actually led to the deaths of individuals who would not otherwise have been subjected to that, had this information not been inappropriately put into the public domain.*[380]

> *- General Michael Hayden*

> *If . . . these newspapers proceed to publish the critical documents and there results therefrom the death of soldiers . . . (the) prolongation of the war and further delay in the freeing of United States prisoners, then the Nation's people will know where the responsibility for these sad consequences rests.*[381]

> *- Supreme Court Justice Harry Blackmun*

One particularly vulnerable source of intelligence is HUMINT, information derived from a human source. As opposed to imagery from a satellite or communications intercepted by a remote listening device, the compromise of a human source may result not only in loss of intelligence, but also loss of life. Advocates of reducing the level of unauthorized disclosures have focused attention on this intelligence source based on the increased sensitivities involved when lives are placed at risk.

When discussing the potential threat to life from unauthorized disclosures, the primary focus has been on Intelligence Community employees, such as Case Officers for the CIA's National Clandestine Service. These are the individuals who collect information concerning an adversary's capabilities and intentions from recruited assets. Unfortunately, there have reportedly been instances in which an unauthorized disclosure by the media contributed to the death of members of the IC.

Counterspy and Covert Action Bulleting

In 1969 Philip Agee resigned from the CIA after a 12-year career as a case officer. Agee indicated that he had become disillusioned with the CIA's overseas activities.[382] After his resignation, Agee published three books, *Inside the Company: CIA Diary* (1975); *Dirty Work: The CIA in Western*

Europe (1978); and *Dirty Work: The CIA in Africa* (1979). The books are reported to contain the names of several thousand CIA employees and other individuals affiliated with the CIA. In response to the disclosure of their identities, the CIA was reportedly required to terminate several active assignments.[383]

In 1975 *Counterspy*, a magazine with which Agee was affiliated, identified Richard Welch as a covert CIA employee.[384] The *Athens Daily News* republished Welch's identity on November 25, 1975. Welch was assigned as the chief of station in Athens, Greece, at the time, the highest-ranking CIA officer in the country. On December 24, 1975, Welch was assassinated outside his home in Athens. Agee had previously been quoted in *Counterspy* as saying, "The most effective and important systematic attempts to combat the CIA that can be undertaken right now are, I think, the identification, exposure, and neutralization of its people working abroad."[385] On December 29, 1975, the *Washington Post* commented that the "public identification of Richard Welch was tantamount to an open invitation to kill him."[386] Though additional factors were identified, DCI William Colby believed that the naming of Welch in *Counterspy* had contributed to his death.[387]

In subsequent Congressional hearings, Agee was accused of revealing to the Soviet Union that Jerzy Pawloski, a Polish national, was working as a U.S. agent.[388] Pawlowski had previously been arrested by the Soviets, convicted for spying on behalf of the CIA and sentenced to 25 years imprisonment. MI6, England's Secret Intelligence Service, also blamed Agee for the death of two of its agents in Poland.

In 1979 Agee began publishing the magazine *Covert Action Bulletin*. On July 2, 1980, the magazine revealed the identities of 15 alleged CIA officials working in Jamaica. They included Richard Kinsman, identified as the chief of station in that country. Two days later, Kinsman and his family survived an attack on their home by men armed with machineguns and a small bomb.[389] An attempt to assassinate another U.S. official in Jamaica occurred three days later.

Agee's exposure of individuals affiliated with the CIA was cited as one of the primary motivations for the enactment of the 1982 Intelligence Identities

Protection Act. The Act makes it a felony to disclose the identity of a covert U.S. agent.

Mossad in Syria

At a 2006 conference, former DCI James Woolsey remarked, "Agents have been blown and people have been killed by press reports . . ."[390] To support this assertion, he identified a second intelligence officer who was executed as the result of an unauthorized disclosure by the press. Woolsey stated that the Israeli press had published an article containing information obtained in Syria by an agent of the Mossad, Israel's intelligence service.[391] Woolsey asserted that the Syrians were able to identify and capture the agent, Eli Cohen, based on the information contained in the article. Cohen was convicted of espionage and hanged on May 18, 1965.

FIGURE 9 – MOSSAD AGENT ELI COHEN [392]
Source of photo on left: CDI Systems. Used with permission.
Source of photo on right: Public domain.

Intelligence officers are not the only individuals endangered by unauthorized disclosures. Disclosures by the media have also been associated with the death of military members off the battlefield. Former Secretaries of Defense, to include William Perry and Donald Rumsfeld, have discussed the additional threat to military personnel posed by disclosures of classified information.[393,394] Unauthorized disclosures linked to the deaths of members of the military include:

Beirut Barracks

As reported by the former CEO of the *Washington Post*, Katharine Graham, the October 1983 bombing of the U.S. Marine barracks in Beirut potentially could have been averted if the media had not disclosed classified information. Graham wrote that, five months prior to the attack, a television network and a newspaper disclosed that the United States had been intercepting encrypted communications between a terrorist group in Syria and Iran.[395] The disclosure was made after 60 people were killed by a bomb attack in April 1983 at the U.S. Embassy in Beirut.

Graham stated that the communications were discontinued shortly after the disclosure (an additional example of the loss of an intelligence source). She added that the same terrorist group apparently carried out the attack on the U.S. Marine Corps barracks in Beirut, killing 241 servicemen. *Washington Post* reporter Bob Woodward also identified this incident as an example of a harmful disclosure. In 1988 Woodward wrote, "I think that was a genuine, serious mistake and intelligence was lost and I think you can argue that some of your colleagues may have died in '84 because that intelligence was lost."[396]

FIGURE 10 – USMC BARRACKS – BEIRUT, 1983 [397]
Source of photo on left: Long Commission Report, commissioned by U.S. Government.
Source of photo on right: U.S. Marine Corps.

TWA Flight 847

On May 12, 1985, the *Washington Post* disclosed that President Reagan had approved a covert operation for the CIA to train and support counterterrorist units in the Middle East.[398] The article reported that one of these units later killed 80 people during a March 1985 attack in Beirut.

Three months later, on June 14, 1985, members of the terrorist group Hezbollah hijacked TWA Flight 847. The hijackers tortured and executed one of the passengers, U.S. Navy diver Robert Stethem, shooting him in the back of the head and dropping his body onto a runway in Beirut.[399] The hijackers reportedly cited the CIA's involvement in the March attack as justification for Stethem's murder.[400] A subsequent investigation by the HPSCI found no evidence that the CIA had encouraged or participated in terrorist activity in Lebanon.

PURPLE and MAGIC

One of the most frequently cited examples of a harmful disclosure of classified information by the media occurred in 1942. While onboard a U.S. Navy ship returning from the Pacific, *Chicago Tribune* reporter Stanley Johnston discovered that the United States had intercepted the Japanese order of battle prior to the Battle of Midway.[401] As a result of this intelligence, Admiral Nimitz was able to ignore a Japanese feint and concentrate the American fleet near Midway Island. The naval victory at Midway is considered one of the most significant of World War II. After learning of the intercepts, Johnston wrote, and the *Tribune* published, an article titled "Navy Had Word of Jap Plan to Strike at Sea." The information in the article was attributed to "reliable sources in naval intelligence."[402]

The inescapable conclusion of the article was that the United States had decrypted the Japanese military code, known as JN-25 or PURPLE. Soon after the article was published, syndicated columnist Walter Winchell asserted that the *Tribune* article was based on decoded Japanese messages.[403] This capability had been one of the most closely guarded secrets of the war and was credited with shortening the war in the Pacific. Intelligence derived from decrypted Japanese communications was classified by the code name MAGIC.

President Roosevelt reportedly had to be dissuaded from sending the Marines to shut down the newspaper and charging *Chicago Tribune* publisher Robert McCormick with treason.[404] The Navy was concerned that a trial would draw additional attention to the article. McCormick, an isolationist and ardent critic of Roosevelt, had opposed U.S. entrance into World War II.[405] A grand jury was empanelled, but the Navy refused to cooperate with the Justice Department. In addition, JN-25 had been decrypted. As described by former DCI James Woolsey in 2006, "That one story could have changed the outcome of World War II in the Pacific."[406]

Other lives may also be placed in jeopardy by unauthorized disclosures. This includes individuals not directly affiliated with the IC or the military, such as American and foreign civilians who voluntarily assist U.S. intelligence agencies. Speaking before the Society of Professional Journalists in 1986, DCI William Casey addressed the threat to foreign assets, stating that recruited sources "have not been heard from after their information has been published in the U.S. press."[407] Director of the CIA Michael Hayden commented in 2007: "[I]n one case, leaks provided ammunition for a government to prosecute and imprison one of our sources, whose family was also endangered. The revelations had an immediate, chilling effect on our ability to collect against a top-priority target."[408]

Examples of the threat to civilians from unauthorized disclosures include:

Disclosure of U.S. Military Field Reports by WikiLeaks

In July 2010, the Internet-based organization WikiLeaks posted information on its website from over 75,000 classified U.S. military field reports concerning the war in Afghanistan. WikiLeaks did not identify its source for the reports. Prior to publishing the information, WikiLeaks allowed the *New York Times*, the British newspaper *The Guardian*, and the German magazine *Der Spiegel* to review the documents. All three media outlets published articles containing information from the classified reports. In October 2010, WikiLeaks posted almost 400,000 additional classified documents related to the war in Iraq.

Soon after WikiLeaks posted information from the classified reports on its website, concerns were raised that the identities of Afghan citizens cooperating with U.S. and NATO forces had been exposed. Though the *New York Times* did not identify any of these individuals in its articles, it reported that "names or other identifying features of dozens of Afghan informants, potential defectors and others who were cooperating with American and NATO troops" could be found on the WikiLeaks website.[409]

Afghan President Harmid Karzai called the disclosures "extremely irresponsible and shocking," adding that the lives of any Afghans identified would be endangered.[410] Admiral Mike Mullen, Chairman of the U.S. Joint Chiefs of Staff, also voiced his concerns that WikiLeaks "might already have on their hands the blood of some young soldier or that of an Afghan family."[411] In apparent confirmation of President Karzai's and Admiral Mullen's fears, a Taliban spokesman stated that the Taliban was studying the disclosed information and would "punish" anyone identified as collaborating with U.S. forces.[412]

Representatives from five human rights organizations—Amnesty International, Campaign for Innocent Victims in Conflict (CIVIC), Open Society Institute (OSI), Afghanistan Independent Human Rights Commission, and the Kabul office of International Crisis Group (ICG)—contacted WikiLeaks to voice their concerns.[413] The representatives urged WikiLeaks to remove or redact the documents containing identifying information.

In the book *WikiLeaks: Julian Assange's War on Secrecy,* a journalist from *The Guardian* documents a conversation with WikiLeaks founder Julian Assange, concerning the identification of foreign nationals in the compromised documents. During the discussion, Assange reportedly remarked: "Well, they're informants. So, if they get killed, they've got it coming to them. They deserve it."[414] Assange has denied making this statement and indicated that he intends to sue *The Guardian* for libel.[415]

In a commentary concerning the potential breadth of harm resulting from the disclosures, former Director of both the CIA and the NSA Michael Hayden remarked:

> What potential sources in Afghanistan will now believe that America can protect them? Why would anyone in that troubled land bet

his family's well-being and future on such a well-intentioned but obviously porous partner, whatever hope or vision for the future this potential source might harbor? And we will never know who will now not come forward, who will not provide us with life-saving information, who will decide he cannot opt for a common effort against a common enemy. But we can be certain that the cost will be great.[416]

U.S. Army Private First Class Bradley Manning has been identified as a person of interest in the disclosure of the Afghan-related military reports to WikiLeaks.[417] As of May 2011, Manning was being held in pre-trial confinement at Fort Leavenworth, Kansas, on charges related to the disclosure of classified information to an unauthorized person.[418]

Koran Desecration

On May 9, 2005, *Newsweek* published an article by Michael Isikoff disclosing that military guards at Guantanamo Bay, Cuba, had desecrated a copy of the Koran by flushing it down the toilet.[419] Isikoff attributed the information to an anonymous senior government official. The desecration of the Koran is reportedly a death penalty offense in Afghanistan and Pakistan. After the allegation was republished on the front page of several newspapers in Pakistan, the Pakistani Parliament passed a unanimous resolution condemning the desecration.[420]

According to National Security Advisor Stephen Hadley, radical Islamic elements used the report as a justification to incite protests in both Pakistan and Afghanistan.[421] These protests resulted in 17 deaths and numerous injuries.[422] After the protests, Isikoff wrote that *Newsweek* was "caught off guard," adding, "We obviously blame ourselves for not understanding the potential ramifications."[423]

Controversy over the disclosure intensified when *Newsweek* retracted the story one week later. In a published statement, it was acknowledged that the single anonymous source had not directly observed the alleged desecration and had "expressed doubt about his own knowledge of the accusation against the guards."[424] A Pentagon investigation was unable to corroborate the desecration. The Chairman of the Joint Chiefs of Staff, General Richard

Myers, stated that Defense Department investigators identified only one uncorroborated incident with any similarities to the allegation.[425] In that case, a detainee reportedly attempted to block a toilet pipe using pages from a Koran. In response to the incident, Assistant Secretary of State for Public Affairs Richard Boucher stated, "It's appalling, really, that an article that was unfounded to begin with has caused so much harm, including loss of life."[426]

Newsweek reportedly issued rigorous new rules for using material from unidentified sources as a result of the article.[427]

CIA Recruiting Iranians

In January 2002 the *Los Angeles Times* published an article by Greg Miller entitled "CIA Looks to Los Angeles for Would-Be Iranian Spies."[428] The article details CIA efforts to recruit U.S. citizens, particularly in the Los Angeles area, with family members still residing in Iran. The article alleges that the CIA had successfully recruited "foreign students and other visitors to America, who return to their home countries and provide valuable information for the United States." Miller identified the potential for harm in the same article, reporting that individuals caught spying in Iran face severe punishment, including execution. Prior to publication, DCI George Tenet urged *Los Angeles Times* managing editor Dean Baquet to withhold the story.[429] Baquet withheld the story for one day but then published the article, stating "They were kidding themselves if they thought it wouldn't get out."[430]

After the story was published, a representative from the CIA Public Affairs Office noted, "The plan to use the Iranian Americans to bring back intelligence had worked quite well, but not since the *Times* story."[431] The officer added, "The press can't have it both ways, criticizing us for not knowing things and then making it harder for us to find out things and do our job." The officer also noted that Iranian expatriates traveling to Iran from the United States would find themselves under much greater scrutiny. Though no causal relationship can be concluded, a 2007 article in *Commentary* magazine reported that four U.S. citizens had been detained in Iran subsequent to the publication of the *Times* article.[432] At least one of the individuals was from Southern California.

Soviet Mechanic

As previously identified, a 1971 article published in the *Washington Post* disclosed the existence of the classified program BROADSIDE, which involved intercepting phone calls made from Soviet limousines. A 2003 article reported that a Soviet mechanic hired by the CIA to install covert listening devices in the limousines had "disappeared" after the *Post* article was published.[433]

Though the Constitution and the Bill of Rights were enacted to safeguard individual liberties, including the First Amendment's right to a free press, the courts and members of Congress have recognized that protecting life is of paramount importance. In ordering the preliminary injunction prohibiting *Progressive* magazine from publishing instructions for constructing a hydrogen bomb, District Judge Robert Warren wrote:

> While it may be true . . . as Patrick Henry instructs us, that one would prefer death to life without liberty . . . one cannot enjoy freedom of speech, freedom to worship or freedom of the press unless one first enjoys the freedom to live.[434]

In the Supreme Court case Kennedy v. Mendoza-Martinez, 372 U.S. 144 (1963), Supreme Court Justice Arthur Goldberg wrote in his opinion, "[W]hile the Constitution protects against invasions of individual rights, it is not a suicide pact."[435] In 2006 Senator Pat Roberts of Kansas remarked: "I am a strong supporter of the First Amendment, the Fourth Amendment and civil liberties, but you have no civil liberties if you are dead."[436] Unauthorized disclosures are also perceived to impact foreign policy negatively, including both the deliberation necessary to shape national policy as well as the implementation of approved policies.

Impact on the Development and Implementation of Foreign Policy

> *[T]he development of considered and intelligent international policies would be impossible if those charged with their formulation could not communicate with each other freely, frankly, and in confidence.*[437]
>
> - Justice Potter Stewart, New York Times v. United States

[W]e cannot invariably install, as the ultimate arbiter of disclosure, even the conscience of the well-meaning employee . . . Vital decisions . . . by elected representatives would be subject to summary derailment at the pleasure of one disgruntled employee.[438]

- Judge Harvie Wilkinson, US v. Morison

Foreign policy decisions are normally preceded by extensive debate. Several options may be proposed and rejected before a final decision is made. Reaching a consensus, particularly in the current climate of political partisanship, is uncommon. Though the deliberative process may not always be conclusive, or even civil, it is vital in the formation of U.S. policy. An unauthorized disclosure during this process damages the opportunity for meaningful dialogue. Potential alternatives may not be supported, or even considered, if officials are concerned about the repercussions of being associated with an unpopular or unsuccessful policy.

This concern is particularly compelling when deliberations involve a covert operation or other IC activity. Policy decisions involving classified programs are controversial by their very nature because they involve concealing information from the public. If a government official has to consider the possibility that a classified operation will be exposed, not only by a foreign adversary but also by a political adversary, the potential to garner his/her support may be diminished. As recently as November 2009, President Barack Obama expressed his frustration over unauthorized disclosures related to ongoing administration deliberations.

Troop Levels in Afghanistan

In mid-2009, the Obama administration was deliberating the deployment of additional troops to augment U.S. forces in Afghanistan. In September 2009, Bob Woodward published an article in the *Washington Post* containing information from a "confidential assessment" prepared by General Stanley McChrystal, the U.S. Commander in Afghanistan.[439] According to the article, McChrystal assessed that, if additional troops were not deployed, the administration risked "mission failure." Three weeks later, the *New York Times* disclosed that Karl Eikenberry, U.S. Ambassador to Afghanistan and McChrystal's predecessor, submitted a classified cable to the White House outlining his reservations about deploying additional U.S. troops, and his concerns regarding the Afghan government.[440] On November 19, 2009, President Obama specifically addressed his frustration over these disclosures:

> I think I am angrier than Bob Gates about it, partly because we have these deliberations in the Situation Room for a reason — because we are making decisions that are life-and-death, that affect how our troops will be able to operate in a theater of war. For people to be releasing information during the course of deliberation – where we haven't made final decisions yet – I think is not appropriate."[441]

In December 2009 the Obama administration elected to deploy approximately 30,000 additional troops to Afghanistan. The disclosures did not end with this decision, however. On January 25, 2010, the *New York Times* published a copy of Ambassador Eikenberry's entire classified cable.[442] The article indicates that an American official had provided a copy of the cable to the *New York Times* "after a reporter requested them."

Several other historical examples illustrate how concern over unauthorized disclosures influenced either the development of a policy or implementation of a policy decision:

National Intelligence Estimate – Iran

As previously discussed, the Bush administration made the decision to declassify findings from a December 2007 National Intelligence Estimate (NIE) related to Iran. Two months prior to the release, Director of National Intelligence Michael McConnell had published a statement which read, "It is the policy of the Director of National Intelligence that KJs [Key Judgments of an NIE] should not be declassified."[443] After the Iran NIE findings were published, the *Washington Post* reported that the decision had been made "out of fear of leaks and charges of a cover-up."[444]

In this instance, it appears that a valid and legal policy decision, not to disclose classified information, had been altered because officials were resigned that the information would eventually be compromised. After these Key Judgments were released, classified information concerning the intelligence underlying the findings was also disclosed by the *Washington Post*[445] and the *New York Times*.[446] These disclosures involved intelligence from both human and technical collection sources.

Covert Action in Pakistan

In January 2008 the *New York Times* reported that President Bush and senior national security advisors were considering expanding the authority of the military and the CIA to conduct covert operations inside Pakistan's borders.[447] The article speculated on the manner in which these "highly classified" covert actions could be carried out and reported that the United States already had approximately 50 members of the military operating inside Pakistan. The article specifically stated that the officials disclosing the information wished to remain anonymous "because of the highly delicate nature of the discussions." The article added that American diplomats and military officials critical of the operations being deliberated believed their exposure could result in a tremendous backlash, including angering the Pakistani Army, increasing support for anti-government militants, and reducing support for Pakistani President Pervez Musharraf.

In response to the unauthorized disclosure, Pakistan's chief military spokesman stated, "It is not up to the U.S. administration, it is Pakistan's government which is responsible for this country."[448] He also rejected the idea that the United States should conduct covert operations inside Pakistan.

Even in cases where an administration is able to conduct sensitive deliberations confidentially, the ability to implement a policy can still be impacted by an unauthorized disclosure. Almost all policy decisions will have detractors. As noted by Judge Wilkinson, unauthorized disclosures may permit the judgments of a single opponent to override the entire policy process. Based on the threat of an unauthorized disclosure, the implementation of complex covert actions can become dependent on the continued good grace of every government official with knowledge of the activity.

At a 1984 conference held at Columbia University, James Schlesinger, former DCI and Secretary of Defense, commented that unauthorized disclosures had become routine and that this breakdown in discipline had made it "virtually impossible" to conduct covert operations.[449] Seventeen years later, Attorney General John Ashcroft confirmed that the unauthorized disclosure of classified government information had hampered legitimate government policies.[450]

Examples of the impact of unauthorized disclosures on the implementation of policies include:

Support to Egyptian Operation

In 1983 Egyptian president Hosni Mubarak requested support from the United States for a joint operation targeting Libya. U.S. support for the operation would include the use of AWACS aircraft to assist Egyptian pilots. Though the policy decision was not unanimous, the Reagan administration agreed to support the operation. As part of the agreement, President Mubarak required that U.S. involvement remain covert.[451] Opponents of the policy reportedly included senators Joseph Biden, Patrick Leahy, and David Durenberger. ABC reporter Brit Hume later reported that Senator Biden threatened on two occasions to expose U.S. involvement in the operation.[452] The *Washington Times* reported that senators Leahy and Durenberger wrote a letter to DCI William Casey, also threatening to expose the operation.[453]

During final preparations for the operation, which had taken over a year to plan, the administration learned that ABC was preparing a story detailing a portion of the operational plan, the movement of the USS Nimitz closer to the Libyan coast. National Security Advisor William Clark met with ABC executives and, without revealing the complete operation, requested that ABC withhold publication. ABC agreed to delay broadcast for 24 hours but then released the story. Other media organizations, including the *Washington Post*, also published articles related to the operation. After the disclosures, the operation was aborted. The *Washington Post* later quoted administration officials who stated that the disclosure revealed U.S. intentions and broke Mubarak's condition that U.S. support remain confidential.[454]

Non-Lethal Presidential Findings

In May 2007 ABC News reported that President Bush had signed a non-lethal "Presidential finding" related to Iran.[455] A Presidential finding is a directive approving the execution of a covert operation. The online article noted that Presidential findings are classified, adding that they are briefed to members of Congress, including the House and Senate Intelligence Committees. The addition of the term "non-lethal" indicates that the CIA was not authorized to use deadly force during the operation. The reported objective of this particular CIA operation was to pressure Iran to discontinue its nuclear program without resorting to military force. The article's author recognized the sensitivity of the Presidential finding, noting that the covert action could lead to Iranian retaliation and a "cycle of escalation."[456]

In a separate disclosure five months after the ABC News article, the British newspaper *The Telegraph* published an article revealing that President Bush had also signed a non-lethal Presidential finding concerning Hezbollah.[457] The finding reportedly authorized the CIA to assist the Lebanese government in preventing increased Iranian influence in the region, including Iranian support for Hezbollah. The article stated that Saudi Arabian officials were included in deliberations and that the U.S. Congress had been briefed on the finding. As previously noted, U.S. and CIA involvement in the Middle East had been identified as a justification for Hezbollah hijackers to execute a member of the U.S. Navy in 1985.

Ironically, even policy decisions concerning unauthorized disclosures are susceptible to disclosure. In January 1982, after a series of disclosures by the media, the Reagan administration published National Security Decision Directive (NSDD) 19, "Protection of Classified National Security Council and Intelligence Information."[458] The directive enacted specific measures in an attempt to reduce disclosures. Disclosures that preceded the directive, and may have led to its creation, related to cost overruns in the Defense Department and a decision not to sell the current generation of jet fighters to Taiwan.

Announcement of the NSDD-19 guidelines had to be rushed because news of its existence was beginning to leak.[459] Whether coincidence or not, the day after the directive was published another disclosure revealed that the United States had detected crates of Soviet aircraft near Havana.[460]

The impact unauthorized disclosures have on policy deliberations and their implementation appears to be among the most frustrating categories of harm for government officials. This is a result of the enormous impact a single discontented individual can have on a lengthy and complex policy process.

FIGURE 11 – UNAUTHORIZED DISCLOSURE SATIRE [461]
Source: Harley Schwadron and www.CartoonStock.com. Used with permission.

Effect on International Alliances

In at least two instances . . . the foreign liaison services refused to share crucial information with the United States because of fear of leaks.[462]

- WMD Commission Report

The massive hemorrhage of state secrets was bound to raise doubts about our reliability and about the stability of our political system.[463]

- Henry Kissinger, former Secretary of State and
National Security Advisor

As complicated as the implementation of domestic policies can be, successfully conducting international diplomacy is almost assuredly more complex. Beyond balancing internal interests, diplomacy requires the ability to achieve consensus with foreign government(s), which have their own, potentially competing, motivations. Fragile negotiations and partnerships can collapse if one party believes their interests are not being served. Supreme Court Justice Potter Stewart believed it was "elementary" that diplomacy required secrecy, and that other nations could not deal with the United States "unless they can be assured that their confidences would be kept."[464]

During June 2000 testimony before the SSCI, Attorney General Janet Reno specifically cited the damage unauthorized disclosures can cause to diplomatic efforts and liaison relationships.[465] In an environment where an increased emphasis has been placed on responding to international incidents with a coalition, rather than through unilateral action, any harm to international relationships resulting from unauthorized disclosures will be magnified.

Cases in which unauthorized disclosures are reported to have damaged relations with a foreign ally include:

Net-Centric Diplomacy

In November 2010, the Internet-based organization WikiLeaks began releasing classified U.S. State Department cables from a reported cache of more than 250,000 documents it had obtained from an unknown source. The diplomatic cables were part of an electronic database referred to as Net-Centric Diplomacy. The cables contained assessments of foreign governments and officials by U.S. embassy and consulate staff.

Mexican President Felipe Calderon described the harm to U.S. relations resulting from the disclosures as "severe."[466] Calderon personally called for the removal of U.S. Ambassador to Mexico Carlos Pascual. Pascual, who had been critical of the Calderon administration in several of the compromised cables, ultimately resigned his position and returned to the United States.[467] In addition to Pascual, the U.S. Ambassador to Ecuador was also expelled from the country and the U.S. Ambassador to Libya recalled to the United States.[468] The Ecuadorian government reportedly expelled the U.S. Ambassador in response to a compromised cable discussing high-level corruption in the police force and possible knowledge by Ecuador's President.

Secretary of State Hillary Clinton denounced WikiLeaks' disclosure of the classified diplomatic cables.[469] Clinton stated that the compromise undermined efforts to work with other countries to solve shared problems and tore "at the fabric of the proper function of responsible government." She added that individuals who dedicated their lives to protecting others faced serious repercussions, including imprisonment, torture, and death. Clinton was confident, though, that U.S. relationships with foreign governments would endure despite the more immediate harm.

Hadley Memo

On November 29, 2006, the *New York Times* published the text of a memorandum prepared by National Security Advisor Stephen Hadley.[470] The article described the memo as a secret document prepared for Cabinet-level officials. In the memo Hadley was critical of Iraqi Prime Minister Nuri al-Maliki, stating he was either unwilling or unable to control the violence in Iraq, or he was possibly ignorant of its true extent.

A second *New York Times* article, published the same day, indicated that the Bush administration was specifically seeking to avoid public criticism of Maliki. The article also reported that a meeting between President Bush and Maliki, scheduled for the day the classified memo was published, had been cancelled at the last minute.[471]

Stinger Missiles to Angola

In 1986 the United States agreed to ship Stinger anti-aircraft missiles to Angola.[472] As part of the operation, DCI William Casey flew to Africa to arrange for the missiles to be shipped through Zaire. Zaire agreed to participate, on the condition that it not be linked to the transfer. Ultimately, information concerning these shipments was disclosed to the *Washington Post*, which published an article exposing the operation. In this case, the government is reported to have identified the U.S. official who provided the information to the *Post*, Assistant Secretary of Defense for Policy Planning Michael Pillsbury. Pillsbury reportedly failed three polygraph tests and was fired from his position in April 1986.[473]

Military Aircraft to Taiwan

On January 11, 1982, the *Washington Post* disclosed that the Reagan administration had agreed to sell F5-E fighter jets to Taiwan, but had denied its request for more advanced fighters.[474] On January 13, White House spokesman Larry Speakes condemned the disclosure because it "did not allow us to conduct foreign policy in an orderly manner." Speakes added that the administration had not concluded consulting with allies or with members of Congress when the disclosure occurred.

As mentioned above, National Security Decision Directive 19, outlining the administration's intention to implement greater control over access to classified information, was published soon after the Taiwan disclosure.[475] When publication of the directive was announced, the Taiwan disclosure was specifically cited as a justification for the enhanced security measures. At a news conference held a week after the Taiwan disclosure, President Reagan complained that leaks "had reached a new high."[476]

Unauthorized disclosures not only harm state-to-state relations, but also relationships between the U.S. Intelligence Community and allied intelligence services. Based on the increased requirement to collect information in support of U.S. interests worldwide, the ability to collaborate with foreign intelligence services continues to be crucial. Historically, many of the most successful intelligence operations have relied on cooperation among allied intelligence services. These include Operation FORTITUDE, a deception operation to conceal the Allies' landing at Normandy in 1944, and ULTRA, the Allied program to decrypt German communications encoded by its Enigma machines.

If allied intelligence services are expected to continue working jointly with the United States, intelligence sources and methods must be protected. If an agency is concerned that its intelligence will be compromised, it may refuse to share valuable information. If the allied intelligence service fears participation in joint operations will be exposed, it may elect not to provide assistance. In 2005 Congressman Peter Hoekstra of New York noted, "The loss of foreign partners would undoubtedly create overwhelming gaps in our ability to collect good intelligence around the globe."[477]

In 1979 DCI Stansfield Turner discussed the harm to relationships resulting from a perception that the U.S. was unable to protect classified information. During testimony in a case involving disclosures contained in a book written by former CIA employee Frank Snepp, Turner stated, "We have had very strong complaints from a number of foreign intelligence services with whom we conduct liaison, who have questioned whether they should continue exchanging information with us, for fear it will not remain secret."[478] In 2007 CIA Director Michael Hayden confirmed that allied intelligence services withheld intelligence as a result of unauthorized disclosures by the U.S. media:

> Several years before the 9/11 attacks, a press leak of liaison intelligence prompted one country's service to stop cooperating with us on counterterrorism for two years. More recently, more than one foreign service has told us that, because of public disclosures, they had to withhold intelligence that they otherwise would have shared with us. That gap in information puts Americans at risk.[479]

Examples of unauthorized disclosures concerning collaboration with allied intelligence services, and the harm to continued relations, include:

Curveball

Among the findings of the WMD Commission, it was reported that foreign intelligence services refused to share intelligence with the United States on at least two occasions because of concerns that their intelligence would be disclosed.[480] One of these cases involved an asset recruited by a foreign intelligence service, codenamed "Curveball." Curveball was reported to be an Iraqi defector with information concerning the status of Iraq's WMD program.

The reliance on erroneous information obtained from Curveball was reported to be one of the causes of the U.S. Intelligence Community's inaccurate assessment of the status of Iraq's weapons program.[481] It was also reported that the foreign intelligence service had refused numerous requests by the CIA for direct access to Curveball.[482] Direct access may have resulted in a better assessment of his credibility, allowing the CIA to conclude that he was unreliable.

During 2006 Senate Judiciary Committee hearings, Gabriel Schoenfeld, senior editor for *Commentary* magazine, testified that the media should be held partially responsible for the flawed intelligence, based on the foreign (identified as German) intelligence service's refusal to grant access to the informant. The refusal to allow access to Curveball was reportedly based on a fear that his identity would be exposed. [483] Validating these concerns, Curveball's identity was later revealed by CBS.[484]

CIA Detention Facilities

On November 2, 2005, the *Washington Post* published an article reporting the existence of a system of covert CIA detention facilities in Eastern Europe,[485] for which journalist Dana Priest was awarded a Pulitzer Prize. In announcing that the HPSCI would be investigating this and other disclosures, Chairman Peter Hoekstra stated that the greatest harm realized was to U.S. relations with countries that conducted joint intelligence operations with the United States.[486] A separate article quoted a government official who stated that the disclosure by Priest caused an "international uproar" and "did significant damage to relationships between the U.S. and allied intelligence agencies."[487] In 2006 it was reported that a senior CIA official was fired as a consequence of her unlawful contact with Priest and the disclosure of classified information to her.[488]

Almost two years after the initial disclosure by the *Washington Post*, a 2007 Council of Europe report disclosed that two of the detention facilities were located in Poland and Romania. The report stated that "sources in the CIA" had confirmed the locations.[489] In this case, not only had information concerning a classified program been disclosed to the American public, but CIA officials are also alleged to have disclosed classified information directly to a foreign government official. A former undersecretary of defense wrote that more than one of the foreign governments that had allowed the CIA facilities in their country had subsequently rescinded their approval.[490]

Pakistani Collaboration with Afghan Insurgents

In June 2010, the *New York Times* published an article alleged to contain information obtained from classified U.S. military field reports.[491] Over 70,000 classified reports relating to the war in Afghanistan had been made available to the *Times*, the British newspaper *The Guardian*, and the German magazine *Der Spiegel* by the Internet-based organization WikiLeaks. WikiLeaks subsequently posted the classified reports on its website. The identity of WikiLeaks' original source for the reports was not identified. In October 2010 WikiLeaks published almost 400,000 additional classified military reports concerning the war in Iraq.

Information contained in the military documents report suspected collaboration between Pakistan's intelligence service, Inter-Services Intelligence (ISI), and elements of the Afghan insurgency. The reports suggest that representatives from ISI met directly with Afghan insurgents, including the Taliban, to provide material support and to review strategies.

Pakistani officials are reported to have reacted angrily to the disclosures, stating that they could have "damaging consequences for Pakistan's relations with the United States."[492] Pakistani officials also questioned whether the United States could be trusted with sensitive information. A senior ISI official suggested that his agency might need to "reexamine its cooperation" with the United States if the CIA did not denounce allegations involving the ISI. A former head of the ISI was also quoted as saying that Pakistan should end its alliance with the United States altogether.

Concern over the impact unauthorized disclosures can have on intelligence relationships is not a recent development. At least four former Directors of Central Intelligence recognized and commented on this threat. In 1979 DCI William Colby confirmed that "Foreign intelligence services were reluctant to share sensitive information with us because they thought it would not be protected."[493] In 1986 DCI Casey wrote:

> Leaders and intelligence services of our closest allies have told us that if we can't tighten up, they will have to pull back on cooperation with us because they have had enough of reading the information they provide in the U.S. media.[494]

DCI Robert Gates made a similar pronouncement two years later. In 1988 he wrote: "Unauthorized disclosures have damaged U.S. relationships with other intelligence services and have dissuaded potential agents from accepting the risks of working on behalf of the United States."[495] DCI Porter Goss also discussed the threat to international alliances in 2006:

> Because of the number of recent news reports discussing our relationships with other intelligence services, some of these partners have even informed the CIA that they are reconsidering their participation in some of our most important antiterrorism ventures.[496]

Because information sharing among governments and intelligence services is particularly crucial during wartime, the consequences of unauthorized disclosures can be all the more devastating. As evidenced by the intelligence successes of World War II, cooperation among intelligence services may ultimately play a decisive role in a U.S. victory, or defeat.

Though not as provocative as the threat to human life or harm to international alliances, the financial cost to the Intelligence Community is also reported to be significant.

Financial Costs

In our classified report, we detail several leaks that have collectively cost the American people hundreds of millions of dollars, and have done grave harm to national security.[497]

- WMD Commission Report, 2005

The harm caused by unauthorized disclosures has been described both in terms of increasing financial costs for the United States and decreasing costs for U.S. adversaries. In separate speeches in 1986, DCI William Casey described both sides of the issue. In an April 1986 speech before the American Society of Newspaper Editors (ASNE), Casey remarked:

> Stories in both the print and electronic media have shown, sometimes in great detail, how to counter capabilities in which we have invested billions of dollars and many years of creative talent and effort.[498]

Five months later, in a September 1986 speech delivered to the Society of Professional Journalists, Casey noted:

> The KGB and other hostile intelligence services each year spend billions of dollars trying to acquire this information (information concerning U.S. sources and methods). But the unauthorized publication of restricted information hands to our adversaries on a silver platter information that their spies, their researchers, and their satellites are working 24 hours a day to uncover and use against us.[499]

Though it is rare for the exact costs for IC programs and equipment to be reported, there have been instances in which the financial impact of unauthorized disclosures by the media has been discussed:

FIGURE 12 – GLOMAR EXPLORER[501]
Source: Courtesy of *Offshore* magazine. Used with permission.

Project *AZORIAN*

As previously identified, Howard Hughes' company, Global Marine, constructed the ship Glomar Explorer in support of Project AZORIAN. The objective of AZORIAN was to salvage a sunken Soviet submarine in the Pacific. The cost to construct the 619-foot-long, 116-foot-wide, 36,000-ton Glomar Explorer was reported to be in excess of $200 million.[500] A submersible barge the size of a football field, HMB-1, was constructed along with the ship.

The cost for the entire operation was estimated at $550 million.[502] Though reports vary regarding the success in recovering the Soviet submarine, the operation was prematurely terminated in March 1975 after being exposed by several media outlets, including the *Los Angeles Times* and *New York Times*. According to DCI William Colby, "The Glomar project stopped because it was exposed."[503]

In December 1976, *Time* magazine reported that the ship was idle and that the government had placed it up for sale.[504] The government was never able to sell the ship. From 1978 to 1980 the Glomar Explorer was leased to a private company. For the next 16 years, from 1980 to 1996, it remained unused in the Navy's mothball fleet. It was leased once again in 1996.[505] In 2006, the government published a notice offering the submersible mining barge, HMB-1, for donation.[506]

Project *GREEK ISLAND*

In May 1992, the *Washington Post* published the article "The Ultimate Congressional Hideaway."[507] The article disclosed that the government had constructed a bunker underneath the Greenbrier Hotel in White Sulphur Springs, West Virginia. The purpose of the bunker was to house members of Congress in the event of a nuclear war or other national crisis. The estimated cost to construct the bunker, in 1960, was $14 million.[508] The government had kept the existence of the 100,000-square foot bunker secret for over 30 years. The article's author, Ted Gup, believed the bunker had become obsolete.

The day after the article was published, Speaker of the House Tom Foley sent a letter to Secretary of Defense, Dick Cheney, recommending that support for the compromised bunker be discontinued. The bunker was subsequently decommissioned. It is unknown whether another facility was constructed to replace the Greenbrier bunker.

Alaskan Airfield

Also previously discussed was a 1958 disclosure by the *New York Times*, revealing that the United States had the ability to monitor the countdowns for Soviet missile launches.[509] After the Soviets reduced the length of the countdowns by four hours, U.S. aircraft were no longer able to reach the landing area to monitor the splashdown. To regain a portion of the lost collection capability, the United States rebuilt and staffed an airfield in Alaska "at a cost of millions of dollars."[510]

In addition to DCI William Casey's 1986 remarks regarding the financial harm caused by unauthorized disclosures, DCIs Robert Gates and Porter Goss discussed the issue in general terms. In 1988 DCI Gates wrote, "Deliberate leaks of intelligence information have . . . required the expenditure of billions of dollars in order to revamp or replace sophisticated technical collection systems that have been compromised."[511] In a 2006 op-ed published in the *New York Times*, DCI Goss concurred with the findings of the WMD Commission regarding the "hundreds of millions of dollars" lost as the result of unauthorized disclosures.[512] Whether measured in hundreds of millions or billions of dollars, the perceived financial cost of unauthorized disclosures has been considerable.

Decrease in Public Knowledge Resulting from Incomplete or Inaccurate Information

The man who never looks into a newspaper is better informed than he who reads them, inasmuch as he who knows nothing is nearer the truth . . .[513]

- Thomas Jefferson

Rather than creating a more knowledgeable citizenry and increasing informed public debate, unauthorized disclosures may have the opposite effect—decreasing or distorting public knowledge. Journalists who obtain classified information often receive only partial details concerning a particular program or operation. Government employees who disclose information often have motivations beyond the desire to increase public awareness. These motivations may include garnering public approval for a program they support or harming a policy sponsored by a political rival. Whether a government source elects only to divulge a specific piece of information or has access only to a portion of an entire program, a journalist is often left with incomplete facts.

If the journalist is unable to obtain the remaining relevant information, he or she is only able to provide one piece of a larger mosaic to the public. The government is then put in an undesirable position of either allowing the public to consider inaccurate or incomplete, and potentially prejudicial, information or disclosing additional classified information to clarify what has already been improperly disclosed.

In almost every instance, a journalist who discloses classified information elects not to identify his or her source. Consequently, the public is unable to judge the source's credibility, which would assist in assessing the reliability of the information disclosed. Similar to the United States' difficulty in assessing the credibility of the discredited foreign asset Curveball, the public has less knowledge with which to make an informed decision.

The media may use this blanket of anonymity to purposefully mislead the public on the credibility of a source. Seymour Hersh, an investigative journalist for the *New Yorker* well-known for publishing articles containing classified information, characterized the use of anonymity to disguise a weak source as a "chronic problem."[514] Hersh added that he was aware of this "very troubling" practice being used at the *New York Times*, the Associated Press, and other media outlets where he had worked. Ironically, a Pentagon spokesman stated in 2006 that Hersh himself had "a solid and well-earned reputation for making dramatic assertions based on thinly sourced, unverifiable anonymous sources."[515]

On at least one occasion, a journalist agreed to misidentify a source. In an article identifying Valerie Plame as a CIA employee, *New York Times* reporter Judith Miller agreed to identify a source, Scooter Libby, chief of staff for Vice President Dick Cheney, as a "former Hill staffer."[516] In this case, Miller reportedly elected to mislead the public in an effort to protect her source.

Though not involving classified information, a 2004 report regarding former President Bush's service in the Air National Guard provides an example of the harm caused by the use of anonymous sources. In this case, a CBS broadcast presented documents that appeared to identify discrepancies with President Bush's service in the National Guard.[517] The CBS report, televised two months prior to the 2004 Presidential election, verified the documents' authenticity but did not identify their source. Shortly after the broadcast it was determined that the documents were almost certainly forgeries.

Because CBS chose not to disclose the identity of its source, the public did not know that the source, Bill Burkett, was a long-time opponent of President Bush, described as an "embittered former officer who will do anything to embarrass the president and retaliate against senior Texas Guard officers."[518]

The alleged desecration of the Koran in 2005 is another example of a disclosure that decreased public knowledge. In this instance, the disclosure resulted not only in a misinformed American public, but also reportedly contributed to several deaths. In response to this article, *USA Today* announced its intention to reduce the use of information from unnamed sources by 75 percent.[519] Three additional articles, published in *New Republic* magazine in 2007, may have also led to a less, rather than more, informed citizenry.

Baghdad Diarist

In 2007 *New Republic* magazine published three articles containing information obtained from an anonymous U.S. soldier. Each of the articles detailed incidents alleged to have occurred in Iraq, including U.S. soldiers desecrating a grave, running over dogs with military vehicles, and ridiculing a disfigured Iraqi woman.[520] After the articles were published, the U.S.

soldier was identified as Private Scott Beauchamp. It was also reported that Beauchamp was romantically involved with a *New Republic* reporter.

A subsequent article, published in another magazine, reported that Beauchamp signed a sworn statement admitting that the information he provided for the articles were "exaggerations and falsehoods."[521] A Pentagon spokesman stated that, after a military investigation, no member of Beauchamp's troop or company was able to substantiate Beauchamp's allegations.[522]

When the U.S. public is provided only with partial information and is unable to evaluate the credibility of a source, the consequence may be a public that is less knowledgeable about government activity. In the Beauchamp case, along with the Bush National Guard and Koran desecration articles, an anonymous source, providing incomplete or inaccurate information, may have led to the American public actually being misinformed rather than informed. In these cases, the benefits of disclosure are particularly questionable.

Journalists contend that the practice of concealing a source's identity is a crucial component of their government oversight function. Without a policy of offering anonymity to a source, members of the media contend that government employees would be more hesitant to provide the information necessary to expose misconduct or illegal activity. In a July 2008 letter to Congress supporting the proposed "Free Flow of Information Act," the American Society of Newspaper Editors (ASNE) emphasized the importance of confidential sources: "[H]istory is replete with examples of news articles critical to the national interest that would have never been written had it not been for the protection of confidential sources."[523]

Because the use of anonymous sources has always been an accepted practice by the American media, any theory of the impact of its discontinuation is purely speculative. It is possible that government sources would still have the conviction to openly disclose classified information exposing illegal activity or abuse. It is also possible that sources might elect to avail themselves of other outlets, such as the procedures established by whistleblower statutes. Perhaps only the disclosures of greatest concern to the government would be impacted, disclosures where the harm to national security is recognized as significant and the benefit to the public considered nominal.

Benefiting U.S. Adversaries While Harming U.S. Interests

The primary beneficiaries of leaks of national security and intelligence secrets are the enemies and potential adversaries of the United States.[524]

- *Attorney General John Ashcroft*

The fact of the matter is, some of the worst damage done to our Intelligence Community has come not from penetration by spies, but from unauthorized leaks by those with access to classified information.[525]

- *Representative Peter Hoekstra, Ranking Member, HPSCI*

Each of the six identified categories of harm may not only damage U.S. capabilities or interests, but also directly benefit U.S. adversaries. Whether providing the Soviet Union with advanced knowledge of the development of Stealth technology, informing Iran of efforts to disrupt its nuclear weapons program, or revealing to Al Qaeda that its computer network had been infiltrated, U.S. adversaries have benefited from the unauthorized disclosure of classified information. Former Russian military intelligence officer Stanislav Lunev, confirmed that adversaries welcome the disclosures and that, in his case, the Soviet Union was "very appreciative" of the classified information disclosed in U.S. newspapers.[526]

Critics of these disclosures contend that the harm not only surpasses any benefit to the U.S. public but also potentially rivals the damage caused by traditional espionage. When classified information is disclosed in a public forum, such as a newspaper or on the Internet, countless foreign governments or other adversaries are provided insight into U.S. capabilities and intentions. In response to President Clinton's 2000 veto of a bill to broaden the Espionage Act, Senator Richard Shelby of Alabama noted, "Where a spy generally serves one customer, media leaks are available to anyone with twenty-five cents to buy the *Washington Post*, or access to an Internet connection."[527]

In his 1985 denial of a motion to dismiss Samuel Morison's indictment under the Espionage Act, Judge Joseph Young identified this concern:

> The danger to the United States is just as great when this information is released to the press as when it is released to an agent of a foreign government. The fear in releasing this type of information is that it gives other nations information concerning the intelligence gathering capabilities of the United States. The fear is realized whether the information is released to the world at large or whether it is released only to specific spies.[528]

Even in cases where a disclosure by the media is perceived to have caused little or no direct harm to national security, critics still oppose the practice. Speaking of the potential harm from information believed "unimportant," Chief Justice Warren Burger wrote:

> Foreign intelligence services have both the capacity to gather and analyze any information that is in the public domain and the substantial expertise in deducing the identities of intelligence sources from seemingly unimportant details. ... [B]its and pieces of data may aid in piecing together bits of other information even when the individual piece is not of obvious importance in itself.[529]

In his opinion in Snepp v. United States, 444 *U.S. 507 (1980)*, Supreme Court Justice John Paul Stevens noted that disclosures which do not directly damage national security can still be harmful. Justice Stevens recognized that all disclosures reinforce a perception that the government is unable to prevent the undesirable behavior.[530] This perception, in turn, increases the likelihood that other government employees will elect to disclose classified information which does cause direct and identifiable harm to national security.

Confirmation Bias and the Media's Ability to Identify Harm

In order to reduce incidence of unauthorized disclosures, members of the media must not only recognize the harm caused by disclosures but also conclude more frequently that this harm outweighs perceived benefits.

Complicating what is already a difficult process, additional obstacles exist that may decrease the likelihood that a journalist will reach this conclusion. These include psychological limitations that affect an individual's ability to perceive and process information. Chief among these limitations is the concept of "confirmation bias."

Confirmation Bias is defined as "a phenomenon wherein decision makers have been shown to actively seek out and assign more weight to evidence that confirms their hypothesis, and ignore or underweigh evidence that could disconfirm their hypothesis."[531] Because government officials are normally unaware of an unauthorized disclosure until a media outlet notifies them of the intent to publish, confirmation bias would likely apply. Consequently, even if government officials offer evidence of harm to national security, the potential for altering the decision would be reduced. Paul Steiger, Managing Editor of the *Wall Street Journal*, discussed this predisposition to publish: "The presumption is that we will publish what we have learned through our reporting, if we think a story is newsworthy."[532] *Washington Times* reporter Bill Gertz shared Steiger's sentiment: "As a reporter, I lean towards publication."[533] Once a journalist concludes that disclosing classified information is beneficial, any attempt to alter this conclusion is immediately disadvantaged by confirmation bias.

It must also be understood that at the same time advocates of reducing the level of unauthorized disclosures are attempting to convince a journalist to alter his or her decision to publish, supporters of the legitimacy of these disclosures may be doing the opposite. Based on the effect of confirmation bias, it can be expected that a member of the media predisposed to publication would give greater credence to arguments favoring disclosure. As will be seen in the next chapter, members of the media may not only give greater credence to information that agrees with their preconceived notions; they may actively seek out this information.

Conclusion

The continued publication of classified information signifies that, at least in those cases, members of the media concluded that the identified motivations and justifications outweighed the recognized categories of harm. In Chapter 1 this cost-benefit analysis was visualized as a "psychological scale." Applying the concepts of Rational Choice Theory with the findings presented in Chapters 2 and 3, a journalist's deliberative process can be visualized in the following manner:

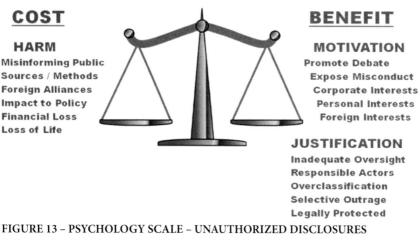

COST

HARM
Misinforming Public
Sources / Methods
Foreign Alliances
Impact to Policy
Financial Loss
Loss of Life

BENEFIT

MOTIVATION
Promote Debate
Expose Misconduct
Corporate Interests
Personal Interests
Foreign Interests

JUSTIFICATION
Inadequate Oversight
Responsible Actors
Overclassification
Selective Outrage
Legally Protected

FIGURE 13 – PSYCHOLOGY SCALE – UNAUTHORIZED DISCLOSURES
Source: Author.

Though not all motivations, justifications, or categories of harm may be applicable in every circumstance, each has the potential to contribute to the cost-benefit analysis. An ability to recognize which is relevant in a specific situation is also essential for understanding a journalist's thought process. This capability will be examined in the final chapter.

If advocates of reducing the frequency of unauthorized disclosures are genuine in their desire to effect change, a successful approach that incorporates Rational Choice Theory must be considered. Before examining the potential for applying such an approach, one final historical case study will be presented. Based on information made available by journalist Bob Woodward in the 1987 book *Veil*, the thought processes of members of the media and their rational weighing of choices can be examined in remarkable detail.

CHAPTER 4

IVY BELLS – Inside the Journalist's Decision-Making Process

We shouldn't publish what others are prosecuted for treason for.

- *Washington Post Executive Editor Ben Bradlee*

The deliberation that preceded the *Washington Post*'s publication of classified information related to Operation IVY BELLS provides an excellent case study of how Rational Choice Theory can be applied to a journalist's decision-making process. This study illustrates how the motivations, justifications, and categories of harm identified in Chapters 2 and 3 are weighed by members of the media.

The case study is based on information made available by journalist Bob Woodward in Chapter 23 of his 1987 book, *Veil: The Secret Wars of the CIA 1981-1987*.[534] Woodward discusses, in considerable detail, the deliberative process performed by officials at the *Post* prior to electing to publish an article containing classified information. The process includes Woodward's initial acquisition of the information, the drafting and editing of articles, and conversations with senior government officials, including President Ronald Reagan. Through Woodward's description of events, it is possible to identify the motivations, justifications, and categories of harm that Woodward and other senior *Post* executives considered prior to reaching the decision to publish.[535]

The Analysis Preceding Publication

In November 1985, former NSA employee Ronald Pelton was arrested and charged with espionage for providing classified information to the Soviet Union. Pelton had worked for the NSA from 1965 to 1979. Among the information compromised by Pelton was a classified operation named IVY BELLS. As reported by Woodward, this operation involved tapping Soviet undersea communication cables in the Sea of Okhotsk. U.S. submarines were used to attach a bell-shaped device to the cables, which could capture and record communications without damaging the outer shell of the cable. Submarines were also used to service the device and retrieve the recorded information.

Operation IVY BELLS was reported to have been active from the late 1970s through 1981 when the Soviets discovered and removed the device. Woodward states that KGB defector Vitaly Yurchenko assisted in identifying Pelton, adding that the United States had not known how the device was compromised prior to Pelton being identified.

Woodward writes that he had been provided with information concerning IVY BELLS prior to Pelton's arrest in 1985, but had withheld publishing the information because "we were not absolutely sure it had been compromised." (**Justification – Responsible Actors**) Once it became apparent that the operation had been compromised, *Washington Post* Editor Ben Bradlee "felt it would be legitimate to explain the details to demonstrate what damage could be done by one of thousands of clerks, technicians, translators and information processors who operated the latest spy technologies." (**Motivation – Promote Informed Debate**)

On December 5, 1985, Bradlee and *Washington Post* Managing Editor Len Downie, Jr., met with the NSA Director, Army Lieutenant General William Odom, to discuss the operation and the *Post*'s intent to publish information concerning its existence. (**Justification – Responsible Actors**) Odom told Bradlee and Downie that the disclosure would "tell the Russians something they did not know" and that "great national-security issues were at stake." (**Harm – Damage to Sources and Methods**) Woodward indicates that another official with whom he spoke was concerned that articles involving IVY BELLS would "launch a competitive feeding frenzy in the news media for more information" and that a "string of stories could follow, revealing a detail here and another there." (**Harm – Damage to Sources and Methods**)

After Woodward located prior publications that referred to the use of submarines to intercept Soviet communications, the decision was made to draft an article for publication. These prior publications included a 1975 article published in the *New York Times* and information contained in the 1975 Pike Committee Congressional Report on intelligence activities. On January 27, 1986, Bradlee and Woodward met with Odom again and showed him a draft of the article they intended to publish. The purpose for the meeting was to have Odom and his aides "point out anything they felt might damage national security." **(Justification – Responsible Actors)**

The next day, Odom informed Woodward that he would not assist them in editing the article, that publication "would generate attention, all destructive and unwanted," and that "even if the Soviets knew (about IVY BELLS) they did not know precisely what the United States knew about what they (the Soviets) knew." Woodward received a similar response from another former senior official with whom he spoke, one of "the elders of the CIA." This official told Woodward that the discovery of the IVY BELLS device "might have been embarrassing to those in charge of the military or KGB" and that the KGB probably did not tell Soviet leader Mikhail Gorbachev because "they conceal fuck-ups in the Soviet system just like ours." The CIA official explained that, in response to the additional attention the article would undoubtedly cause, "a general alarm would go off in the Soviet military or the KGB requiring a full investigative response." The official explained that the resulting investigation "might lead to the compromise of other U.S. operations." **(Harm – Damage to Sources and Methods)**

Woodward describes the meeting with the CIA elder as "sobering," adding that it "served the purpose of reminding us that this story was not simple," and could have "unintended consequences." Bradlee advised Woodward that he "wanted to slow down to see clearly what might be coming." **(Justification – Responsible Actors)**

After this meeting, Woodward indicated that they began "shopping the story around town to see whether we could get someone with impeccable authority to tell us it would be all right to publish." **(Confirmation Bias)** He took an updated draft of the story to the White House and gave it to a "well-placed official" to determine if there were still objections. Four details in the earlier draft had been removed because "further reporting by us suggested it was conceivable that the Soviets might not know them." **(Justification – Responsible Actors)**

On February 26 the updated draft was discussed by several senior Reagan administration officials, including Secretary of State George Shultz, Secretary of Defense Casper Weinberger, National Security Advisor John

Poindexter, and Chief of Staff Donald Regan. Woodward writes that they concluded the article, if published, would damage national security by "harming the political relationship between the United States and Soviet Union." (Harm – Effect on International Alliances)

After the administration officials completed their review, Woodward and Bradlee met again to discuss the issue. Bradlee told Woodward that six drafts of the article had been written, each containing fewer details. Bradlee confirmed that "the first drafts could have caused trouble" and that they "shouldn't publish what others are prosecuted for treason for." Bradlee asked Woodward, "What social purpose is there in this story?" Woodward responded that his rationale was "to find out, and tell our readers, what he (Pelton) had sold" and "also show how easy it was to walk into the Soviet Embassy here and sell American secrets." Woodward indicated that "Pelton was one of the biggest spies the Russians ever had" and that "he had given away crown-jewel intelligence-gathering operations, not just IVY BELLS." (Motivation – Promote Informed Debate) Woodward wrote that "the editors remained uncertain."

In mid-March a "senior FBI official" told Woodward that the administration had come close to declining to prosecute Pelton "because of fears that a trial would expose secrets." The official explained that "any reporting on the nuts and bolts of how information is obtained raises consciousness" which "might uncork counterintelligence forces we want bottled up." (Harm – Damage to Sources and Methods)

On March 21, Woodward spoke with Director of Central Intelligence William Casey at a reception hosted by the *New York Times*. Woodward asked Casey why the administration was opposed to publication of the IVY BELLS article. Casey responded that, if classified information related to IVY BELLS was disclosed, "public opinion will build, could build, so we can't do it." Woodward's impression was that Casey was referring to the concern that the public might not support "cable-tapping or submarine operations close to the Soviet coast."

Woodward related the conversation to Bradlee, who "made it clear that, for the moment, he was unhappy we were still pursuing the story." Woodward explained to Bradlee that he believed failing to pursue the story was a "serious mistake." Bradlee again asked Woodward, "What is the social purpose of reporting this?" In response, Woodward identified several concerns related to Intelligence Community activities.

Woodward indicated that "many intelligence people and others who use it are uneasy" over "the possibility that the United States is pressing too much" and that the result may be "a declaration of a kind of intelligence war against the Soviets." He also told Bradlee that "at some earlier point . . . the U.S. had plans to send a U.S. nuclear submarine not only into their (Soviets) territorial waters, but up one of their rivers." Woodward said that there was "contradictory information whether it had happened" and that "maybe it never happened."

Bradlee asked Woodward if things in the Intelligence Community were "under control." Woodward answered that the NSA was "getting into non-Soviet undersea cables worldwide" and that "serious people" were concerned that the U.S. allowed the Soviets to "vacuum up telephone conversations from microwave towers all over Washington," a "massive invasion of the privacy of U.S. citizens." **(Motivation – Expose Government Misconduct)** Woodward added that "as well as I could piece it together there was a tacit understanding that, in return, the U.S. could operate electronic intelligence-gathering from the U.S. Embassy in Moscow." After discussing these issues, Woodward reported that Bradlee "wasn't buying" it and was still concerned that they were going to "cross legitimate national security." **(Justification – Responsible Actors)**

Bradlee and Woodward agreed that Bradlee should speak directly with one of Woodward's original sources of information on IVY BELLS, a "former senior intelligence official." Woodward felt the official was "someone who could say confidently that the IVY BELLS story would not tell the Russians anything they did not know." Bradlee met with the "senior official" in late April 1986. The official convinced Bradlee that "the story as now drafted would not tell the Soviets anything they did not already know." **(Confirmation Bias)**

On April 25, Bradlee instructed Woodward to contact the White House and inform officials there that the story would be running in two days. The next day, NSA Director Odom called Bradlee. Odom told Bradlee that he was still opposed to the story being published because he "was really worried about other countries that didn't know about the capability." **(Harm – Damage to Sources and Methods)** Bradlee agreed to meet with Odom again. During this meeting, Odom told Bradlee that some in the administration were "looking into the possibility of using a 1950 law that provides criminal penalties for anyone who 'publishes' anything classified about communications intelligence."

Woodward wrote that William Casey met with the head of the Justice Department Criminal Division on May 2, and "proposed that the department consider bringing criminal charges." Casey also wanted the Justice Department to consider "going to court to get an order to stop the *Post* from publishing the IVY BELLS story." After meeting with the Justice Department, Casey met with Bradlee and Managing Editor Downie. Casey told Downie that if the IVY BELLS story was published Casey would "recommend that you be prosecuted." Casey requested that Bradlee and Downie hold the story for another week and told them he would request that President Reagan talk with Bradlee. Bradlee asked if the story was "that important." Casey responded that "lives could conceivably be in danger if that is published." **(Harm – Potential Loss of Life)**

Based on the meeting with Casey, Bradlee and Downie again agreed to postpone publication. **(Justification – Responsible Actors)** Though Bradlee and Downie agreed to withhold the IVY BELLS article, they did publish an article on May 7 reporting that the administration was considering prosecuting the *Washington Post* for disclosing classified information. The article stated that the *Post* was holding back on "another story it has prepared concerning U.S. intelligence capabilities."

On May 10, Katharine Graham, chairman of the board of the *Washington Post*, received a phone call from President Reagan. Reagan insisted to Graham that the story on Pelton would harm national security. Reagan reportedly told Graham that "good intelligence had prevented 125 terrorist incidents over the last year," creating an impression that preventing these attacks was somehow tied to IVY BELLS. **(Harm – Potential Loss of Life)** Graham responded to the President that she would speak with Bradlee. She later told Bradlee that she "was impressed with the president's argument" and "wondered why we had to write this story." (**Justification – Responsible Actors**)

Ultimately, on May 19, 1986, the day jury selection for Pelton's trial was scheduled to begin, NBC reported on the *Today* show that "Pelton apparently gave away one of the NSA's most sensitive secrets – a project with the code name 'IVY BELLS,' believed to be a top-secret underwater eavesdropping operation by American submarines inside Soviet harbors." After being informed of the disclosure, Casey issued a statement saying he was referring NBC's broadcast to the Justice Department for possible prosecution.

On May 21, after the NBC story was broadcast, the *Washington Post* published its article concerning IVY BELLS. The article was titled "Eavesdropping System Betrayed, High-Technology Device Disclosed by Pelton Was Lost to Soviets." Casey issued another statement indicating that the *Post* story was also "being reviewed to see whether prosecution would be initiated." The *Post* subsequently published articles with additional details, including the location of the operation in the Sea of Okhotsk.

In response to the *Washington Post* articles, Casey and Odom issued a joint public statement. The statement "cautioned against speculation and reporting details beyond the information actually released at trial," adding that "such speculations and additional facts are not authorized disclosures and may cause substantial harm to the national security."

Ultimately, no charges were brought against NBC or the *Washington Post* for the disclosures. On May 29, 1986, Casey told the Associated Press, "I think that certainly the press has been very hysterical about the thing, saying we're trying to tear up the First Amendment and scuttle the freedom of the press. We're not trying to do that."

Conclusion

The IVY BELLS incident demonstrates how identified motivations, justifications, and categories of harm apply in a real-world scenario. The deliberations by the *Post* prior to its decision to publish, as revealed by Bob

Woodward, also illustrate how these variables are applied to the decision-making process, as described by Rational Choice Theory.

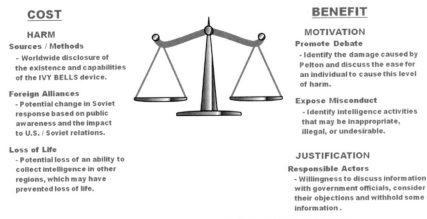

COST

HARM

Sources / Methods
 - Worldwide disclosure of
 the existence and capabilities
 of the IVY BELLS device.

Foreign Alliances
 - Potential change in Soviet
 response based on public
 awareness and the impact
 to U.S. / Soviet relations.

Loss of Life
 - Potential loss of an ability to
 collect intelligence in other
 regions, which may have
 prevented loss of life.

BENEFIT

MOTIVATION

Promote Debate
 - Identify the damage caused by
 Pelton and discuss the ease for
 an individual to cause this level
 of harm.

Expose Misconduct
 - Identify intelligence activities
 that may be inappropriate,
 illegal, or undesirable.

JUSTIFICATION

Responsible Actors
 - Willingness to discuss information
 with government officials, consider
 their objections and withhold some
 information.

FIGURE 14 – PSYCHOLOGICAL SCALE – IVY BELLS DISCLOSURE
Source: Author.

In this case, the assessment of cost and benefit changed several times before a final decision was reached. These changes were based on additional information the media obtained from government officials who expressed their concerns. This additional information increased the identified harm, which altered the media's cost-benefit analysis, at least in the short term. In the end, conversations with other anonymous sources (and the possible impact of confirmation bias) led to the decision to publish.

In addition to supporting the applicability of Rational Choice Theory, the IVY BELLS incident demonstrates how legal authorities are ineffective in preventing disclosures. Not only was the threat of criminal prosecution unsuccessful in deterring the media, it appears to have been detrimental to government efforts. By publishing the government's threat of prosecution, the media effectively placed the government on the defensive. Rather than focusing on the message that disclosures "may cause substantial harm to the national security," officials were placed in the undesirable position of having to respond to the perception that the First Amendment and freedom of the press were being attacked.

Though preventing an unauthorized disclosure by altering a journalist's cost-benefit analysis was not completely successful, Woodward confirmed that the *Post* did elect to withhold facts that would otherwise have been disclosed. Publication of the remaining classified information was also delayed for several months.

Considering the "psychological scale" one final time, this case study allows for the most detailed depiction of a journalist's rational weighing of choices. Actual events surrounding the IVY BELLS disclosure can be applied to the identified elements of a journalist's cost-benefit analysis. It is important to note that, because this case study is presented from the media's point of view, only those elements Woodward elected to discuss can be identified. There may be other elements that Woodward either did not recognize, or recognized but consciously withheld from his narrative, such as advancing corporate or personal interests.

After considering the information contained in Chapters 1-4, one final question remains: whether the perceived harm from unauthorized disclosures can be effectively reduced through an approach that proactively applies the principles of Rational Choice Theory.

CHAPTER 5

A Proactive Application of Rational Choice Theory

Leaks are like prostitution and gambling. You can control them and contain them a bit – but you're not going to eliminate them.[536]

- Patrick Buchanan

Unauthorized disclosures of classified information by the U.S. media continue to occur. Completely eliminating these disclosures is not a realistic goal for the U.S. government. A more reasonable objective is to reduce disclosures perceived to cause the greatest harm to national security. Past efforts to prevent unauthorized disclosures, focused primarily on a legislative solution, have proven ineffective. Other approaches involved activities which exceeded statutory authorities. Considering these past failures, a more innovative approach is required, an approach that recognizes the value of a free press outside the government, information sharing within the government, and secrecy in the interest of national security.

One potential resolution to this conflict was described by University of Chicago Law Professor Cass Sunstein in 1986. Sunstein referred to this solution as an "Equilibrium Model" of disclosures:

[T]he absence of a right of access to information held by the government is balanced by the power to publish almost all information that has been lawfully obtained. The self-interested behavior of countervailing forces, it is thought, will produce an equilibrium that benefits the citizenry as a whole.[537]

Sunstein's colleague, Professor Geoffrey Stone, described this laissez-faire approach as follows:

The solution, which has stood us in good stead for more than two centuries, is to reconcile the conflicting values of secrecy and accountability by guaranteeing both a strong authority of the government to prohibit leaks and an expansive right of the press to publish them.[538]

Unfortunately, several concerns have been identified that prevent the Equilibrium Model from being widely accepted as a solution.

Professor Sunstein notes that the Equilibrium Model allows the government potentially to suppress information in response to concerns other than national security (perhaps to conceal politically harmful or illegal activity), and for the press to publish information in which a substantial national security interest actually exists (possibly to advance corporate or personal interests).[539] The model also assumes, perhaps incorrectly, that either side has the ability to overcome the other's less desirable motivations. The government's ability to prevent or respond to past disclosures has reportedly been affected by a reluctance to disclose the additional information necessary to demonstrate the true extent of harm. This issue was specifically cited in the 1942 *Chicago Tribune* disclosure involving Japanese naval codes and the 1975 *New York Times* disclosures related to Operation HOLYSTONE. Furthermore, Sunstein points out that no empirical evidence exists to justify the validity of the Equilibrium Model. While the Equilibrium Model may initially appear to be an aesthetic and logical approach, it fails to offer an acceptable solution.

If the desire to reduce the perceived harm from unauthorized disclosures is genuine and a legislative or administrative solution is ineffective, illegal activity unacceptable, and the "Equilibrium Model" inadequate, an alternative approach must be considered. Rational Choice Theory offers one such alternative.

Applying Rational Choice Theory to the Dilemma of Disclosures

Attorney General John Ashcroft recognized the need to "deter" those who reveal classified information while Principal Deputy Assistant Attorney General Matthew Friedrich spoke of working cooperatively with journalists to "persuade" them not to publish classified information. The 1982 Willard Group wrote that changing the status quo would require "a sense of discipline and self-restraint by those who work with or obtain classified information." The use of terms such as "deter," "persuade," and "self-restraint" denotes an appreciation for the significance psychological processes play in the disclosure of classified information.

Developing an effective approach that incorporates Rational Choice Theory requires an improved understanding of the thought process of members of the media. The findings presented in Chapters 2 and 3 confirm that it is possible to identify the underlying motivations, justifications, and categories of harm that comprise a journalist's cost-benefit analysis. The events described in Chapter 4 demonstrate that Rational Choice Theory's rational weighing of alternatives can be applied to the behavior of publishing classified information. Collectively, these facts support the premise that a "Rational Choice" model would be a valid approach to the dilemma of unauthorized disclosures, one which may ultimately succeed in reducing its perceived harm. Unfortunately, recognizing that an approach has the potential to be effective and achieving the desired results are not the same. Applying Rational Choice Theory would be neither a simple nor swift solution.

Complicating what would already be a complex approach are the internal and external obstacles previously identified. Internal barriers include the psychological limitation of "confirmation bias" (discussed in Chapter 3) and anxiety caused by "performance pressure" (discussed in Chapter 2). These factors affect a journalist's ability to perform the cost-benefit analysis in a rational manner. External barriers to success involve those factors that may actually create an atmosphere more conducive to an increase rather than a decrease in disclosures. These include the increased number of world events that impact U.S. interests (globalization), increased Intelligence Community collection capabilities and requirements, the increased number of media outlets (along with the advent of the 24-hour news cycle), the politicization of intelligence by government officials, and an increased desire by the public to remain aware of government activity during a time of war.

Considering just one of these factors, it was reported in 1987 that there had been a 400 percent increase in the number of radio and television reporters operating in Washington, DC, over the prior two decades.[540] This equates to approximately 10,000 journalists representing over 3,000 news organizations. Because the Internet did not become widely available until the following decade, these levels are also likely to have increased.

As long as journalists continue to provide the demand for classified information and government employees remain willing to supply this information, successfully impacting the "leak economy" will remain difficult. No significant change can occur however, unless proactive action is taken to alter this status quo.

The Process

For a proactive application of a Rational Choice model to be effective, journalists would have to conclude more frequently that the costs associated with the perceived harm outweigh the identified motivations and justifications for publishing classified information. If journalists were persuaded to reevaluate their cost-benefit analysis in cases that would have otherwise resulted in an unauthorized disclosure, incidents could be decreased, along with the associated harm.

As presented, the motivations and justifications that comprise the benefit side of the cost-benefit analysis are:

Potential Motivations

1. Promote informed debate

2. Expose government misconduct

3. Advance corporate interests

4. Advance personal interests

5. Advance foreign interests

Potential Justifications

1. Government overclassification

2. Government toleration for advantageous disclosures

3. Legal protection under the First Amendment

4. Inadequacy of Congressional oversight

5. Media's ability to handle classified information responsibly

The six categories of harm that make up the cost side of the cost-benefit analysis are:

Potential Harm

1. Damage to sources and methods

2. Potential loss of life

3. Impact to the development and implementation of foreign policy

4. Effect on international alliances

5. Financial costs

6. Decrease in public knowledge from disclosures of incomplete or inaccurate information

Once the relevance of Rational Choice Theory is recognized, the additional barriers to success understood, and the components of a journalist's cost-benefit analysis identified, four additional steps remain. These steps involve identifying:

- which of the motivations, justifications, and categories of harm are applicable to a specific disclosure or category of disclosures

- the relative significance of the applicable variables for members of the media

- whether the government has both the ability and desire to impact the identified variables

- appropriate venues for implementing this approach

Relevancy of Variables

If an attempt is made to prevent publication involving a specific classified operation/program, or an entire category of classified information (e.g., intelligence derived from a human source), the motivations and justifications the media would consider applicable in those instances must be identified. Not all motivations and justifications would apply to every operation or program. Similarly, it is unlikely that the media would perceive all six categories of harm to be relevant.

Relative Significance of Variables

Once the applicable motivations, justifications, and categories of harm are identified, the relative weight members of the media attribute to each must be considered. Altering the cost-benefit analysis, to a point where the decision to perform an undesirable action is no longer reached, requires an understanding of the significance of each variable on both sides of the equation.

Decreasing the value of a specific motivation or increasing the recognition of a particular category of harm would be irrelevant if the variable selected represented only a fraction of a journalist's overall estimation. For example, convincing the media that Congressional oversight was robust for a particular program may be pointless if other motivations or justifications were perceived to hold significantly more value. The same issue would apply if members of the media were persuaded that a disclosure would almost certainly have a negative impact on foreign policy, but this single category of harm was not considered significant enough to overcome the multiple recognized benefits.

Government Ability and Desire to Effect Change

Consideration must also be given to the Executive Branch's willingness and ability to impact a perceived motivation, justification, or category of harm. Even if the proper variables were identified which, if successfully modified, could alter the balance of journalists' cost-benefit analyses, it must be determined whether the government was capable of affecting these variables. Beyond this ability, the government must also have both the desire and political will to perform the necessary actions.

For example, if reducing disclosures perceived to be condoned for political reasons would result in a similar decrease in all disclosures, politicians and other senior government officials would have to be willing to discontinue disclosing information to influence policy. Similarly, if a media outlet was willing to withhold classified information that potentially threatened the life of a government employee or source, it would have to be determined if the government could make such an assertion (and if it was willing to provide that information to the media). This difficulty was discussed by former CIA Director Michael Hayden:

> [T]here is sometimes an instinct on the part of the media to take a story into the darkest corner of the room. ... And here we are fill in the blank, NSA, CIA – in a very real sense unable to defend ourselves publicly, because we can't enter into the debate about the story, because to enter into the debate would actually reveal even more information that would be helpful to those who would do the republic harm.[541]

Appropriate Venues for Implementation

Finally, once the above three steps are completed, a forum conducive to applying this approach must be identified. Ultimately, success or failure may depend on the government's ability to engage members of the media. Possible venues include one-on-one discussions between a senior agency official and a senior editor, meetings between a group of senior agency and media officials, working groups comprised of mid-level intelligence officers and journalists, and indirect engagement through the public. Some of these venues have been utilized in the past, though not as part of a unified approach.

Past Forums for Engaging with the Media: SIGINT 101 and the Dialogue Group

The most commonly used method for engaging with the media has been direct one-on-one discussions between high-ranking government officials and senior members of the media. Several examples were previously cited in which CIA Directors spoke directly with senior editors and journalists to attempt to prevent the publication of classified information. This interaction represents the least strategic and most reactive option.

Considering a more strategic approach, there have been past attempts to engage members of the media proactively. Between 2002 and 2004, the

National Security Agency held several half-day, off-the-record seminars labeled "SIGINT 101." The stated purpose of these seminars was to "talk to journalists regarding our mission and the sensitivities of our mission in an unclassified way."[542] The belief was that, through education, journalists could be discouraged from publishing classified information harmful to NSA programs. The course outline included sessions with high-ranking NSA officials, including then-Lieutenant General Michael Hayden, NSA Director during this period. The intent of these sessions was to discuss how past articles could have been edited to remove the most objectionable portions without significantly altering the intent of the articles. This program appears to have been discontinued in 2004 due to staffing changes in NSA's Public Affairs Office.

SIGINT 101 represents one example of a venue in which a journalist's decision-making process was discussed in a group setting. One other group forum used by government officials to discuss a journalist's cost-benefit analysis was the "Dialogue Group."

In early 2001, after President Clinton vetoed the Shelby Amendment to the 2001 Intelligence Authorization Act, there were discussions regarding the possible reintroduction of the legislation. Ultimately, the bill was not reintroduced. As an alternative, an interagency task force (Interagency Task Force Concerning Protections against Unauthorized Disclosures) was established and an informal dialogue between government and media officials was initiated. Former CIA General Counsel Jeffrey Smith and former *Washington Post* reporter Scott Armstrong are credited with the group's formation.[543]

In a *Los Angeles Times* article, journalist Jack Nelson described this "Dialogue Group" as a forum to discuss "ways to protect the most sensitive national security secrets without abridging the public's right to know."[544] Meetings, held every few weeks at the Metropolitan Club in Washington, DC, were attended by senior government officials from the CIA, NSA, Department of Justice, Department of Defense, and National Security Council.[545] Media representatives included senior officials from the *Los Angeles Times* and the *Washington Post*. The group was cited as a contributing factor in the Bush administration's decision not to pursue broader anti-leak legislation.[546]

Specific elements of the journalist's cost-benefit analysis described as being discussed during the meetings include the justification of government overclassification and the harm resulting from the loss of sources and methods.[547] During meetings, government officials identified specific articles that had been published and discussed the harm each had caused. Similar to the SIGINT 101 seminars, alternatives were suggested that would have diminished the harm to national security interests without compromising the overall intent for publication. The most recent reporting regarding the Dialogue Group was published in May 2006.[548]

As opposed to reactive meetings precipitated by the media informing the government of its intent to publish classified information, the Dialogue Group and SIGINT 101 represent a more proactive approach. Forums such as these offer an opportunity for members of the government and the media to discuss government concerns informally and examine the journalist's decision-making process in a constructive, less adversarial manner.

Proactive discussions between the government and media, similar to the Dialogue Group, have been successfully utilized outside the United States. For the past 99 years, the Defence Press and Broadcasting Advisory Committee (DPBAC) has provided a mechanism for the UK government to engage formally with British media organizations. The DPBAC, whose membership includes senior government and media officials, issues guidance on the publication of classified information. The goal of the Committee is to prevent harm to national security resulting from the disclosure of sensitive information.

The British Model – Defence Advisory Committee and the Official Secrets Act

Formed in 1912, the Defence Press and Broadcasting Advisory Committee provides a forum for the government of the United Kingdom to work jointly with media organizations on matters involving national security. The Committee is comprised of five government employees, representing four government agencies, and sixteen representatives from the British media. The Committee is chaired by the Under-Secretary of State for Defence.

The DPBAC was established one year after the passage of the Official Secrets Act of 1911, which broadly proscribed the disclosure of "official government information" without authorization. Unlike the 1917 U.S. Espionage Act, the Official Secrets Act was not constrained by the provisions of the First Amendment to the U.S. Constitution. In 1989, the Official Secrets Act was amended to significantly narrow its scope. The amended Act identifies six specific categories of government information illegal to disclose without authorization.[549] It also designates an intra-government review board for government employees to report unlawful, abusive, or fraudulent activity.

Guidance issued by the DPBAC to the media is referred to as Defence Advisory (DA) Notices. There are currently five standing DA Notices, which identify categories of information that the Committee recommends the media not disclose in the interest of national security. These categories are:

DA Notice 01: Military Operations, Plans, and Capabilities

DA Notice 02: Nuclear and Non-Nuclear Weapons and Equipment

DA Notice 03: Ciphers and Secure Communications

DA Notice 04: Sensitive Installations and Home Addresses

DA Notice 05: United Kingdom Security and Intelligence Special Services

In addition to the standing notices, the DPBAC also issues letters to provide guidance in response to specific incidents. These letters are issued when the Committee is notified or has reason to believe a media organization may publish information involving national security. The most recent "Letter of Advice" from the DPBAC was issued on November 26, 2010.[550] The letter concerned British media reporting on the disclosure of classified U.S. State Department cables by the website WikiLeaks. DA Notices, such as the November 2010 letter, are advisory in nature and are not legally binding. Media organizations ultimately retain the right to publish and are under no legal obligation to participate in the DA Notice system.

In addition to the UK, Israel also reportedly maintains an "Honest Broker" system similar to the DA Notice process.[551] In 1952 Australia also formed an Advisory Committee to provide guidance to the media.[552] This Committee was active for 30 years before the discontinuation of meetings in 1982. In November 2010, Australian Attorney General Robert McClelland proposed the reestablishment of a "formal mutually agreed arrangement with the media on the handling of sensitive national security information." The intent of the agreement was to "facilitate reporting in a manner that avoids risk . . . or compromises important investigations or operations," as well as to "strike a balance between national security and the public's right to know."[553]

Because the United Kingdom and Australia have no direct equivalent to the U.S. Constitution's First Amendment, a more formal "Advisory Committee" model may be both more feasible and publicly accepted. In the political, legal, and social climate of the United States, where freedoms such as those guaranteed in the First Amendment are jealously guarded and the seed of a "credibility gap" has been cultivated, a less formal "Dialogue Group" concept is more likely to succeed.

The Road Ahead

Proactively engaging with the media to examine the costs and benefits associated with unauthorized disclosures represents the greatest potential for reducing the perceived harm to national security. Maintaining the status quo or attempting to legislate a solution both have proven to be ineffective methods for resolving the dilemma. True change can only occur if the Executive Branch is willing to invest the time and resources necessary to implement an approach focused on engagement with the media. Past efforts, including the informal Dialogue Group, and current systems, such as the formal British Advisory Committee, offer a roadmap for the implementation of such an approach.

After expressing his belief that leaks could not be prevented through legislation, former DCI Robert Gates spoke of this more appropriate, yet difficult, approach. Gates wrote: "The answer, if there is one, is the slower, more mundane and frustrating process of again instilling discipline through education and developing broad support . . ."[554] The 1982 House Judiciary Committee Report on Unauthorized Disclosures (Willard Group) similarly concluded that a "fundamental change in prevailing attitudes . . . will not be achieved easily or quickly" but that "without a change in attitudes, no program to deal with unauthorized disclosures can possibly be effective."[555] Regardless of the difficulties in persuading journalists that the benefits of an unauthorized disclosure may not outweigh its harm, advocates of reducing the frequency of unauthorized disclosures will likely continue their efforts.

General Michael Hayden, former director of the CIA and NSA, understands the crucial role of a proactive and sustained dialogue with the media. He offered the following advice to his former colleagues in the Intelligence Community:

> I'm telling people to talk to the press when the press is accusing us of something. An additional lesson I would draw for my friends in the Intelligence Community, especially talk to the press when they aren't accusing you of something. Go out of your way to establish communication and openness with all sorts of media.

> Talk to the press when you're not being accused. There's a lot more that can be done, not when you're fighting a fire but in more peaceful times, to have open dialog with members of the press.[556]

Reducing the perceived harm of unauthorized disclosures can be achieved through a proactive approach that incorporates the principles of Rational Choice Theory. Ultimately, success or failure will depend on the government's willingness to pursue this "frustrating" process and effect a "fundamental change in prevailing attitudes."

APPENDIX

The Legal Framework Underlying Unauthorized Disclosures

Because freedom of the press can be no broader than the freedom of reporters to investigate and report the news, the prosecutorial power of the government should not be used in such a way that it impairs a reporter's responsibility to cover as broadly as possible controversial public issues.[557]

- Section 50.10 of Title 28 of the Code of Federal Regulation

A comprehensive understanding of the conflict between freedom of the press and national security would not be complete without an analysis of the legal foundations underlying the issue. This appendix examines the framework, including the U.S. Constitution and the Bill of Rights, enacted and proposed legislation, Executive Orders, and case law.

Legal Framework: Executive Branch

The basis for Executive Branch authority to withhold information from public dissemination has been interpreted through case law related to Article II of the U.S. Constitution. In the 1988 Supreme Court ruling in Department of Navy v. Egan 484 U.S. 518 (1988) Justice Harry Blackmun wrote: "His (the President's) authority to classify and control access to information bearing on national security . . . flows primarily from this constitutional investment of power in the President (Article II)."[558] In an earlier ruling in the "Pentagon Papers" case, New York Times v. United States 403 U.S. 713 (1971), Supreme Court Justice Potter Stewart wrote: "Under the Constitution, the Executive must have the largely unshared duty to determine and preserve the degree of internal security necessary to exercise that power (the conduct of foreign affairs and the maintenance of our national defense) successfully."[559]

FIGURE 15 – CLASSIFIED DOCUMENT COVER SHEETS – SF 703, 704 and 705
Source: U.S. Government.

Beyond the interpreted authority of Article II, the responsibility to protect classified information within the Intelligence Community (IC) has been delegated by legislation on two occasions. In the National Security Act of 1947, the Director of Central Intelligence, the designated head of the IC, was charged with protecting intelligence sources and methods from unauthorized disclosure.[560] This duty was transferred to the Director of National Intelligence (DNI) in 2004 through the Intelligence Reform and Terrorism Prevention Act, codified under Title 50, Section 403. As the head of a reorganized IC, the DNI was similarly tasked to protect intelligence sources and methods.[561]

Federal regulations governing the procedures for safeguarding intelligence sources and methods are contained in Executive Order (EO) 13526, signed by President Barack Obama on December 29, 2009. EO 13526 replaced EO 12958, which was enacted in 1995. EO 12958 was preceded by EO 12356 (1982), EO 12065 (1979), and EO 10501 (1953).

EO 13526 establishes three classification levels for information. These levels are specifically defined based on the harm that would result if the information were disclosed without authorization. Information classified "Confidential" would "cause damage" to national security, while the disclosure of "Secret" information would cause "serious damage." The disclosure of information classified "Top Secret" would, by definition, result in "exceptionally grave" damage to national security.[562] Documents classified in accordance with EO 13526 require additional safeguards to prevent unauthorized disclosure. These safeguards include specific storage requirements and the use of cover sheets and classification markings to identify the classification level of a document.

Beyond these collateral classification levels, there are additional instructions and procedures for handling information related to particularly sensitive programs, which are categorized by "compartments." These include Special Access Programs (SAP) and Sensitive Compartmented Information (SCI). SAP and SCI information requires additional safeguards that exceed protections for information with a collateral classification.

Executive Order 13526 identifies eight specific categories of information eligible for classification. In addition to an expectation that national security would be harmed if the information were disclosed, the information must also relate to one of the following eight categories to be considered suitable for classification:

1. Military plans, weapons systems, or operations;

2. Foreign government information;

3. Intelligence activities (including covert action), intelligence sources or methods, or cryptology;

4. Foreign relations or foreign activities of the United States, including confidential sources;

5. Scientific, technological, or economic matters relating to the national security;

6. United States Government programs for safeguarding nuclear materials or facilities;

7. Vulnerabilities or capabilities of systems, installations, infrastructures, projects, plans, or protection services relating to the national security; or

8. The development, production, or use of weapons of mass destruction.

Executive Order 13526 defines the term "Unauthorized Disclosure" as "a communication or physical transfer of classified information to an unauthorized recipient."[563] In recognition of the conflicting issues raised by withholding information in a democracy, the following statement is included in the Executive Order:

> Our democratic principles require that the American people be informed of the activities of their Government. Also, our Nation's progress depends on the free flow of information both within the Government and to the American people. Nevertheless, throughout our history, the national defense has required that certain information be maintained in confidence in order to protect our citizens, our democratic institutions, our homeland security, and our interactions with foreign nations.[564]

EO 12065, the 1979 predecessor to EO 13526, similarly identified the need to "balance the public's interests in access to Government information with the need to protect certain national security information from disclosure."[565]

EO 13526 identifies three prerequisites for an individual to be granted access to classified information. They include a favorable determination of eligibility, the completion of an approved non-disclosure agreement, and a "need to know" the classified information.[566] Sanctions for the knowing, willful, or negligent disclosure of properly classified information to unauthorized persons are also prescribed in the Executive Order. These penalties include the loss of access to classified information, the termination of employment, and "other sanctions in accordance with applicable law and agency regulation."[567]

The authority for an agency to take administrative action against an employee, such as the removal of access to classified information or termination of employment, is codified under Title 5 of the U.S. Code, Section 7532. Section 7532 grants the head of an agency broad discretion to terminate an employee when he considers that action necessary in the interests of national security.[568]

Though the "applicable" criminal laws are not specifically identified in EO 13526, they are enumerated in the non-disclosure agreement required by the Executive Order. Standard Form 312, the "Classified Information Nondisclosure Agreement," identifies eight criminal statutes under which an individual could potentially be prosecuted for the unauthorized disclosure of classified information.[569] These statutes will be discussed in the next section.

Executive Orders have not been used solely to limit the dissemination of information. In addition to establishing procedures for protecting information, Executive Order 13526 also expressly prohibits the classification of information "to conceal violations of law, inefficiency, or administrative error," "prevent embarrassment to a person, organization, or agency," "restrain competition," or "prevent or delay the release of information that does not require protection in the interests of national security."[570] The penalties identified in the Executive Order for the unauthorized disclosure of classified information, including the loss of access to classified information, termination of employment, or "other sanctions" also apply to the improper classification of information.

Current Executive Branch policy shows great deference for the role of the press in the United States. Section 50.10 of Title 28 of the Code of Federal Regulation (CFR) governs the Department of Justice's policy regarding the issuance of subpoenas to members of the news media. Section 50.10 states:

> Because freedom of the press can be no broader than the freedom of reporters to investigate and report the news, the prosecutorial power of the government should not be used in such a way that it impairs a reporter's responsibility to cover as broadly as possible controversial public issues.[571]

The guidelines, first proposed by Attorney General William French Smith in 1980, were established in an attempt to strike a balance between "the public's interest in the free dissemination of ideas and information and the public's interest in effective law enforcement and the fair administration of justice."[572] In accordance with this policy, the Department of Justice will not issue a subpoena to a member of the media unless all reasonable attempts are made to obtain the desired information from alternative sources. The policy further states that negotiations with the media should be pursued when the Department is considering subpoenaing a journalist. The Attorney General must also directly authorize the issuance of a subpoena for a member of the media.

Legal Framework: Legislative Branch

The criminal statutes identified by the non-disclosure agreement include the following sections of Titles 18 and 50 of the U.S. Code:

18 USC 641 - Prohibits the theft or conversion of government property for personal use.

18 USC 952 - Prohibits the unauthorized publication or disclosure of a diplomatic code or coded correspondence.

18 USC 1924 - Prohibits the unauthorized removal, retention, or storage of classified information.

50 USC 421 - Prohibits the disclosure of the identity of a covert U.S. agent to unauthorized persons.

50 USC 783 - Prohibits the communication of classified information to the agent of a foreign government by a government employee or employee of a corporation in which the government is a majority owner.

The remaining three statutes, 18 USC 793, 794, and 798 are part of the Espionage Act, the most comprehensive statute relating to unauthorized disclosures. Section 793 prohibits the disclosure of "national defense information" to "any person not entitled to receive it,"[573] while Section 794 specifically proscribes disclosures to "any foreign government."[574] Sections 793 and 794 both include a requirement that the disclosure be committed "with intent or reason to believe that the information is to be used to the injury of the United States, or to the advantage of any foreign nation."

Section 798, a 1950 amendment to the Act, contains several key distinctions from its predecessors. Section 798 criminalizes the disclosure of "classified information," specifically involving cryptographic or communications intelligence.[575] Section 798 does not include an "intent" provision, only a requirement that the disclosure be performed "knowingly" and "willfully." Section 798 is also the only section that expressly prohibits the publication of classified information.

The severity of the penalties for violating Sections 793, 794, and 798 vary widely. The sentence for a conviction under Section 793 or 798 includes a fine and imprisonment for up to ten years, while a violation of Section 794 is punishable by imprisonment for up to life. Section 794 also includes provisions for seeking the death penalty under certain circumstances, including the disclosure of information resulting in the death of an individual, the disclosure of military plans during time of war, or a disclosure concerning nuclear weaponry or early warning systems. In accordance with the 1954 Hiss Act, codified under Title 5 of the U.S. Code, Section 8312, an individual convicted under Sections 793, 794, or 798 of the Espionage Act (or comparable provisions of the Uniform Code of Military Justice) forfeit any federal annuity or other retirement benefits.[576]

When initially proposed, the Espionage Act included a provision which would have made it unlawful, during time of war, to publish any information determined to be "of such character that it is or might be useful to the enemy."[577] Congress debated whether the provision would do more to protect national security (potentially preventing the enemy from sinking a U.S. vessel as the result of published information) or stifle legitimate criticism (possibly concealing an epidemic among U.S. troops).

In response to opposition, the provision was amended to specify "nothing in this section shall be construed to limit or restrict any discussion, comment, or criticism of the acts or policies of the Government."[578] President Woodrow Wilson, a Democrat, addressed Congress directly, arguing that the provision was necessary for public safety. Despite both the amendment and President Wilson's personal appeal, the provision was defeated on May 31, 1917, by a vote of 184 to 144. Of the 184 votes against the provision, 148 were cast by Republicans.[579]

There is one additional legal prohibition related to unauthorized disclosures not identified in the non-disclosure agreement. Section 224 of the Atomic Energy Act of 1954 criminalizes the communication, transmission, or disclosure of "Restricted Data" to any person "with intent to injure the United States or with intent to secure an advantage to any foreign nation."[580] The term "Restricted Data" is defined as information related to the design, manufacture, or utilization of atomic weapons or the production or use of special nuclear material. The relevant portion of the Atomic Energy Act is codified under Title 42 of the U.S. Code, Section 2274.

Between 1946 and 2010, there have been at least 18 unsuccessful proposals to amend existing statutes related to unauthorized disclosures. In 1946 the Joint Congressional Committee for Investigation of the Attack on Pearl Harbor recommended legislation akin to the British Official Secrets Act, broadly prohibiting the unauthorized disclosure of classified information.[581] The Secretary of War submitted a comparable proposal to the Attorney General, also in 1946. The Secretary of War's proposal was based on the results of a joint study conducted by Army and Navy Intelligence and the FBI. Neither proposal became law. Secretary of Defense Robert Lovett again proposed the enactment of broad legislation in 1952. The Justice Department drafted legislation, though it was never voted on by Congress.

The 1957 Wright Commission on Government Security recommended enacting legislation that would have made it a crime for "any person willfully to disclose without proper authorization, for any purpose whatever, information classified 'secret' or 'top secret,' knowing, or having reasonable grounds to believe, such information to have been so classified."[582] The proposal was ultimately rejected by the Senate. Similar initiatives during the Eisenhower administration in 1958 and the Johnson administration in 1966 were also unsuccessful.[583]

The next proposal, Senate Bill S.1400, was introduced in March 1973. Section 1124 of the bill criminalized the communication of "classified information" by individuals who were authorized to have possession of the information to "a person not authorized to receive it."[584] This proposal focused solely on the individual with authorized access, indicating that the recipient of the classified information would not be subject to prosecution under the provision. No action was taken on the bill. Section 1124 was eventually reintroduced as part of Senate Bill S.1 in 1975. Though additional procedural safeguards were added, controversy over the section led to its withdrawal. In 1976 legislation drafted by the CIA was proposed by the Ford administration. The legislation was strongly criticized by the media and civil liberties organizations and never enacted.

The next four proposals were included in draft intelligence authorization bills for fiscal years 1984, 1986, 1987, and 1993.[585] Both expansive and narrowly written proposals were considered. Two proposals broadly proscribed the unauthorized disclosure of all classified information. Another provided for civil remedies in cases involving the disclosure of signals intelligence, while one other allowed for an affirmative defense and an *ex parte* determination by a judge whether the relevant information was classified appropriately. The 1993 proposal only related to disclosures of TOP SECRET information involving technical collection systems or capabilities. Ultimately, all were removed from the final bill submitted to Congress due to legal and/or political concerns and a perceived lack of support.

In 2000, a provision to amend Section 798(a) of the Espionage Act was included in the final version of the Intelligence Authorization Act for 2001. Section 304 of the Act, introduced by Senator Richard Shelby of Alabama, broadly criminalized the disclosure of classified information to unauthorized persons. After Congress approved a final version of the Act containing the "Shelby Amendment," President Bill Clinton vetoed the bill. The veto occurred four days before the November 8, 2000, Presidential election. In a published statement, President Clinton identified the Shelby Amendment as the sole reason for the veto, citing both a lack of public hearings as well as its potentially chilling effect on legitimate activities.[586] Six years later, in August 2006, Senator Kit Bond introduced Senate Bill S.3774, which duplicated the provisions of the Shelby Amendment. It was heavily criticized and never enacted.

The next two attempts to enact legislation were proposed in 2007 by Senator Jon Kyl of Arizona. In February 2007, Senator Kyl attached an amendment to the "Federal Agency Data Mining Reporting Act," S.236. The amendment prohibited the communication, transmission, or publication of classified information "concerning efforts by the United States to identify, investigate, or prevent terrorist activity."[587] Violations of this provision were punishable by imprisonment for up to 20 years. As the result of strong opposition, Senator Kyl removed the amendment, modified the text, and reintroduced it as an amendment to Senate Bill S.4, "Improving America's Security Act of 2007."[588] The new amendment criminalized the unauthorized disclosure of classified information contained in reports submitted to Congress. The amendment specified that the statute would apply to members and employees of both the House of Representatives and the Senate. This provision also faced significant opposition and was never enacted.

The most recent attempt to amend existing legislation, the "Securing Human Intelligence and Enforcing Lawful Dissemination (SHIELD) Act," was introduced in the Senate in December 2010. The proposal amended Section 798 of the Espionage Act, adding two additional categories of information illegal to disclose without authorization. This information includes the identity of a classified informant or source associated with the U.S. Intelligence Community, and information concerning the human intelligence activities of the United States or a foreign government. A similar bill was also introduced in the House of Representatives. Neither bill was approved prior to the conclusion of the 111th Congress.

Beyond the government's recognition of a necessity to protect information in the interest of national security, the responsibility to maintain an enlightened citizenry in a democracy is also acknowledged. The foundation for this principle is found in the U.S. Bill of Rights, which contains the first ten amendments to the U.S. Constitution. Though not as prominent in the public consciousness as the preamble to the U.S. Constitution, the preamble to the Bill of Rights similarly captures the Founding Fathers' sentiments. The preamble declares that the Bill of Rights was established "in order to prevent misconstruction or abuse of its [U.S. Constitution] powers . . . And as extending the ground of public confidence in the Government."[589]

This desire to instill confidence in the government and prevent abuse is further reinforced by the protections guaranteed under the First Amendment to the U.S. Constitution. In order to ensure the public remain free to, among other things, openly debate the propriety of government activity, the First Amendment declares that the government

will "make no law . . . abridging the freedom of speech . . . of the press
. . ."[590] Two documents that precede the Bill of Rights, the Virginia
Declaration of Rights (1776) and the Constitution of the Commonwealth
of Massachusetts (1780), appear to have influenced the author of the Bill
of Rights, James Madison.

Article 12 of the Virginia Declaration of Rights states: "The freedom
of the press is one of the greatest bulwarks of liberty and can never be
restrained but by despotic governments."[591] Article 16 of the Constitution
of the Commonwealth of Massachusetts reads: "The liberty of the press is
essential to the security of freedom in a state; it ought not, therefore, to be
restrained in this commonwealth."[592] In an early draft of the Bill of Rights,
Madison wrote: "The people shall not be deprived or abridged of their right
to speak, to write, or to publish their sentiments, and the freedom of the
press, as one of the great bulwarks of liberty, shall be inviolable."[593]

Beyond the ability of the press to provide oversight from a position outside
of the government, legislation has also been enacted to allow those inside
a government "of the people" to report items of concern. This authority is
codified in two "Whistleblower" acts. The Whistleblower Protection Act
(WPA) of 1989 establishes provisions for government employees to report
activity they believe violates a law, rule, or regulation; evidences an abuse
of authority or a waste of funds; or creates a substantial danger to health
or safety.[594] The legislation also provides protection for the government
employee against retaliation by his or her employing agency.

Four venues for a government employee to report undesirable activities
are identified in the WPA: the Office of Special Counsel, U.S. Congress,
an agency's Inspector General Office, or an employee designated by the
head of the agency. The WPA is codified under Title 5 of the U.S. Code,
Section 2302. It was amended in 1994 to provide additional protections for
government employees against adverse actions.

In 1998 a provision of the proposed Intelligence Authorization Act of
1999 expanded the coverage of the WPA to employees and contractors
of Intelligence Community agencies. These individuals were previously
precluded from protection under the WPA. The WPA had also specifically
prohibited the disclosures of information "required by Executive Order to

be kept secret in the interest of national defense or the conduct of foreign affairs."[595] The 1998 provision was enacted as the Intelligence Community Whistleblower Protection Act (ICWPA) of 1998. In accordance with the ICWPA, IC employees can report prohibited actions, including allegations containing classified information, to their agency's Inspector General, an authorized official of the covered agency, or members of Congressional intelligence committees (HPSCI or SSCI).[596]

The provisions of the WPA and ICWPA do not apply to disclosures to the media. The processes and protections enumerated in the Acts relate specifically to reports made through approved government channels.

A proposal introduced in Congress in 2007, but never enacted, would have had a considerable impact on the oversight role of the press. The "Free Flow of Information Act" would have provided journalists with a federal privilege protecting them from being compelled to disclose the identity of a confidential source.[597] The proposal did contain a possible exception in cases involving national security. Advocates continue to support the reintroduction and passage of the Act. One particular point of contention in the 2007 proposal appears to have been the definition of a "journalist."

As of 2011, 36 states offered at least some level of privilege for journalists to protect the identity of a source. Questions regarding an individual's status as a journalist also appear to be present at the state level. In April 2010, the New Jersey Court of Appeals ruled that an online blogger was not eligible for journalist protections available at the state level.[598]

Legal Framework: Judicial Branch

The Supreme Court has recognized a compelling government interest to protect information related to national security. Consequently, the Court has found that restricting provisions of the First Amendment in certain circumstances may be justified. In Pickering v. Board of Education, 391 U.S. 563 (1968) and National Federation of Federal Employees v. United States, 695 F. Supp. 1196 (1988), the courts ruled that First Amendment restrictions of government employees are permissible when there is a substantial government interest and the restrictions are narrowly drawn.[599, 600]

In the 1980 case Snepp v. United States, 444 U.S. 507 (1980), the Supreme Court affirmed the authority of the CIA to require current and former employees to submit articles and books for pre-publication review in the interests of national security.[601] One year later, in Haig v. Agee, 453 U.S. 280 (1981), the court ruled that the Executive Branch could decline to issue a passport to an individual in response to national security concerns.[602] In Department of Navy v. Egan, 484 U.S. 518 (1988), the Supreme Court also ruled that Executive Branch agencies had the discretion to deny a security clearance based on a compelling need to protect classified information.[603] In each of these cases the defense argued, unsuccessfully, that the government's actions infringed on its client's First Amendment rights.

University of Chicago law professor Geoffrey Stone provides an excellent overview of permissible limitations to First Amendment protections in the article "Government Secrecy vs. Freedom of the Press."[604] Stone identifies three instances in which a law may limit speech: content restrictions, restrictions other than content (time and location), and restrictions of conduct incidental to speech.

Professor Stone wrote that restrictions related to content are presumptively unconstitutional and "held to the highest degree of First Amendment scrutiny" as a result of the potential negative impact to public debate. The courts analyze non-content legal restrictions, such as time or location prohibitions, by weighing the government interest against the impact to speech. Restrictions of "non-communicative" activities *incidental* to speech, such as wiretapping, breaking and entering, or bribery, are presumptively constitutional because they do not expressly restrict speech.

Stone indicates that a court will only invalidate incidental restrictions if the impact on speech is substantial and significantly outweighs the government's interest in enforcing the law.[605] An example of a non-communicative restriction with only incidental impact to speech would include the enforcement of traffic laws. Though it could be argued that citing an individual for speeding to a protest rally restricts his or her speech, the incidental impact to speech does not outweigh the government's interest in enforcing traffic laws to prevent injury.

When these criteria are applied to a law that prohibits the publication of classified information, two standards would appear to apply. Stone writes that, because such a law regulates content, it would require the highest level of scrutiny for validity. However, because publication by the media is necessarily preceded by the non-communicative removal of classified information by a government employee, and possibly the solicitation of the government employee to disclose classified information, Stone asserts that the latter criteria may also be applicable. A prohibition against unlawful acts, such as the removal of classified information by a government employee or the solicitation of a government employee for classified information, would be presumptively constitutional. This presumption would only be invalidated if it was determined that the government's interest was significantly outweighed by the impact to speech.

In two 1974 Supreme Court cases related to access to government information, Saxbe v. Washington Post Co. 417 U.S. 843 (1974)[606] and Pell v. Procunier, 417 U.S. 817 (1974),[607] the court ruled that the First Amendment does not provide the media with an absolute right to access government information. In these decisions, the Court found that the media's ability to access information is no greater than that of the general public.

In the 1972 Supreme Court case Branzburg v. Hayes (408 U.S. 665), the Court ruled that journalists did not have a federal privilege to refuse to identify a source during grand jury proceedings. The case combined three incidents in which journalists were subpoenaed to testify before the grand jury regarding criminal activity they had witnessed. The first case involved a journalist's knowledge of the manufacture and use of hashish while the other two involved knowledge of the activities of the Black Panther Party, an African American organization founded to promote civil rights. In a five-to-four decision, the Court ruled that the First Amendment did not provide authority for a journalist to refuse to comply with a valid grand jury subpoena.

Between 1991 and June 2007, the Department of Justice reported subpoenaing journalists on 19 occasions.[608] This equates to approximately one subpoena per year over a 16-year period. Of the 19 subpoenaed journalists, at least three were imprisoned for refusing to comply with the subpoena. In 2001 freelance reporter Vanessa Leggett was jailed for 168 days for refusing to reveal unpublished information relevant to a murder trial.[609] In 2005 *New York Times* reporter Judith Miller was sentenced to 18 months incarceration, serving 85 days before agreeing to identify her source of information concerning the identity of a CIA employee.[610] Most recently, in 2006, freelance videographer Joshua Wolf was imprisoned for 226 days. Wolf refused to provide authorities with video footage from a street protest related to the July 2005 G-8 economic summit.[611]

As previously discussed, there have been four attempted prosecutions specifically for the unauthorized disclosure of classified information to the media. In 1971 Daniel Ellsberg and Anthony Russo, employees of the Rand Corporation, were indicted for providing portions of a TOP SECRET Defense Department study to the *New York Times* and the *Washington Post*. The indictment included eight counts under the Espionage Act, six counts of theft, and one count of conspiracy. On May 11, 1973, the cases against Ellsberg and Russo were dismissed due to government misconduct.[612]

In the second case involving an unauthorized disclosure to the media, Navy analyst Samuel Morison was indicted and successfully convicted in 1985 under section 793 of the Espionage Act.[613] Morison, with the Navy's approval, was a part-time contributor to the British magazine *Jane's Defence Weekly*. In an apparent attempt to garner favor with *Jane's* and obtain a full-time position, Morison provided three classified satellite images to an editor at the magazine. The imagery, from the U.S. KH-11 reconnaissance satellite, showed the first Soviet Kiev-class nuclear powered aircraft carrier still under construction. *Jane's* subsequently published one of the images on the cover of its August 11, 1984, edition.

During the trial, Morison's attorneys argued that the Espionage Act did not apply to unauthorized disclosures to the media, that provisions of the Act were vague and overbroad, and that Morison's motivation was actually patriotic. The judge and jury rejected these arguments. Morison was found guilty on all counts and was sentenced to two years' incarceration. The conviction was upheld by the Court of Appeals and the Supreme Court declined to hear the appeal. After serving his sentence, Morison was pardoned by President Bill Clinton in January 2001, his final day in office.[614]

In August 2010, Stephen Jin-Woo Kim, a State Department contractor, was indicted under Section 793 of the Espionage Act for disclosing the contents of a TOP SECRET intelligence report to a journalist working for a national news organization.[615] As of May 2010, the case was pending in the U.S. District Court for the District of Columbia. The most recent criminal indictment for an unauthorized disclosure to the media occurred in December 2010. Former CIA Operations Officer Jeffrey Sterling was indicted, also under Section 793, for disclosing classified information to a member of the media.[616] The information reportedly concerned a covert CIA operation involving Iran. As of May 2010, the case was pending in U.S. District Court, Eastern District of Virginia.

Though not specifically charged for disclosing classified information to the media, former NSA employee Thomas Drake was indicted in April 2010 for activities related to unauthorized disclosures to a member of the media.[617] According to the indictment, multiple articles published between February 2006 and November 2007 contained classified information provided by Drake. Drake was indicted under Section 793 of the Espionage Act for the unlawful possession and retention of classified information. He was also charged with obstruction of justice (18 USC 1519) and making a false statement to a special agent of the FBI (18 USC 1001(a)). Drake's trial was scheduled to begin in June 2011 in U.S. District Court, Maryland District.

There are four additional notable instances in which portions of the Espionage Act were used to prosecute individuals for unauthorized disclosures to recipients other than a foreign government. In 2006, Larry Franklin, a Defense Department analyst, pled guilty under Section 793 of the Espionage Act for disclosing classified information to U.S. employees of the American Israel Public Affairs Committee (AIPAC).[618] The classified information concerned U.S. policies toward Iran. Based on the terms of the plea agreement, Franklin was sentenced to 12½ years imprisonment. Franklin cooperated with prosecutors and the FBI and his sentence was later reduced to 10 months house arrest, community service, and probation.

The guilty plea included one count for the conspiracy to communicate national defense information to persons not entitled to receive it. Included in the overt acts in furtherance of the conspiracy were disclosures made to members of the media.[619]

In December 2009, former FBI linguist Samuel Leibowitz pled guilty under Section 798 of the Espionage Act for providing five classified FBI documents to the owner of an Internet blog site. The unidentified documents "contained classified information concerning the communication intelligence activities of the United States."[620] Information from the documents was subsequently posted to the blog site. In May 2010, in accordance with the terms of the plea agreement, Leibowitz was sentenced to 20 months incarceration.

One other conviction not involving a disclosure to a foreign government resulted from charges brought by the Navy under the Uniform Code of Military Justice (UCMJ). In 2007, Lieutenant Commander Matthew Diaz was found guilty during a general court-martial for the disclosure of classified information to an individual not authorized to receive it.[621] While assigned to the U.S. detention camp in Guantanamo Bay, Cuba, Diaz mailed a classified list of detainees to the Center for Constitutional Rights, a legal advocacy group. Criminal charges were preferred under Article 134 of the UCMJ, which provides for the application of federal criminal statutes to members of the military. Diaz was sentenced to six months confinement and was discharged from the Navy. Diaz had served in the military for over 20 years.

In July 2010, charges for an unauthorized disclosure were also preferred under the UCMJ against Private First Class Bradley Manning.[622] Manning was charged with communicating national defense information to an unauthorized recipient, exceeding his authorized access on a classified computer network, and improperly storing classified information on his personal computer. Information alleged to have been disclosed by Manning includes a video of a military operation in Iraq and more than 50 classified State Department cables. The unauthorized recipient of the information is reported to be the Internet-based organization WikiLeaks, an international organization reportedly dedicated to publishing documents revealing misconduct by governments or corporations. Similar to the case involving LCDR Diaz, violations of Section 793 of the Espionage Act were brought under Article 134 of the UCMJ. As of May 2011 Manning remained in pre-trial confinement at Fort Leavenworth, Kansas.

Beyond criminal prosecution, the most significant case involving the conflict between the government's authority to withhold information and the ability of the press to publish this information is the previously discussed Supreme Court case New York Times v. United States, 403 U.S. 713 (1971), better known as the "Pentagon Papers" case.[623] The principal issue in this case involved "prior restraint," the government's ability to prevent the publication of information it believes will harm national security.

On June 13, 1971, the *New York Times* published a front-page article containing classified information from a TOP SECRET Department of Defense study concerning Vietnam. Daniel Ellsberg, an employee of the RAND Corporation, had provided the study to *Times* reporter Neil Sheehan without authorization. After refusing a request from the Nixon administration to discontinue the disclosures, the *New York Times* published articles on each of the next two days.

In response to the *Times'* refusal to cooperate, the government obtained a federal injunction to prevent further disclosures. After the injunction was issued, Ellsberg provided portions of the study to the *Washington Post*, which began publishing its own articles. The government subsequently enjoined the *Washington Post* from publishing additional articles. Both newspapers appealed the injunctions, the appeals were combined, and the Supreme Court agreed to hear the joint case.

On June 30, 1971, the Supreme Court ruled, six to three, that the government had not overcome the "heavy presumption" against prior restraint.[624] In his concurring opinion, Justice Stewart wrote that prior restraint could only be justified when a disclosure "will surely result in direct, immediate, and irreparable damage to our Nation or its people."[625] The Court relied partially on the precedent established in the 1931 Supreme Court case Near v. Minnesota, 283 U.S. 697 (1931). In the Near case, the Court determined that prior restraint was unconstitutional except for extremely limited circumstances.[626]

Though the Supreme Court ruled that prior restraint was not warranted in this instance, subsequent courts have identified at least two instances in which they believed prior restraint was justified. In the 1979 case United States v. Progressive Inc., 467 F Supp 990 (1979), the District Court for the Western District of Wisconsin issued an injunction to prevent the magazine *The Progressive* from publishing an article detailing the instructions for constructing a hydrogen bomb.[627] The Court found that prior restraint was necessary in this case to prevent "irreparable harm to the national security of the United States." The government ultimately dropped the case when the information was disclosed in another publication.

FIGURE 16 – NOVEMBER 1979 PROGRESSIVE MAGAZINE [628]
Source: *The Progressive*, November 1979. Used with permission.

In the second case, the U.S. District Court for the Southern District of Florida issued an injunction in 1990 to prevent CNN from broadcasting recorded conversations between former Panamanian dictator Manuel Noriega and his attorneys.[629] CNN defied the court order, broadcasting excerpts from the conversations 11 times while appealing the injunction. CNN reported that it chose to defy the court order because it believed that the injunction was an invalid prior restraint.[630] The Supreme Court denied CNN's appeal of the injunction, even though the information had already been broadcast.[631] CNN was convicted of contempt of court in 1994 and ordered to broadcast an apology for defying the court. CNN was also ordered to reimburse the government $85,000 in attorney fees. CNN's apology read, in part, "On further consideration . . . CNN realizes that it was in error in defying the order of the court . . . while appealing the court's order."[632]

In the 2001 Supreme Court case Bartnicki v. Vopper, 532 U.S. 514 (2001), the Court ruled that a member of the media could not be held liable for broadcasting information he or she had obtained lawfully, even if the information was provided by an individual who had acquired the information through a violation of federal law.[633] In this case, a radio station had broadcast excerpts from a phone conversation that a private citizen had unlawfully recorded. The Court found that the media outlet could not be held liable because it had not performed an illegal act to obtain the recording. This decision did not discuss the additional legal issues raised when the media obtain and publish classified information.

The government has considered criminal prosecution for a journalist or media outlet on at least four occasions. In August 1942, a grand jury was empanelled after a June 7, 1942, *Chicago Tribune* article disclosed that the U.S. Navy had access to Japanese operational plans prior to the Battle of Midway. No indictment was returned, largely because the Navy refused to cooperate with the investigation. The Navy's decision was reportedly based on concern over the additional attention the disclosed information would receive during criminal proceedings.[634] The government was also reportedly concerned that additional classified information would be disclosed during a trial.

In the wake of the Supreme Court's 1971 decision to allow the continued publication of the "Pentagon Papers" articles, the U.S. Attorney for New York reportedly rejected a request by the Nixon administration to convene a grand jury to indict the *New York Times*.[635] In 1975, the Ford administration considered filing criminal charges against the *New York Times* for its disclosure of a classified program to intercept Soviet communications.[636] The operation, code-named HOLYSTONE, utilized specially equipped submarines to enter the territorial waters of the Soviet Union. Dick Cheney, then a White House aide, prepared a memorandum for White House Chief of Staff Donald Rumsfeld after the disclosure. The memorandum outlined potential courses of action, including the prosecution of the *New York Times* and/or Seymour Hersh, the author of the article.[637]

The Attorney General also prepared a "Memorandum for the President," outlining the Justice Department's position regarding legal action. The memorandum discussed all potential legal options, concluding that "the most promising course of action, for the moment, would be to discuss the problem of publication of material detrimental to the national security with leading publishers."[638] Ultimately, neither the *New York Times* nor Hersh was indicted and no further legal action was pursued. Similar to the 1942 *Tribune* disclosure, the decision was also partially based on concerns that criminal proceedings would draw additional attention to the classified program.[639]

Most recently, in May 1986, Director of Central Intelligence William Casey reportedly requested that the Justice Department consider prosecuting NBC for broadcasting a news report containing classified information.[640] The request was in response to a broadcast detailing the NSA operation IVY BELLS, in which the United States is reported to have intercepted Soviet communications by tapping undersea cables. Similar to the prior two cases, no legal action against NBC was taken.

Conclusion

Though he recognized that the law failed to offer an adequate resolution, Justice Potter Stewart identified the role of the law in establishing a foundation for the "contest" between a free press and national security. In a 1974 speech delivered at Yale Law School, Justice Stewart remarked:

> So far as the Constitution goes, the autonomous press may publish what it knows, and may seek to learn what it can.
>
> But this autonomy cuts both ways. The press is free to do battle against secrecy and deception in government. But the press cannot expect from the Constitution any guarantee that it will succeed. There is no constitutional right to have access to particular government information, or to require openness from the bureaucracy. The

public's interest in knowing about its government is protected by the guarantee of a Free Press, but the protection is indirect. The Constitution itself is neither a Freedom of Information Act nor an Official Secrets Act.

The Constitution, in other words, establishes the contest, not its resolution. Congress may provide a resolution, at least in some instances, through carefully drawn legislation. For the rest, we must rely, as so often in our system we must, on the tug and pull of the political forces in American society.[641]

Stewart's sentiments are reminiscent of Thomas Jefferson's second inaugural address. Jefferson also asserted that recourse for undesirable behavior by the media "must be sought in the censorship of public opinion" and not in the law.[642] Alexander Hamilton, one of Jefferson's greatest political rivals, shared his belief. In 1788 Hamilton wrote that the "liberty of the press" was dependent on "public opinion and on the general spirit of the people . . ."[643] Though an examination of the legal system can aid in framing the debate over the impact of unauthorized disclosures, it ultimately fails to offer an adequate solution to the dilemma.

Endnotes

1 New York Times Co. v. United States, 403 U.S. 713 (1971) (per curiam).

2 *Id.* at 719 (Black, J., concurring).

3 Terminiello v. City of Chicago, 337 U.S. 1, 37 (1949) (Jackson, J., dissenting). In a book that borrows Jackson's phraseology, Judge Richard Posner offered an analysis of the risks posed by transnational terrorism quite analogous to that offered by Ross. See RICHARD A. POSNER, NOT A SUICIDE PACT: THE CONSTITUTION IN TIMES OF EMERGENCY (2006).

4 For a thoughtful framing of the problem, see Note, Mechanisms of Secrecy, 121 HARV. L. REV. 1556 (2008).

5 See Harold Edgar & Benno C. Schmidt, Jr., *The Espionage Statutes and Publication of Defense Information*, 73 COLUM. L. REV. 929 (1973); see also Harold Edgar & Benno C. Schmidt, Jr., *Curtiss-Wright Comes Home: Executive Power and National Security Secrecy*, 21 HARV. C.R.-C.L. L. REV. 349 (1986) (updating their earlier analysis). For a more recent analysis, see Stephen I. Vladeck, *Inchoate Liability and the Espionage Act: The Statutory Framework and the Freedom of the Press*, 1 HARV. L. & POL'Y REV. 219 (2007).

6 See, for example, Stephen I. Vladeck, *The Espionage Act and National Security Whistleblowing After Garcetti*, 57 AM. U. L. REV. 1531 (2008).

7 See, for example, *Geoffrey R. Stone, Top Secret: When Our Government Keeps Us In The Dark* (2007).

8 See, for example, Neal Kumar Katyal, *Internal Separation of Powers: Checking Today's Most Dangerous Branch from Within*, 115 YALE L.J. 2314 (2006).

9 See, for example, Eric Lichtblau, *The Education of a 9/11 Reporter: The Inside Drama Behind the Times' Warrantless Wiretapping Story*, SLATE.COM, Mar. 26, 2008, *available at http://www.slate.com/id/2187498.*

10 Bruce, James, *How Foreign Adversaries Learn to Degrade U.S. Intelligence, and the Steps that Can be Take to Counter It.* Based on a shorter article appearing in *Strategic Denial and Deception: The Twenty-First Century Challenge*, Roy Godson and James Wirtz, eds. (New Brunswick, NJ: Transaction Books, 2002).

11 Esther Addley, "Assange claims WikiLeaks is more accountable than governments," *The Guardian*, April 9, 2011. http://www.guardian.co.uk/media/2011/apr/09/julian-assange-wikileaks-public-debate (accessed April 11, 2011).

12 Though the *New York Times* had been given access to the U.S. military reports prior to their release, WikiLeaks did not offer *The Times* advanced access the to U.S. State Department cables. The refusal was reportedly in retaliation for *The Times'* decision not to include a link to the WikiLeaks website in its earlier articles discussing U.S. military reports, as well as its publication of an article critical of Julian Assange. *The Times* ultimately obtained a copy of the cables from a separate source prior to their release by WikiLeaks.

13 Anne Kornblut, "Guantanamo documents revive debate," *Washington Post*, April 25, 2011. *http://www.washingtonpost.com/world/national-security/guantanamo_documents_revive_debate/2011/04/25/AF15ySlE_story.html?wprss=rss_homepage* (accessed April 26, 2011).

14 "A Superpower's View of the World," *Spiegel Online International*, November 28, 2010. *http://www.spiegel.de/international/world/0,1518,731580,00.html* (accessed February 21, 2011).

15 "I Enjoy Crushing Bastards," *Spiegel Online International*, July 26, 2010. *http://www.spiegel.de/international/world/0,1518,708518,00.html* (accessed November 2, 2010).

16 "WikiLeaks' Julian Assange, Pt. 2," *60 Minutes*, January 30, 2011. *http://www.cbsnews.com/video/watch/?id=7300036n&tag=contentBody;housing* (accessed February 21, 2011).

17 "I Enjoy Crushing Bastards," Spiegel Online International, July 26, 2010.

18 "The Iraq Archive: The Strands of War," New York Times, October 22, 2010. *http://www.nytimes.com/2010/10/23/world/middleeast/23intro.html* (accessed October 29, 2010).

19 Anne Kornblut, "Guantanamo documents revive debate," *Washington Post*, April 25, 2011.

20 "A Note to Readers: The Decision to Publish Diplomatic Documents," *New York Times*, November 28, 2010. *http://www.nytimes.com/2010/11/29/world/29editornote.html* (accessed February 21, 2011).

21 "The Defense Department's Response," *New York Times*, October 22, 2010. *http://www.nytimes.com/2010/10/23/world/middleeast/23response.html* (accessed October 29, 2010).

22 "Public Sees WikiLeaks as Harmful," Pew Research Center, December 8, 2010. *http://pewresearch.org/pubs/1823/poll-wikileaks-harm-serve-public-interest-press-handling* (accessed March 29, 2011).

23 Richard Spencer, "Wikileaks: Nick Clegg backs calls for investigation," *The Telegraph*, October 24, 2010. *http://www.telegraph.co.uk/news/worldnews/middleeast/iraq/8084116/Wikileaks-Nick-Clegg-backs-calls-for-investigation.html* (accessed October 29, 2010).

24 Joshua Partlow and Greg Jaffe, "Karzai calls WikiLeaks disclosures 'shocking' and dangerous to Afghan informants," The *Washington Post*, July 29, 2010. http://www.washingtonpost.com/wp-dyn/content/article/2010/07/29/AR2010072901762.html (accessed October 29, 2010).

25 Joshua Partlow and Karin Brulliard, "Pakistan decries WikiLeaks release of U.S. military documents on Afghan war," The *Washington Post*, July 27, 2010. *http://www.washingtonpost.com/wp-dyn/content/article/2010/07/26/AR2010072602393_pf.html* (accessed July 27, 2010).

26 Mary Beth Sheridan, "Calderon: WikiLeaks caused severe damage to U.S-Mexican relations," *Washington Post*, March 3, 2011. *http://www.washingtonpost.com/wp-dyn/content/article/2011/03/03/AR2011030302853.html?referrer=emailarticle* (accessed March 7, 2011).

27 Adam Thomson, "WikiLeaks spat leads to US diplomat resigning," Financial Times, March 20, 2011. http://www.ft.com/cms/s/0/00911f6e-530b-11e0-86e6-00144feab49a.html#axzz1HF2PtLkD (accessed March 21, 2011).

28 Steven Stalinsky, "American-Yemeni Al-Qaeda Cleric Anwar Al-Awlaki Highlights the Role and Importance of Media Jihad, Praises Al-Jazeera TV Journalists and WikiLeaks," The Middle East Media Research Institute, March 15, 2011. http://www.thememriblog.org/blog_personal/en/35529.htm (accessed March 18, 2011).

29 Robert Mackey, "Taliban Study Wikileaks to Hunt Informants," New York Times, July 30, 2010. http://thelede.blogs.nytimes.com/2010/07/30/taliban-study-wikileaks-to-hunt-informants (accessed October 29, 2010).

30 Jeanne Whalen, "Rights Groups Join Criticism of WikiLeaks," The Wall Street Journal, August 9, 2010. http://online.wsj.com/article/SB10001424052748703428604575419580947722558.html (accessed February 21, 2011).

31 "The Data Revolution: How WikiLeaks is changing journalism," Frontline Club, August 12, 2010. http://frontlineclub.com/events/2010/08/the-data-revolution-how-wikileaks-is-changing-journalism.html (accessed February 23, 2011).

32 Luke Harding and David Leigh, "WikiLeaks: How US political invective turned on 'anti-American' Julian Assange," The Guardian, February 3, 2011. http://www.guardian.co.uk/world/2011/feb/03/wikileaks-julian-assange-us-reaction (accessed February 23, 2011).

33 "Julian Assange extended interview," Australian Broadcasting Corporation, November 4, 2011. http://www.abc.net.au/7.30/content/2011/s3188451.htm (accessed April 11, 2011).

34 "WikiLeaks website publishes classified military documents from Iraq," CNN, October 22, 2010. http://articles.cnn.com/2010-10-22/us/wikileaks.iraq_1_wikileaks-website-classified-documents-iraq-wiki-leaks-iraqis?_s=PM:US (accessed February 22, 2011).

35 Mark Landler and Scott Shane, "U.S. Sends Warning to People Named in Cable Leaks," *New York Times*, January 6, 2011. *http://www.nytimes.com/2011/01/07/world/07wiki.html* (accessed February 22, 2011).

36 Simon Romero, "Ecuador Expels U.S. Ambassador over WikiLeaks Cable," *New York Times*, April 5, 2011. *http://www.nytimes.com/2011/04/06/world/americas/06ecuador.html* (accessed April 9, 2011).

37 "Secretary Clinton's remarks on WikiLeaks documents," *The Hill*, November 29, 2010. *http://thehill.com/blogs/congress-blog/lawmaker-news/130973-secretary-clintons-remarks-on-wikileak-documents* (accessed April 9, 2011).

38 "DoD News Briefing with Secretary Gates and Adm. Mullen from the Pentagon," November 30, 2010. *http://www.fas.org/sgp/news/2010/11/dod113010.html* (accessed February 26, 2011).

39 Mark Hosenball, "US officials privately say WikiLeaks damage limited," Reuters, January 18, 2011. *http://www.reuters.com/article/2011/01/18/wikileaks-damage-idUSN1816319120110118* (accessed February 26, 2011).

40 Robert Gates, Secretary of Defense to Carl Levin, Chairman, Senate Armed Services Committee, August 16, 2010, *http://www.fas.org/sgp/othergov/dod/gates-wikileaks.pdf* (accessed October 29, 2010).

41 "Julian Assange answers your questions," *The Guardian*, December 3, 2010. *http://www.guardian.co.uk/world/blog/2010/dec/03/julian-assange-wikileaks* (accessed February 26, 2011).

42 "Judith Miller: Julian Assange is a 'bad journalist'," *Fox News*, January 3, 2011. *http://www.politico.com/blogs/onmedia/0111/Judith_Miller_Julian_Assange_is_a_bad_journalist.html* (accessed February 26, 2011).

43 Dana Priest, "The Evolving Nature of the Relationship Between The Media and National Security," Standing Committee on Law and National Security Breakfast Program, American Bar Association, March 3, 2011.

44 Bill Keller, "Dealing With Assange and the WikiLeaks Secrets," *New York Times*, January 26, 2011. *http://www.nytimes.com/2011/01/30/magazine/30Wikileaks-t.html* (accessed February 26, 2011).

45 Hagit Limor, "The consensus on WikiLeaks: there is no consensus," Society of Professional Journalists, December 2, 2010. *http://blogs.spjnetwork.org/president/?p=370* (accessed February 26, 2011).

46 "The Defense Department's Response," *New York Times*, October 22, 2010.

47 "The Man Who Spilled the Secrets," *Vanity Fair*, February 2011. *http://www.vanityfair.com/politics/features/2011/02/the-guardian-201102* (accessed February 26, 2011).

48 "Bradley Manning Charge Sheet," *Cryptome*, May 29, 2010. *http://cryptome.org/manning-charge.pdf* (accessed October 29, 2010).

49 David S. Cloud, "Army private charged in earlier leak had access to latest WikiLeak papers," The *Los Angeles Times*, July 28, 2010. *http://articles.latimes.com/2010/jul/28/world/la-fg-wikileaks-20100728* (accessed November 2, 2010).

50 Charlie Savage, "Soldier Faces 22 New WikiLeaks Charges," *New York Times*, March 2, 2011. *http://www.nytimes.com/2011/03/03/us/03manning.html* (accessed March 7, 2011).

51 Kevin Poulson and Kim Zetter, "'I Can't Believe What I'm Confessing to You': The Wikileaks Chats," *Wired.com*, June 10, 2010. *http://www.wired.com/threatlevel/2010/06/wikileaks-chat/* (accessed October 29, 2010).

52 Michael Calderone, "NY Times considers creating an 'EZ Pass lane for leakers'," *The Cutline*, January 25, 2011. *http://news.yahoo.com/s/yblog_thecutline/20110125/ts_yblog_thecutline/ny-times-considers-creating-an-ez-pass-lane-for-leakers* (accessed February 26, 2011).

53 "This house believes whistleblowers make the world a safer place: Part II," *New Statesman*, April 10, 2011. *http://www.newstatesman.com/blogs/the-staggers/2011/04/assange-murray-speech* (accessed April 11, 2011).

54 "WikiLeaks' Julian Assange, Pt. 2," *60 Minutes*, January 30, 2011. *http://www.cbsnews.com/video/watch/?id=7300036n&tag=contentMaincontentBody* (accessed February 26, 2011).

55 18 U.S.C. 798 (1982).

56 *U.S. Constitution*, amend. 1.

57 "The James Madison Center: Quotes on Various Issues," James Madison University. *http://www.jmu.edu/madison/center/main_pages/madison_archives/quotes/great/issues.htm* (accessed June 4, 2008).

58 *U.S. Constitution*, amend. 1.

59 Executive Order 13526 defines an unauthorized disclosure as "a communication or physical transfer of classified information to an unauthorized recipient."

60 J. William Leonard, "Managing Secrets in a Changing World," First Amendment Center, March 16, 2004. http://www.firstamendmentcenter.org/commentary.aspx?id=12878&printer-friendly=y (accessed June 4, 2008).

61 Moncure Daniel Conway, *The Life of Thomas Paine* (New York, NY: Knickerbocker Press, 1893), http://www.thomaspaine.org/bio/ConwayLife.html (accessed June 4, 2008).

62 Moncure Daniel Conway, *The Life of Thomas Paine.*

63 "Thomas Jefferson on Politics and Government: Freedom of the Press," University of Virginia Online Library. http://etext.virginia.edu/jefferson/quotations/jeff1600.htm (accessed June 3, 2008).

64 "Thomas Jefferson on Politics and Government: Freedom of the Press."

65 "Thomas Jefferson Second Inaugural Address," The Avalon Project at Yale Law School, *http://avalon.law.yale.edu/19th_century/jefinau2.asp* (accessed June 3, 2008).

66 "Thomas Jefferson Second Inaugural Address."

67 Elie Abel, *Leaking: Who Does It? Who Benefits At What Cost?* (New York, NY: Priority Press Publications, 1987).

68 New York Times v. United States, 403 U.S. 713 (1971).

69 Bill Keller, "Letter From Bill Keller on The Times's Banking Records Report," *New York Times*, June 25, 2006. *http://www.nytimes.com/2006/06/25/business/media/25keller-letter.html* (accessed January 2, 2010).

70 The sixteen member agencies of the Intelligence Community include the four branches of the military; Defense Department organizations National Security Agency (NSA), National Reconnaissance Office (NRO), National Geospatial-Intelligence Agency (NGA), and Defense Intelligence Agency (DIA); and non-Defense Department agencies Central Intelligence Agency (CIA), Federal Bureau of Investigation (FBI), Drug Enforcement Administration, Department of Homeland Security (DHS), Coast Guard, Department of Energy (DOE), Department of Treasury, and Department of State.

71 Dennis Blair, "Unauthorized Disclosures of Classified Information," July 1, 2009.

72 Commission on the Intelligence Capabilities of the United States Regarding Weapons of Mass Destruction, *Report of the Commission on the Intelligence Capabilities of the United States Regarding Weapons of Mass Destruction.* Washington DC: Government Printing Office, 2005, http://www.gpoaccess.gov/wmd/index.html (accessed June 4, 2008).

73 William Casey, "Remarks Before the Society of Professional Journalists," September 24, 1986.

74 Steven Aftergood, "Secrecy and Accountability in U.S. Intelligence," Federation of American Scientists, http://www.fas.org/sgp/cipsecr.html (accessed June 8, 2008).

75 Katharine Graham, "Safeguarding Our Freedoms As We Cover Terrorist Acts," *Washington Post*, April 20, 1986. http://www.washingtonpost.com/ac2/wp-dyn/A4577-2001Jul16 (accessed June 3, 2008).

76 Tom Brokaw, Walter Cronkite, and Ted Koppel to SSCI, May 25, 2006. *http://www.naa.org/~/media/3570430F97464C018CA4177BD022DBDD. ashx* (accessed June 4, 2008).

77 "Leaks Seen as Motivated More by Personal Than Political Reasons," The Pew Research Center, April 5, 2007. *http://pewresearch.org/pubs/446/news-leaks-remain-divisive-but-libby-case-has-little-impact* (accessed June 4, 2008).

78 "Leaks Seen as Motivated More by Personal Than Political Reasons."

79 "State of the First Amendment 2006," First Amendment Center. *http://www.firstamendmentcenter.org/about.aspx?item=state_first_amendment_2006* (accessed June 4, 2008).

80 Plato, *The Republic*, trans. R.E. Allen (New Haven, CT: Yale University Press, 2006).

81 Plato, *The Republic*.

82 U.S. National Security Council, National Security Council Meeting Minutes, October 7, 1974. *http://fordlibrarymuseum.gov/library/document/nscmin/mscmin.html* (accessed June 3, 2008).

83 Joel Garreau, "Up To Their Keisters in Leaks," *Washington Post*, January 16, 1983.

84 Howard Kurtz, "President Wants a Plumber," *Washington Post*, November 19, 2009. *http://www.washingtonpost.com/wp-dyn/content/article/2009/11/19/AR2009111901008.html* (accessed November 20, 2009).

85 "Up To Their Keisters in Leaks."

86 Richard Nixon, "Address to the Nation About the Watergate Investigations," August 15, 1973. *http://www.pbs.org/wgbh/amex/presidents/37_nixon/psources/ps_water2.html* (accessed June 3, 2008).

87 U.S. National Security Council, National Security Council Meeting Minutes, October 7, 1974.

88 "Lid on Leaks," *Time Magazine*, January, 25, 1982. *http://www.time.com/time/magazine/article/0,9171,925218,00.html* (accessed June 3, 2008).

89 Daniel Schorr, "Whistle-blower's intent is pure," *Christian Science Monitor*, May 2, 2006. *http://findarticles.com/p/articles/mi_qn4188/is_20060502/ai_n16211140* (accessed June 3, 2008).

90 Robert Gates, "Unauthorized Disclosures: Risks, Costs, and Responsibilities," in "Intelligence Leaks," special issue, *American Intelligence Journal* (1988).

91 David Ignatius, "When Does Blowing Secrets Cross the Line?" *Washington Post*, July 2, 2000. *http://pqasb.pqarchiver.com/washingtonpost/access/55923003.html* (accessed June 3, 2008).

92 Janet Reno, "Statement Before the Senate Select Committee on Intelligence Concerning Unauthorized Disclosures of Classified Information," Federation of American Scientists. *http://www.fas.org/sgp.othergov/renoleaks.html* (accessed June 3, 2008).

93 Janet Reno, "Statement Before the Senate Select Committee on Intelligence Concerning Unauthorized Disclosures of Classified Information."

94 Ronald Weich, Assistant Attorney General to Patrick Leahy, Chairman, Senate Judiciary Committee, April 8, 2010. http://www.fas.org/irp/agency/doj/intel-leak.pdf (accessed June 22, 2010).

95 "Button Your Lip," *Time Magazine*, July 28, 1980. http://www.time.com/time/magazine/article/0,9171,922071,00.html (accessed June 3, 2008).

96 George Church, "Plugging the Leak of Secrets," *Time Magazine*, January 28, 1985. *http://www.time.com/time/magazine/article/0,9171,959281,00.html* (accessed June 3, 2008).

97 Brian A. Benczkowski, Principal Deputy Assistant Attorney General to John D. Rockefeller, Chairman, SSCI, February 4, 2008. *http://www.fas.org/irp/congress/2007_hr/threat.pdf* (accessed July 30, 2009).

98 James Bruce, "The Consequences of Permissive Neglect: Laws and Leaks of Classified Intelligence," *Studies in Intelligence* 47, no. 1 (2003) *https:// www.cia.gov/library/center-for-the-study-of-intelligence/csi-publications/csi-studies/studies/vol47no1/article04.html* (accessed June 4, 2008).

99 Michael Gordon and David Cloue, "U.S. Knew of China's Missile Test, but Kept Silent," *New York Times*, April 23, 2007. http://www.nytimes.com/2007/04/23/washington/23satellite.html (accessed June 3, 2008).

100 L. Britt Snider, "Recollections from the Church Commission," *Studies in Intelligence* (Winter 1999-2000). *https://www.cia.gov/library/center-for-the-study-of-intelligence/csi-publications/csi-studies/studies/winter99-00/art4.html* (accessed June 8, 2008).

101 Dana Priest, "CIA Holds Terror Suspects in Secret Prisons," *Washington Post*, November 2, 2005. *http://www.washingtonpost.com/wp-dyn/content article/2005/11/01/AR2005110101644.html* (accessed June 3, 2008).

102 James Risen and Eric Lichtblau, "Bush Lets U.S. Spy on Callers Without Courts," *New York Times*, December 16, 2005. *http://www.nytimes.com/2005/12/16/politics/16program.html* (accessed June 3, 2008).

103 Eric Lichtblau and James Risen, "Bank Data is Sifted by U.S. in Secret to Block Terror," *New York Times*, January 23, 2006. *http://www.nytimes.com/2006/06/23/washington/23intel.html* (accessed January 2, 2010).

104 "ODNI Announces Establishment of Open Source Center," Office of the Director of National Intelligence. *http://www.dni.gov/press_releases/20051108_release.htm* (accessed June 3, 2008).

105 "Today's spies find secrets in plain sight," *USA Today*, April 1, 2008. *http://www.usatoday.com/tech/news/surveillance/2008-03-31-internet-spies_N.htm* (accessed June 3, 2008).

106 Today's spies find secrets in plain sight.

107 Geoffrey Stone, "Government Secrecy vs. Freedom of the Press." *Harvard Law and Policy Review* 1, no. 1 (Winter 2007).

108 New York Times v. United States, 403 U.S. 713 (1971).

109 Branzburg v. Hayes, 408 U.S. 665 (1972).

110 New York Times v. United States, 403 U.S. 713 (1971).

111 Ronald Weich, Assistant Attorney General to Patrick Leahy, Chairman, Senate Judiciary Committee, April 8, 2010. *http://www.fas.org/irp/agency/doj/intel-leak.pdf* (accessed June 22, 2010).

112 18 U.S.C. 793 (1982).

113 Gabriel Schoenfeld, "Has the 'New York Times' Violated the Espionage Act?" *Commentary*, March 2006. *http://www.commentarymagazine.com/viewarticle.cfm/has-the-new-york-times-violated-the-espionage-act-10036* (accessed June 4, 2008).

114 "Pentagon Papers Case Dismissed," *Time Magazine*, May 21, 1973. *http://www.time.com/time/magazine/article/0,9171,907273,00.html* (accessed June 3, 2008).

115 "Supreme Court Denies Freedom in Spy Case," *New York Times*, June 12, 1988. *http://www.nytimes.com/1988/06/12/us/supreme-court-denies-freedom-in-spy-case.html* (accessed January 2, 2010).

116 Spencer Hsu, "State Dept. contractor charged in leak to news organizations," *Washington Post*, August 28, 2010. *http://www.washingtonpost.com/wp-dyn/content/article/2010/08/27/AR2010082704602.html* (accessed October 21, 2010).

117 Charlie Savage, "Ex-C.I.A. Officer Named in Disclosure Indictment," *New York Times*, January 6, 2011. *http://www.nytimes.com/2011/01/07/us/07indict.html* (accessed March 30, 2011).

118 Janet Reno, "Statement Before the Senate Select Committee on Intelligence Concerning Unauthorized Disclosures of Classified Information."

119 Committee on Classified Information, Report to the Secretary of Defense by the Committee on Classified Information, November 8, 1956. *http://www.thememoryhole.org/foi/coolidge.html* (accessed June 3, 2008).

120 Report of the Subcommittee on Secrecy and Disclosure to the Senate Select Committee on Intelligence, 1978. *http://intelligence.senate.gov/pdfs/95national_security_secrets.pdf* (accessed April 15, 2011).

121 Report of the Interdepartmental Group on Unauthorized Disclosures of Classified Information, March 31, 1982. *http://www.fas.org/sgp/library/willard.pdf* (accessed June 3, 2008).

122 Robert Gates, "Unauthorized Disclosures: Risks, Costs, and Responsibilities."

123 Interagency Task Force Concerning Protections Against Unauthorized Disclosures of Classified Information, Report to the Attorney General of the United States, Washington DC: Government Printing Office, 2002.

124 John Ashcroft, Attorney General, to Dennis Hastert, Speaker of the House, October 15, 2002. *http://www.fas.org/sgp/othergov/dojleaks.html* (accessed July 30, 2009).

125 William Cohen, "National Secrets, Too Frequently Told," *New York Times*, September 5, 2001. *http://www.nytimes.com/2001/09/05/opinion/national-secrets-too-frequently-told.html* (accessed January 2, 2010).

126 Interagency Task Force Concerning Protections Against Unauthorized Disclosures of Classified Information, Report to the Attorney General of the United States.

127 Report of the Commission on the Intelligence Capabilities of the United States Regarding Weapons of Mass Destruction.

128 Report of the Interdepartmental Group on Unauthorized Disclosures of Classified Information.

129 Report of the Subcommittee on Secrecy and Disclosure to the Senate Select Committee on Intelligence, 1978.

130 Committee on Classified Information, *Report to the Secretary of Defense by the Committee on Classified Information.*

131 Daniel P. Altman, Special Agent in Charge, U.S. Agency for International Development, Office of Inspector General, interview by author, July 3, 2010, Bethany Beach, DE.

132 *United States Intelligence Community Information Sharing Strategy,* February 22, 2008. *http://www.dni.gov/reports/IC_Information_Sharing_Strategy.pdf* (accessed June 3, 2008).

133 James Clapper, "Remarks and Q&A by Director of National Intelligence James Clapper," November 2, 2010. *http://www.fas.org/irp/news/2010/11/dni-geoint.pdf* (accessed April 17, 2011).

134 Peter Grier, "Soldier arrested in WikiLeaks classified Iraq video case," *Christian Science Monitor,* June 7, 2010. *http://www.csmonitor.com/USA/Military/2010/0607/Soldier-arrested-in-WikiLeaks-classified-Iraq-video-case* (accessed June 7, 2010).

135 28 CFR 50.10, "Policy with regard to the issuance of subpoenas to member of the news media," (1980). *http://edocket.access.gpo.gov/cfr_2003/julqtr/pdf/28cfr50.10.pdf* (accessed June 4, 2008).

136 Ronald Weich, Assistant Attorney General to Patrick Leahy, Chairman, Senate Judiciary Committee.

137 John Ashcroft, Attorney General to Dennis Hastert, Speaker of the House, October 15, 2002.

138 Ronald Weich, Assistant Attorney General to Patrick Leahy, Chairman, Senate Judiciary Committee.

139 5 U.S.C. 7532 (1966).

140 In accordance with the "Garrity Rule," a government employee may be compelled to provide a statement or face disciplinary action, such as the termination of employment. Any information obtained as the result of a

compelled interview cannot be used against the employee during criminal proceedings.

141 "Up To Their Keisters in Leaks."

142 Central Intelligence Agency, "Family Jewels Memorandum," May 16, 1973. *http://www.gwu.edu/...nsarchiv/NSAEBB/NSAEBB222/index.htm* (accessed June 3, 2008).

143 Central Intelligence Agency, "Family Jewels Memorandum," May 16, 1973.

144 Central Intelligence Agency, "Family Jewels Memorandum," May 16, 1973.

145 "Pentagon Papers Case Dismissed," *Time Magazine*, May 21, 1973. *http://www.time.com/time/magazine/article/0,9171,907273,00.html* (accessed June 3, 2008).

146 For the purposes of this book, the term "journalist" refers to an individual who gathers information concerning matters of public interest for dissemination to the public for a substantial portion of his or her livelihood. The term "press" includes the local and national organizations that employ journalists and are primarily responsible for the dissemination of matters of public interest.

147 Report of the Interdepartmental Group on Unauthorized Disclosures of Classified Information, March 31, 1982. *http://www.fas.org/sgp/library/willard.pdf* (accessed June 3, 2008).

148 Richard Hertling to Patrick Leahy, March 1, 2007. *http://www.scribd.com/doc/334133/Letter-from-Hertling-to-Senator-Leahy?ga_related_doc=1* (accessed June 3, 2008).

149 John Ashcroft, "Statement Before the United States Senate Select Committee on Intelligence Concerning Unauthorized Disclosure of Classified Information."

150 Neal Shover and Andy Hochstetler, *Choosing White Collar Crime* (New York, NY: Cambridge University Press, 2006

151 Neal Shover and Andy Hochstetler, *Choosing White Collar Crime.*

152 Senate, Report of the Commission on Protecting and Reducing Government Secrecy, 103rd Cong., 1997, S. Doc. 105-2: Government Printing Office, 1997. http://www.access.gpo.gov/congress/commissions/secrecy/index.html (accessed June 3, 2008).

153 Edward Xanders, "A Handyman's Guide to Fixing National Security Leaks: An Analytical Framework for Evaluating Proposals to Curb Unauthorized Publication of Classified Information."

154 Michael Hayden, "Remarks of Central Intelligence Agency Director at the Council on Foreign Relations," September 7, 2007. *http://www.fas.org/irp/cia/product/dcia090707.html* (accessed December 9, 2009).

155 "Motivation," Word Reference. http://www.wordreference.com/definition/motivation (accessed June 8, 2008).

156 Branzburg v. Hayes, 408 U.S. 665 (1972).

157 Committee on Classified Information, Report to the Secretary of Defense by the Committee on Classified Information.

158 Committee on Classified Information, Report to the Secretary of Defense by the Committee on Classified Information.

159 "Code of Ethics," Society of Professional Journalists. *http://www.spj.org/ethicscode.asp* (accessed June 8, 2008).

160 Newspaper Association of America and National Newspaper Association to HPSCI, May 23, 2006.

161 Neil Sheehan, "Vietnam Archive: Pentagon Study Traces 3 Decades of Growing U. S. Involvement," *New York Times*, June 13, 1971. *http://select.nytimes.com/gst/abstract.html?res=F10B1FFD3D5813748DDDAA0994DE405B818BF1D3* (accessed June 8, 2008).

162 New York Times v. United States, 403 U.S. 713 (1971).

163 Katharine Graham, Personal History (New York, NY: Random House, 1997).

164 Rachel Patron, "Does the media have freedom of speech," Florida Sun-Sentinel, March 28, 2008. *http://pqasb.pqarchiver.com/sun_sentinel/results.ht ml?st=advanced&QryTxt=%22here%27s+an+example+of+how+one+of+the+g reat+political+scoops%22&type=current&sortby=REVERSE_CHRON&datety pe=0&frommonth=01&fromday=01&fromyear=1985&tomonth=06&today=0 8&toyear=2008&* (accessed June 8, 2008).

165 Rachel Smolkin, "Judgment Calls: How top editors decide whether to publish national security stories based on classified information."

166 Rachel Smolkin, "Judgment Calls: How top editors decide whether to publish national security stories based on classified information."

167 Dean Baquet, "Why We Ran the Bank Story," Los Angeles Times, June 27, 2006. http://www.democraticunderground.com/discuss/duboard. php?az=view_all&address=364x1514165 (accessed June 8, 2008).

168 Bill Keller, "Letter From Bill Keller on The Times's Banking Records Report," New York Times, June 25, 2006. http://www.nytimes.com /2006/06/25/business/media/25keller-letter.html (accessed June 8, 2008).

169 Bill Keller, "Letter From Bill Keller on The Times's Banking Records Report."

170 Senate Committee on the Judiciary, Examining DOJ's Investigation of Journalists Who Publish Classified Information: Lessons from the Jack Anderson Case, 109th Congress, 2nd sess., June 6, 2006. http://www.fas. org/irp/congress/2006_hr/journalists.html (accessed June 8, 2008).

171 "The Pentagon Papers: Secrets, Lies and Audiotapes," The National Security Archive, George Washington University. http://www.gwu. edu/~nsarchiv/NSAEBB/NSAEBB48/ (accessed July 27, 2010).

172 Pentagon Papers Case Dismissed, *Time Magazine*, May 21, 1973. *http://www.time.com/time/magazine/article/0,9171,907273,00.html* (accessed June 3, 2008).

173 "The CIA's Family Jewels," George Washington University, The National Security Archive. *http://www.gwu.edu/...nsarchiv/NSAEBB/NSAEBB222/* (accessed June 8, 2008).

174 Scott Shane, "There are Leaks. And Then There are Leaks," *New York Times*, April 30, 2006. *http://www.nytimes.com/2006/04/30/weekinreview/30shane.html?ex=1304049600&en=68008f1a247c9b9c&ei=5088&partner=rssnyt&emc=rss* (accessed June 8, 2008).

175 L. Britt Snider, "Recollections from the Church Commission."

176 Library of Congress, Congressional Research Service, CRS Report for Congress: Assassination Ban and E.O. 12333: A Brief Summary (Washington, DC: Government Printing Office, January 4, 2002). *http://www.fas.org/irp/crs/RS21037.pdf* (accessed June 8, 2008).

177 Central Intelligence Agency, "Family Jewels Memorandum," May 16, 1973.

178 Tim Weiner, "Guatemalan Agent of C.I.A. Tied to Killing of American," *New York Times*, March 23, 1995. http://query.nytimes.com/gst/fullpage.html?res=990CE4D7173EF930A15750C0A963958260 (accessed June 9, 2008).

179 Tim Weiner, "C.I.A. Agent's Tie to Deaths In Guatemala Is Still Hazy," *New York Times*, July 27, 1995. *http://query.nytimes.com/gst/fullpage.html?res=990CEED8113AF934A15754C0A963958260* (accessed June 9, 2008).

180 Thomas Powers, "Computer Security: The Whiz Kid vs. the Old Boys," *New York Times*, December 3, 2000. *http://query.nytimes.com/gst/fullpage.html?res=9E0CEFDA163DF930A35751C1A9669C8B63* (accessed June 9, 2008).

181 Tim Geraghty, "A Brief History of Classified Leaks," National Review Online, October 1, 2003. *http://www.nationalreview.com/geraghty/geraghty200310010843.asp* (accessed June 9, 2008).

182 Tim Geraghty, "A Brief History of Classified Leaks."

183 Tim Weiner, "CIA Severs Ties to 100 Foreign Agents," *New York Times*, March 3, 1997. *http://query.nytimes.com/gst/fullpage.html?res=9406E2D71F3 1F930A35750C0A961958260&scp=59&sq=%22Tim+Weiner%22+and+% 22guatemala%22&st=nyt* (accessed June 9, 2008).

184 Jack Nelson, "U.S. Government Secrecy and the Current Crackdown on Leaks."

185 Lyle Denniston, "The Constitution That Delicate Balance: National Security and Freedom of the Press" (panel interview conducted at Columbia University Seminar on Media and Society, New York, New York, 1984). *http://www.learner.org/resources/series72.html* (accessed June 4, 2008).

186 Katharine Graham, "Safeguarding Our Freedoms As We Cover Terrorist Acts."

187 "'New York Times' Stirs Controversy in Exposing Government Secrets," National Public Radio. *http://www.npr.org/templates/story/story. php?storyId=5515699* (accessed June 10, 2008).

188 Congress, House of Representatives, Rep. Dennis Oxley of Indiana speaking for the Resolution Supporting Intelligence and Law Enforcement Programs to Track Terrorists and Terrorist Financing, H.Res. 895, 109th Cong., 2nd sess. *http://www.fas.org/irp/congress/2006_cr/h062906.html* (accessed June 8, 2008).

189 James Bruce, "The Consequences of Permissive Neglect: Laws and Leaks of Classified Intelligence."

190 "Internet Security Advisory Group Publications," Internet Security Advisory Group. *http://www.isag.com/library/index.html* (accessed June 5, 2008).

191 Ben Bradlee, *A Good Life: Newspapering and Other Adventures*.

192 Katharine Graham, *Personal History*.

193 New York Times v. United States, 403 U.S. 713 (1971).

194 "Free Speech, Reporting on National Security," PBS Online News Hour.

195 Robert Kaiser, "Public Secrets."

196 Rachel Smolkin, "Judgment Calls: How top editors decide whether to publish national security stories based on classified information."

197 Kathryn Olmsted, Challenging the Secret Government: The post-Watergate investigations of the CIA and FBI.

198 "CBS Ousts 4 for Bush Guard Story," CBS.

199 Congress, House of Representatives, Rep. Pete Hoekstra, "Opening Statement Before the House Permanent Select Committee on Intelligence: Hearing on the Role and Responsibilities of the Media in National Security," May 26, 2006. *http://www.globalsecurity.org/intell/library/congress/2006_hr/060526-hoekstra.pdf* (accessed June 8, 2008).

200 "Two Gulf Coast newspapers win Pulitzer Prize," [*USA Today*], April 17, 2006. *http://www.usatoday.com/life/2006-04-17-katrina-pulitzers_x.htm?POE=LIFISVA* (accessed June 10, 2008).

201 Brent Baker, "Cokie and Steve Roberts Hail Pulitzer Prize Winning Stories on Bush's 'Abuse of Power'," Newsbusters. *http://newsbusters.org/node/5071* (accessed June 10, 2008).

202 Tim Hackler, "The Press and National Security Secrets."

203 Tim Hackler, "The Press and National Security Secrets."

204 Tim Hackler, "The Press and National Security Secrets."

205 Byron Calame, "Behind the Eavesdropping Story, a Loud Silence," *New York Times*, January 1, 2006. *http://www.nytimes.com/2006/01/01/opinion/01publiceditor.html* (accessed January 2, 2010).

206 Thomas Joscelyn, "Source Code," *The Daily Standard*. http://www.weeklystandard.com/Content/Public/Articles/000/000/006/541acool.asp (accessed June 10, 2008).

207 Philip Shenon, "Times Reporter Subpoenaed Over Source for Book," *New York Times*, February 1, 2008. *http://www.nytimes.com/2008/02/01/washington/01inquire.html* (accessed January 2, 2010).

208 Neal Shover and Andy Hochstetler, *Choosing White-Collar Crime*.

209 "Secretive website WiliLeaks may be posting more U.S. military video," CNN.com, June 21, 2010. *http://articles.cnn.com/2010-06-21/tech/wikileaks.assange_1_wikileaks-documents-video?_s=PM:TECH* (accessed April 25, 2011).

210 "WikiLeaks Founder Julian Assange on the 'War Logs'," Der Spiegel Online, July 26, 2010. *http://www.spiegel.de/international/world/0,1518,708518,00.html* (accessed April 25, 2011).

211 FBI says spies working in State Department media, Reuters, May 13, 2000. *http://www.turkishdailynews.com.tr/archives.php?id=17331* (accessed June 10, 2008).

212 FBI says spies working in State Department media, Reuters.

213 Christopher Ruddy, "Russia Defector: Large Number of Spies Act as Journalists," Newsmax. *http://archive.newsmax.com/articles/?a=2000/5/14/143832* (accessed June 10, 2008).

214 Pat Holt, *Secret Intelligence and Public Policy: A Dilemma of Democracy*.

215 Ben Bradlee, *A Good Life: Newspapering and Other Adventures*.

216 "Justification," Dictionary.com. *http://dictionary.reference.com/browse/justification* (accessed June 9, 2008).

217 New York Times v. United States, 403 U.S. 713 (1971).

218 Elie Abel, *Leaking: Who Does It? Who Benefits At What Cost?*

219 Congress, House of Representatives, Rep. Jane Harman, "Opening Statement Before the House Permanent Select Committee on Intelligence: Hearing on the Role and Responsibilities of the Media in National Security," May 26, 2006. *http://www.fas.org/irp/congress/2006_hr/052606harman.pdf* (accessed June 8, 2008).

220 Jack Nelson, "U.S. Government Secrecy and the Current Crackdown on Leaks."

221 Congress, House of Representatives, Rep. Jane Harman, "Opening Statement Before the House Permanent Select Committee on Intelligence: Hearing on the Role and Responsibilities of the Media in National Security."

222 Information Security Oversight Office, Report to the President, May 31, 2007. *http://www.fas.org/sgp/isoo/2006rpt.pdf* (accessed June 8, 2008).

223 Dana Priest and William Arkin, "A hidden world, growing beyond control," *Washington Post*, July 19, 2010. *http://projects.washingtonpost.com/top-secret-america/articles/a-hidden-world-growing-beyond-control/* (accessed July 23, 2010).

224 Edward Xanders, "A Handyman's Guide to Fixing National Security Leaks: An Analytical Framework for Evaluating Proposals to Curb Unauthorized Publication of Classified Information."

225 Steven Aftergood, "Secrecy and Accountability in U.S. Intelligence."

226 William Casey, "Remarks Before the Society of Professional Journalists," September 24, 1986.

227 "Plugging Media Leaks," News Hour with Jim Lehrer. *http://www.pbs.org/newshour/bb/media/jan-june00/leaks_6-29.html* (accessed June 9, 2008).

228 Congress, Senator Richard Shelby of Alabama speaking for the Intelligence Authorization Act for Fiscal Year 2001.

229 Senate Committee on the Judiciary, *Examining DOJ's Investigation of Journalists Who Publish Classified Information: Lessons from the Jack Anderson Case.*

230 Report to the Secretary of Defense by the Committee on Classified Information, 1956.

231 Bob Woodward, "A Journalist's Perspective on Public Disclosures."

232 Ben Bradlee, *A Good Life: Newspapering and Other Adventures* (New York, NY: Simon and Schuster, 1996).

233 "National Declassification Center," Society for History in the Federal Government. *http://shfg.org/shfg/federal-history-work/declassification* (accessed April 25, 2011).

234 Kevin Kosar, "The Reducing Over-Classification Act Becomes Law," Society for History in the Federal Government. *http://shfg.org/shfg/federal-history-work/declassification* (accessed April 25, 2011).

235 Scott Shane, "Increase in the Number of Documents Classified by the Government," *New York Times,* July 3, 2005. *http://www.nytimes.com/2005/07/03/politics/03secrecy.html* (accessed January 2, 2010).

236 Murray Waas, "Is There a Double Standard On Leak Probes?

237 Report of the Senate Select Committee on Intelligence, Subcommittee on Secrecy and Disclosure, 1978.

238 Report to the National Security Council on Unauthorized Media Leak Disclosures by the National Counterintelligence Policy Board, 1996.

239 Congress, House of Representatives, Rep. Louis Slaughter of New York speaking for the Resolution Supporting Intelligence and Law Enforcement Programs to Track Terrorists and Terrorist Financing, H.Res. 895, 109th Cong., 2nd sess. *http://www.fas.org/irp/congress/2006_cr/h062906.html* (accessed June 8, 2008).

240 Jack Nelson, "U.S. Government Secrecy and the Current Crackdown on Leaks."

241 Murray Waas, "Is There a Double Standard On Leak Probes?"

242 Colin Powell, "A Policy of Evasion and Deception," *Washington Post*, February 5, 2003. *http://www.washingtonpost.com/wp-srv/nation/transcripts/powelltext_020503.html* (accessed June 9, 2008).

243 "Weapons of Mass Destruction." *http://www.globalsecurity.org/wmd/library/news/iraq/2003/iraq-030205-powell-un-17300pf.html* (accessed April 7, 2010).

244 Robert Novak, "Mission to Niger," *Washington Post*, July 14, 2003. *http://www.washingtonpost.com/wp-dyn/content/article/2005/10/20/AR2005102000874.html* (accessed March 14, 2010).

245 Murray Waas, "Is There a Double Standard On Leak Probes?"

246 David Sanger and David Barstow, "Iraq Findings Leaked by Cheney's Aide Were Disputed," *New York Times*, April 9, 2006. *http://www.nytimes.com/2006/04/09/washington/09leak.html* (accessed January 2, 2010).

247 David Sanger and David Barstow, "Iraq Findings Leaked by Cheney's Aide Were Disputed."

248 Jim Cunningham, "Cracks in the Black Dike: Secrecy, the Media and the F-117A," *Airpower Journal* (Fall, 1991). *http://www.airpower.maxwell.af.mil/airchronicles/apj/apj91/fal91/cunn.htm* (accessed June 9, 2008).

249 Jim Cunningham, "Cracks in the Black Dike: Secrecy, the Media and the F-117A."

250 George Church, "Chronicle of a Security Leak," *Time*, September 29, 1980. *http://www.time.com/time/magazine/article/0,9171,952775-2,00.html* (accessed June 9, 2008).

251 Jim Cunningham, "Cracks in the Black Dike: Secrecy, the Media and the F-117A."

252 Jim Cunningham, "Cracks in the Black Dike: Secrecy, the Media and the F-117A."

253 George Church, "Chronicle of a Security Leak."

254 Jim Cunningham, "Cracks in the Black Dike: Secrecy, the Media and the F-117A."

255 Jim Cunningham, "Cracks in the Black Dike: Secrecy, the Media and the F-117A."

256 Congress, House of Representatives, Rep. Jane Harman, "Opening Statement Before the House Permanent Select Committee on Intelligence: Hearing on the Role and Responsibilities of the Media in National Security."

257 "Frontline: Newswar - Interview, James Risen," PBS. *http://www.pbs.org/wgbh/pages/frontline/newswar/interviews/risen.html* (accessed June 8, 2008).

258 Lee Hamilton, "Being a Partner and Critic to the Congress," CongressLink. *http://www.congresslink.org/print_expert_hamilton.htm* (accessed June 10, 2008).

259 Edward Xanders, "A Handyman's Guide to Fixing National Security Leaks: An Analytical Framework for Evaluating Proposals to Curb Unauthorized Publication of Classified Information."

260 Committee on Government Reform, Minority Staff, Special Investigations Division, "Congressional Oversight of the Bush Administration," January 17, 2006. *http://oversight.house.gov/Documents/20060117103554-62297.pdf* (accessed June 8, 2008).

261 Senate Committee on the Judiciary, Examining DOJ's Investigation of Journalists Who Publish Classified Information: Lessons from the Jack Anderson Case.

262 "Frontline: Newswar - Interview, Eric Lichtblau," PBS.

263 "Frontline: Newswar - Interview, Eric Lichtblau," PBS.

264 "House committee weighs press' role in intelligence leaks," Reporters Committee for Freedom of the Press. *http://www.rcfp.org/news/2006/0530-prr-housec.html* (accessed June 10, 2008).

265 Ellen Nakashima, "Former NSA executive Thomas A. Drake may pay high price for media leak," *Washington Post*, July 14, 2010. *http://www.washingtonpost.com/wp-dyn/content/article/2010/07/13/AR2010071305992_pf.html* (accessed July 23, 2010).

266 Bob Woodward, "A Journalist's Perspective on Public Disclosures."

267 Dana Priest, "National Security Secrets and Democracy: Leaks, Whistleblowers and the Press" (panel interview at 2006 American Bar Association 16th Annual Review of the Field of National Security Law, Washington, DC December 1, 2006). *http://38.105.88.161/Search/basic.asp?BasicQueryText=security+whistleblowers&SortBy=bestmatch* (accessed June 10, 2008).

268 "Frontline: Newswar - Interview, Eric Lichtblau," PBS. *http://www.pbs.org/wgbh/pages/frontline/newswar/interviews/lichtblau.html* (accessed June 10, 2008).

269 James Goodale, "The First Amendment and Freedom of the Press," U.S. Department of State, Bureau of International Information Programs. *http://usinfo.state.gov/journals/itdhr/0297/ijde/goodale.htm* (accessed June 10, 2008).

270 United States v. Morison, 844 F.2d 1057 (4th Cir. April 1, 1988).

271 New York Times v. United States, 403 U.S. 713 (1971).

272 *Huffington Post*, May 21, 2006. *http://www.huffingtonpost.com/geoffrey-r-stone/freedom-of-the-press-v-n_b_21382.html* (accessed June 4, 2008).

273 Jack Nelson, "U.S. Government Secrecy and the Current Crackdown on Leaks."

274 James Risen, "Reporting National Security under Threat of Indictment" (panel interview at 2006 Media Law Resource Center Annual Dinner, Washington, DC, November 9, 2006). *http://www.medialaw.org/*

Template.cfm?Section=Archive_by_Date1&Template=/ContentManagement/ ContentDisplay.cfm&ContentID=4730 (accessed June 8, 2008).

275 United States v. Morison, 844 F.2d 1057 (4th Cir. April 1, 1988).

276 United States v. Morison, 844 F.2d 1057 (4th Cir. April 1, 1988).

277 William Casey, "Remarks Before the Society of Professional Journalists."

278 Katharine Graham, "Safeguarding Our Freedoms as We Cover Terrorist Acts."

279 Newspaper Association of America and National Newspaper Association to HPSCI, May 23, 2006.

280 Tom Brokaw, Walter Cronkite, Ted Koppel to SSCI, May 25, 2006.

281 Dean Baquet and Bill Keller, "When Do We Publish a Secret," *New York Times*, July 1, 2006. *http://www.nytimes.com/2006/07/01/ opinion/01keller.html* (accessed January 2, 2010).

282 "Piecing Together the Reports, and Deciding What to Publish," *New York Times*, July 25, 2010. *http://www.nytimes.com/2010/07/26/ world/26editors-note.html?pagewanted=all* (accessed July 26, 2010).

283 House Permanent Select Committee on Intelligence, Espionage Laws and Leaks, 96th Cong., 1st sess., January 24, 25, and 31, 1979.

284 Robert Gates, "Unauthorized Disclosures: Risks, Costs, and Responsibilities."

285 R. Jeffrey Smite, "Having Lifted CIA's Veil, Deutch Sums Up: I Told You So."

286 Rachel Smolkin, "Judgment Calls: How top editors decide whether to publish national security stories based on classified information."

287 Ben Bradlee, *A Good Life: Newspapering and Other Adventures.*

288 Bob Woodward, "A Journalist's Perspective on Public Disclosures."

289 Dean Baquet and Bill Keller, "When Do We Publish a Secret."

290 Tim Hackler, "The Press and National Security Secrets."

291 Pat Holt, *Secret Intelligence and Public Policy: A Dilemma of Democracy*.

292 Rachel Smolkin, "Judgment Calls: How top editors decide whether to publish national security stories based on classified information."

293 James Hansen, "Soviet Deception in the Cuban Missile Crisis," CIA, Center for the Study of Intelligence. *https://www.cia.gov/library/center-for-the-study-of-intelligence/csi-publications/csi-studies/studies/vol46no1/article06.html* (accessed June 10, 2008).

294 Rachel Smolkin, "Judgment Calls: How top editors decide whether to publish national security stories based on classified information."241 "Free Speech, Reporting on National Security," PBS Online News Hour. *http://www.pbs.org/newshour/bradlee/transcript_security.html* (accessed June 10, 2008).

295 Rachel Smolkin, "Judgment Calls: How top editors decide whether to publish national security stories based on classified information."

296 Rachel Smolkin, "Judgment Calls: How top editors decide whether to publish national security stories based on classified information."

297 Rachel Smolkin, "Judgment Calls: How top editors decide whether to publish national security stories based on classified information."

298 Tim Hackler, "The Press and National Security Secrets."

299 Tim Hackler, "The Press and National Security Secrets."

300 Rachel Smolkin, "Judgment Calls: How top editors decide whether to publish national security stories based on classified information."

301 Tim Hackler, "The Press and National Security Secrets."

302 Tim Hackler, "The Press and National Security Secrets."

303 Tim Hackler, "The Press and National Security Secrets."

304 Katharine Graham, "Safeguarding Our Freedoms As We Cover Terrorist Acts."

305 "Frontline: Newswar - Interview, Ben Bradlee," PBS. *http://www.pbs.org/wgbh/pages/frontline/newswar/interviews/bradlee.html* (accessed June 8, 2008).

306 Katharine Graham, *Personal History*.

307 Dana Priest, "National Security Secrets and Democracy: Leaks, Whistleblowers and the Press."

308 Rachel Smolkin, "Judgment Calls: How top editors decide whether to publish national security stories based on classified information."

309 Rachel Smolkin, "Judgment Calls: How top editors decide whether to publish national security stories based on classified information."

310 Dean Baquet and Bill Keller, "When Do We Publish a Secret."

311 Gabriel Schoenfeld, "Has the 'New York Times' Violated the Espionage Act?"

312 "'New York Times' Stirs Controversy in Exposing Government Secrets," National Public Radio.

313 Bill Keller, "Letter From Bill Keller on The Times's Banking Records Report," *New York Times*, June 25, 2006.

314 Bill Keller, "Making Tough Calls on National Security" (panel interview at 2007 American Society of Newspaper Editors, First Amendment Summit, Washington DC, January 18, 2007). *http://www.asne.org/index.cfm?id=6420* (accessed June 5, 2008).

315 "U.S. 'Making Matters Worse?' U.S. Supports Terrorism; Americans First and Reporters Second; Limbaugh's 'Cheerfully Right-Wing Views'."

Media Research Center, *http://www.mediaresearch.org/cyberalerts/2001/ cyb20011010.asp* (accessed June 10, 2008).

316 "U.S. 'Making Matters Worse?'; U.S. Supports Terrorism; Americans First and Reporters Second; Limbaugh's 'Cheerfully Right-Wing Views'."

317 Ben Bradlee, *A Good Life: Newspapering and Other Adventures.*

318 Ben Bradlee, *A Good Life: Newspapering and Other Adventures.*

319 Ben Bradlee, *A Good Life: Newspapering and Other Adventures.*

320 Ben Bradlee, *A Good Life: Newspapering and Other Adventures.*

321 Elie Abel, *Leaking: Who Does It? Who Benefits At What Cost?*

322 Elie Abel, *Leaking: Who Does It? Who Benefits At What Cost?*

323 Elie Abel, *Leaking: Who Does It? Who Benefits At What Cost?*

324 Elie Abel, *Leaking: Who Does It? Who Benefits At What Cost?*

325 Elie Abel, *Leaking: Who Does It? Who Benefits At What Cost?*

326 John Ashcroft to Dennis Hastert, October 15, 2002, *www.fas.org/sgp/ othergov/dojleaks.html* (accessed June 4, 2008).

327 Newspaper Association of America and National Newspaper Association to HPSCI, May 23, 2006, *http://www.naa.org/~/media/0CB927 2EDCA64213A4991CD8DA066D3A.ashx* (accessed June 4, 2008).

328 Gerhard Casper, "Comment - Government Secrecy and the Constitution," *California Law Review* 74, no. 3 (1986).

329 Jack Nelson, "U.S. Government Secrecy and the Current Crackdown on Leaks," The Joan Shorenstein Center on the Press, Politics and Public Policy (Fall 2002), *http://www.hks.harvard.edu/presspol/research_publications/ papers/working_papers/2003_1.pdf* (accessed June 8, 2008).

330 Newspaper Association of America and National Newspaper Association to HPSCI, May 23, 2006.

331 Robert Gates, "Unauthorized Disclosures: Risks, Costs, and Responsibilities."

332 Bill Clinton, "Statement by the President to the House of Representatives," November 4, 2000.

333 United States v. Morison, 844 F.2d 1057 (4th Cir., April 1, 1988).

334 "Up to Their Keisters in Leaks."

335 R. Jeffrey Smith, "Having Lifted CIA's Veil, Deutch Sums Up: I Told You So," *Washington Post*, December 26, 1996, *http://www.csun.edu/coms/ben/news/cia/961226.wp.html* (accessed June 4, 2008).

336 George H.W. Bush, "Remarks by George Bush at the Dedication Ceremony for the George Bush Center for Intelligence," April 26, 1999, *https://www.cia.gov/news-information/speeches-testimony/1999/bush_speech_042699.html* (accessed June 4, 2008).

337 Several historical examples of the perceived harm caused by unauthorized disclosures will be presented in this chapter. Though it can be assumed that the media outlets considered the disclosures to be appropriate, based on some combination of the motivations and justifications presented in the previous chapter, the intent of this chapter is to discuss the recognized harm.

338 Tim Hackler, "The Press and National Security Secrets," Association of Former Intelligence Officers, *The Intelligence Professional Series*, no. 8 (1992).

339 Porter Goss, "Testimony of DCI Goss Before Senate Armed Services Committee," March 17, 2005, *http://www.cia.gov/news-information/speeches-testimony/2005/Goss_testimony_03172005.html* (accessed June 3, 2008).

340 Dennis Blair, "Unauthorized Disclosures of Classified Information," July 1, 2009.

341 Report of the Commission on the Intelligence Capabilities of the United States Regarding Weapons of Mass Destruction.

342 Len Downie, "Making Tough Calls on National Security" (panel interview at 2007 American Society of Newspaper Editors, First Amendment Summit, Washington, DC, January 18, 2007), *http://www. asne.org/index.cfm?id=6420* (accessed June 5, 2008).

343 Katharine Graham, "Safeguarding Our Freedoms as We Cover Terrorist Acts."

344 James Bruce, "The Consequences of Permissive Neglect: Laws and Leaks of Classified Intelligence."

345 James Bruce, "The Consequences of Permissive Neglect: Laws and Leaks of Classified Intelligence."

346 Jeffrey Richelson, *The U.S. Intelligence Community* (Boulder, CO: Westview Press, 1999).

347 "Plugging the Leak: The Case for a Legislative Resolution of the Conflict Between the Demands of Secrecy and the Need for an Open Government," *Virginia Law Review* 71, no. 5 (June 1985).

348 "Plugging the Leak: The Case for a Legislative Resolution of the Conflict Between the Demands of Secrecy and the Need for an Open Government."

349 Kathryn Olmsted, *Challenging the Secret Government: The Post-Watergate Investigations of the CIA and FBI* (Chapel Hill, NC: University of North Carolina Press, 1996).

350 Tim Hackler, "The Press and National Security Secrets."

351 Tim Hackler, "The Press and National Security Secrets."

352 Katharine Graham, "Safeguarding Our Freedoms as We Cover Terrorist Acts."

353 James Bruce, "The Consequences of Permissive Neglect: Laws and Leaks of Classified Intelligence."

354 James Bruce, "The Consequences of Permissive Neglect: Laws and Leaks of Classified Intelligence."

355 Jeffrey Richelson, *The U.S. Intelligence Community* (Boulder, CO: Westview Press, 1999).

356 "Plugging the Leak: The Case for a Legislative Resolution of the Conflict Between the Demands of Secrecy and the Need for an Open Government," *Virginia Law Review* 71, no. 5 (June 1985).

357 "Plugging the Leak: The Case for a Legislative Resolution of the Conflict Between the Demands of Secrecy and the Need for an Open Government."

358 Porter Goss, "Loose Lips Sink Spies," *New York Times*, February 10, 2006, *http://www.nytimes.com/2006/02/10/opinion/10goss.html* (accessed June 5, 2008).

359 Donald Rumsfeld, "The Impact of Leaking Classified Information," July 12, 2002, *http://www.fas.org/sgp/bush/dod071202.pdf* (accessed June 5, 2008).

360 "Al Qaeda Manual Eleventh Lesson," The Disaster Center, *http://www.disastercenter.com/terror/Al_Qaeda_Manual_ELEVENTH_LESSON.htm* (accessed July 28, 2010).

361 "MSM Leaks," Never Yet Melted, *http://neveryetmelted.com/2006/07/11/msm-leaks/* (accessed April 7, 2010).

362 Brian Ross, "New Videotape from Bin Laden; Al Qaeda's No. 1 Still Alive," ABC News, September 7, 2007, *http://blogs.abcnews.com/theblotter/2007/09/new-videotape-f.html* (accessed June 5, 2008).

363 Eli Lake, "Qaeda Goes Dark After a U.S. Slip," *New York Sun*, October 9, 2007, *http://www.nysun.com/foreign/qaeda-goes-dark-after-a-us-slip/64163/* (accessed June 5, 2008).

364 Sarah Dilorenzio, "Group: U.S. officials leaked secret info on al-Qaeda video, putting intelligence methods at risk," Associated Press.

October 9, 2007, *http://www.signonsandiego.com/news/nation/20071009-1257-us-al-qaidatapeleak.html* (accessed June 5, 2008).

365 Eli Lake, "Qaeda Goes Dark After a U.S. Slip."

366 Eric Lichtblau and James Risen, "Bank Data is Sifted by U.S. in Secret to Block Terror."

367 Rachel Smolkin, "Judgment Calls: How top editors decide whether to publish national security stories based on classified information," *American Journalism Review* (October/November 2006), *http://www.ajr.org/Article.asp?id=4185* (accessed June 5, 2008).

368 Supporting Intelligence and Law Enforcement Programs to Track Terrorists and Terrorist Finances, H.Res.895, 109th Cong, 1st sess, (June 2006), *http://www.govtrack.us/data/us/bills.text/109/hr/hr895.pdf* (accessed June 5, 2008).

369 Supporting Intelligence and Law Enforcement Programs to Track Terrorists and Terrorist Finances, H.Res.895, 109th Cong, 1st sess, (June 2006).

370 Gabriel Schoenfeld, "Not Every Leak Is Fit to Print," *Weekly Standard*, February 18, 2008, *http://www.weeklystandard.com/Content/Public/Articles/000/000/014/714othkb.asp?pg=2* (accessed June 5, 2008).

371 Gabriel Schoenfeld, "Not Every Leak Is Fit to Print."

372 Howard Kurtz, "After reporter's subpoena, critics call Obama's leak-plugging efforts Bush-like," *Washington Post*, April 30, 2010, *http://www.washingtonpost.com/wp-dyn/content/article/2010/04/29/AR2010042904656.html* (accessed May 5, 2010).

373 Phillip Shenon, "Times Reporter Subpoenaed Over Source for Book," *New York Times*, February 1, 2008, *http://www.nytimes.com/2008/02/01/washington/01inquire.html* (accessed June 5, 2008).

374 Charlie Savage, "Ex-C.I.A. Officer Named in Disclosure Indictment," *New York Times*, January 6, 2011. *http://www.nytimes.com/2011/01/07/us/07indict.html* (accessed March 30, 2011).

375 Peter Baker and Dafna Linzer, "Diving Deep, Unearthing a Surprise," *Washington Post*, December 8, 2007, *http://www.washingtonpost.com/wp-dyn/content/article/2007/12/07/AR2007120702418.html* (accessed June 5, 2008).

376 Peter Baker and Dafna Linzer, "Diving Deep, Unearthing a Surprise."

377 David Sanger and Steven Lee Myers, "Details in Military Notes Led to Shift on Iran, U.S. Says," *New York Times*, December 6, 2007, *http://www.nytimes.com/2007/12/06/world/middleeast/06intel.html?hp* (accessed June 5, 2008).

378 William Perry, "Unauthorized Disclosures of Intelligence," July 31, 1996, *http://www.fas.org/sgp/clinton/perry.html* (accessed June 5, 2008).

379 Harley Schwardon, "This one is for not leaking any military secrets," Cartoonstock, *http://www.cartoonstock.com/cartoonview.asp?catref=hsc1279* (accessed April 7, 2010).

380 "Transcript of General Hayden's Interview with WTOP's J.J. Green," Central Intelligence Agency, *https://www.cia.gov/news-information/press-releases-statements/press-release-archive-2007/transcript-of-general-haydens-interview-with-wtop.html* (accessed June 5, 2008).

381 New York Times v. United States, 403 U.S. 713 (1971).

382 Phillip Agee, *London Times*, January 9, 2008, *http://www.timesonline.co.uk/tol/comment/obituaries/article3162281.ece* (accessed June 5, 2008).

383 Phillip Agee, *London Times*, January 9, 2008.

384 Samuel Francis, "The Intelligence Identities Protection Act," The Heritage Foundation, *http://www.heritage.org/Research/NationalSecurity/IB70.cfm* (accessed June 5, 2008).

385 Phillip Agee, London Times, January 9, 2008.

386 Samuel Francis, "The Intelligence Identities Protection Act."

387 Frederick W. Whatley, "Reagan, National Security, and the First Amendment: Plugging Leaks by Shutting Off the Main," The CATO Institute, *http://www.cato.org/pubs/pas/pa037.html* (accessed June 5, 2008).

388 Phillip Agee, *London Times*, January 9, 2008.

389 Samuel Francis, "The Intelligence Identities Protection Act."

390 R. James Woolsey, "National Security and Freedom of the Press" (panel interview at 2006 American Enterprise Institute Conference, Washington, DC, September 7, 2006), *http://www.aei.org/events/filter.,eventID.1383/transcript.asp* (accessed June 5, 2008).

391 R. James Woolsey, "National Security and Freedom of the Press" (panel interview at 2006 American Enterprise Institute Conference, Washington, DC, September 7, 2006).

392 "Eli Cohen," *Wikipedia, http://en.wikipedia.org/wiki/Eli_Cohen* (accessed June 5, 2008).

393 William Perry, "Unauthorized Disclosures of Intelligence," July 31, 1996.

394 Donald Rumsfeld, "U.S. Department of Defense News Briefing," September 12, 2001, *http://www.fas.org/sgp/news/2001/09/dod091201.html* (accessed June 5, 2008).

395 Katharine Graham, "Safeguarding Our Freedoms as We Cover Terrorist Acts."

396 Bob Woodward, "A Journalist's Perspective on Public Disclosures," in "Intelligence Leaks," Special Issue, *American Intelligence Journal* (1988).

397 "1983 Beirut Barracks Bombing," *Wikipedia, http://en.wikipedia.org/wiki/1983_Beirut_barracks_bombing* (accessed June 5, 2008).

398 Tim Hackler, "The Press and National Security Secrets."

399 "The Long Arm of the Law," Federal Bureau of Investigation, *http://www.fbi.gov/page2/jan06/longarm010506.htm* (accessed June 5, 2008).

400 Tim Hackler, "The Press and National Security Secrets."

401 "Reporting in the Time of Conflict: Secrecy vs. the Story," Newseum, *http://www.newseum.org/warstories/essay/secrecy.htm* (accessed June 5, 2008).

402 "Reporting in the Time of Conflict: Secrecy vs. the Story."

403 "Reporting in the Time of Conflict: Secrecy vs. the Story."

404 "Reporting in the Time of Conflict: Secrecy vs. the Story."

405 "Robert McCormick," *New World Encyclopedia*, *http://www.newworldencyclopedia.org/entry/Robert_McCormick* (accessed June 5, 2008).

406 R. James Woolsey, "National Security and Freedom of the Press" (panel interview at 2006 American Enterprise Institute Conference, Washington, DC, September 7, 2006).

407 William Casey, "Remarks Before the Society of Professional Journalists," September 24, 1986.

408 Michael Hayden, "Remarks of Central Intelligence Agency Director at the Council on Foreign Relations," September 7, 2007.

409 Eric Schmitt and Charlie Savage, "U.S. Military Scrutinizes Leaks for Risks to Afghans," *New York Times*, July 28, 2010, *http://www.nytimes.com/2010/07/29/world/asia/29wikileaks.html?_r=1&pagewanted=all* (accessed July 30, 2010).

410 Eric Schmitt and Charlie Savage, "U.S. Military Scrutinizes Leaks for Risks to Afghans."

411 Adam Levine, "Top U.S. military official: WikiLeaks founder may have 'blood' on his hands," CNN, July 30, 2010, *http://edition.cnn.com/2010/US/07/29/wikileaks.mullen.gates/index.html#fbid=1wi0HJ6QJqN* (accessed July 31, 2010).

412 Robert Mackey, "Taliban Study WikiLeaks to Hunt Informants," *New York Times*, July 30, 2010, *http://thelede.blogs.nytimes.com/2010/07/30/taliban-study-wikileaks-to-hunt-informants/* (accessed July 30, 2010).

413 Jeanne Whalen, "Rights Groups Join Criticism of WikiLeaks," *Wall Street Journal*, August 9, 2010. *http://online.wsj.com/article/SB10001424052748703428604575419580947722558.html* (accessed February 21, 2011).

414 Luke Harding and David Leigh, "WikiLeaks: How US political invective turned on 'anti-American' Julian Assange," *The Guardian*, February 3, 2011. *http://www.guardian.co.uk/world/2011/feb/03/wikileaks-julian-assange-us-reaction* (accessed February 23, 2011).

415 "Julian Assange extended interview," Australian Broadcasting Corporation, November 4, 2011. *http://www.abc.net.au/7.30/content/2011/s3188451.htm* (accessed April 11, 2011).

416 Michael Hayden, "WikiLeaks disclosures are a 'tragedy'," CNN, July 30, 2010., *http://www.cnn.com/2010/OPINION/07/30/hayden.wikileaks.secrets/index.html?hpt=T2* (accessed July 30, 2010).

417 David S. Cloud, "Army private charged in earlier leak had access to latest WikiLeak papers," *Los Angeles Times*, July 28, 2010, http://articles.latimes.com/2010/jul/28/world/la-fg-wikileaks-20100728 (accessed November 2, 2010).

418 "Charge Sheet, Bradley Manning," *Cryptome*, May 29, 2010, *http://cryptome.org/manning-charge.pdf* (accessed July 30, 2010).

419 "Newsweek retracts Quran story," CNN, May 16, 2005, *http://www.cnn.com/2005/WORLD/asiapcf/05/16/newsweek.quran/* (accessed June 5, 2008).

420 Katharine Seelye and Neil Lewis, "Newsweek backs off Quran desecration story," *New York Times*, May 17, 2005. *http://www.nytimes.com/2005/05/17/politics/17koran.html?pagewanted=print* (accessed June 5, 2008).

421 Katharine Seelye and Neil Lewis, "Newsweek Retracts Account of Koran Abuse by U.S. Military," *New York Times*, May 17, 2005, *http://www. nytimes.com/2005/05/17/politics/17koran.html?_r=1&oref=slogin* (accessed June 5, 2008).

422 Katharine Skelve and Neil Lewis, "Newsweek Retracts Account of Koran Abuse by U.S. Military."

423 Charles McGrath, "Reporter on Retracted Newsweek Article Put Monica on the Map," *New York Times*, May 17, 2005, *http://www.nytimes. com/2005/05/17/politics/17isikoff.html* (accessed June 5, 2008).

424 Christine Hauser and Katharine Seelye, "Newsweek Retracts Account of Koran Abuse by U.S. Military," *New York Times*, May 16, 2005, *http:// www.nytimes.com/2005/05/16/international/16cnd-koran.html* (accessed June 5, 2008).

425 "Newsweek retracts Quran story," CNN, May 16, 2005.

426 Katharine Seelye and Neil Lewis, "Newsweek Retracts Account of Koran Abuse by U.S. Military," *New York Times*, May 17, 2005.

427 Daniel Schorr, "Standing up for news leaks," Christian Science Monitor, May 27, 2005, *http://www.csmonitor.com/2005/0527/p09s02-cods. html* (accessed June 5, 2008).

428 Greg Miller, "CIA Looks to Los Angeles for Would-Be Iranian Spies," *Los Angeles Times*, January 15, 2002, *http://articles.latimes.com/2002/jan/15/ news/mn-22685* (accessed June 5, 2008).

429 Jack Nelson, "U.S. Government Secrecy and the Current Crackdown on Leaks."

430 Jack Nelson, "U.S. Government Secrecy and the Current Crackdown on Leaks."

431 Jack Nelson, "U.S. Government Secrecy and the Current Crackdown on Leaks."

432 Gabriel Schoenfeld, "The Price of One Leak," *Commentary* magazine (June 11, 2007), *http://www.commentarymagazine.com/blogs/index.php/schoenfeld/523* (accessed June 5, 2008).

433 Fred Kaplan, "The Goods on Saddam," *Slate* (January 31, 2003), *http://www.slate.com/toolbar.aspx?action-print&id=2077961* (accessed June 5, 2008).

434 United States v. Progressive Inc., 467 F. Supp. 990 (1979).

435 Kennedy v. Mendoza-Martinez, 372 U.S. 144 (1963).

436 Senate Select Committee on Intelligence, Hearing of the Committee on the Nomination of General Michael Hayden to be the Director of the Central Intelligence Agency.

437 New York Times v. United States, 403 U.S. 713 (1971).

438 United States v. Samuel Loring Morison, 604 F. Supp. 655 (1985).

439 United States v. Samuel Loring Morison, 604 F. Supp. 655 (1985).

440 Bob Woodward, "McChrystal: More Forces or 'Mission Failure'," *Washington Post*, September 21, 2009, *http://www.washingtonpost.com/wp-dyn/content/article/2009/09/20/AR2009092002920.html* (accessed January 29, 2010).

441 Elisabeth Bumiller and Mark Landler, "U.S. Envoy Urges Caution on Forces for Afghanistan," *New York Times*, November 11, 2009, *http://www.nytimes.com/2009/11/12/us/politics/12policy.html* (accessed January 29, 2010).

442 Howard Kurtz, "President Wants a Plumber," *Washington Post*, November 19, 2009, *http://www.washingtonpost.com/wp-dyn/content/article/2009/11/19/AR2009111901008.html* (accessed November 20, 2009).

443 Eric Schmitt, "U.S. Envoy's Cables Show Worries on Afghan Plans," *New York Times*, January 25, 2010, *http://www.nytimes.com/2010/01/26/world/asia/26strategy.html* (accessed January 29, 2010).

444 Michael McConnell, "Guidance on the Declassification of National Intelligence Estimate Key Judgments," October 24, 2007, *http://www.fas.org/irp/dni/nie-declass.pdf* (accessed June 4, 2008).

445 Peter Baker and Dafna Linzer, "Diving Deep, Unearthing a Surprise."

446 Peter Baker and Dafna Linzer, "Diving Deep, Unearthing a Surprise."

447 "Details in Military Notes Led to Shift on Iran, U.S. Says," *New York Times*, December 6, 2007.

448 Steven Lee Myers, David E. Sanger and Eric Schmitt, "U.S. Considers New Covert Push Within Pakistan," *New York Times*, January 6, 2008, *http://www.nytimes.com/2008/01/06/washington/06terror.html?ex=1357275600&en=d2b610da0c92dd8d&ei=5088&partner=rssnyt&emc=rss* (accessed June 5, 2008).

449 Isambard Wilkinson, "Pakistan rejects 'covert action plans by US'," *London Times*, January 15, 2008, *http://www.telegraph.co.uk/news/worldnews/1574844/Pakistan-rejects-'covert-action-plans-by-US'.html* (accessed June 5, 2008).

450 James Schlesinger, "The Constitution That Delicate Balance: National Security and Freedom of the Press" (panel interview conducted at Columbia University Seminar on Media and Society, New York, New York, 1984), *http://www.learner.org/resources/series72.html* (accessed June 4, 2008).

451 John Ashcroft, "Statement Before the United States Senate Select Committee on Intelligence Concerning Unauthorized Disclosure of Classified Information."

452 Tim Hackler, "The Press and National Security Secrets."

453 "Purposeful Leaks," *National Review* (September 11, 1987), *http://www.thefreelibrary.com/Purposeful+leaks.+(Congressional+leaks+to+press)-a05169250* (accessed June 4, 2008).

454 "Purposeful Leaks," *National Review*.

455 Brian Ross, "Bush Authorizes New Covert Action Against Iran," ABC News, May 22, 2007, *http://blogs.abcnews.com/theblotter/2007/05/bush_authorizes.html* (accessed June 5, 2008).

456 Brian Ross, "Bush Authorizes New Covert Action Against Iran."

457 Toby Harnden, "CIA gets the go-ahead to take on Hizbollah," *Daily Telegraph*, January 10, 2007, *http://www.telegraph.co.uk/news/worldnews/1539095/CIA-gets-the-go-ahead-to-take-on-Hizbollah.html* (accessed June 5, 2008).

458 "Protection of Classified National Security Council and Intelligence Information (NSDD 19)," January 12, 1982, *http://www.fas.org/irp/offdocs/nsdd019.htm* (accessed June 5, 2008).

459 Lid on Leaks, *Time Magazine Online.*

460 Stephen Hess, The Government/Press Connection: Press Officers and *Their Offices* (Washington, DC: The Brookings Institution, 1984).

461 Harley Schwardon, "Someone today leaked information to the media about the government's new 'no leak' policy," Cartoonstock, *http://www.cartoonstock.com/cartoonview.asp?catref=hsc3221* (accessed April 7, 2010).

462 Report of the Commission on the Intelligence Capabilities of the United States Regarding Weapons of Mass Destruction.

463 Henry Kissinger, "The China Connection," *Time*, October 1, 1979, *http://www.time.com/time/magazine/article/0,9171,947490,00.html* (accessed June 6, 2008).

464 New York Times v. United States, 403 U.S. 713 (1971).

465 Janet Reno, "Statement Before the Senate Select Committee on Intelligence Concerning Unauthorized Disclosures of Classified Information."

466 Mary Beth Sheridan, "Calderon: WikiLeaks caused severe damage to U.S-Mexican relations," *Washington Post*, March 3, 2011. *http://www.*

washingtonpost.com/wp-dyn/content/article/2011/03/03/AR2011030302853. html?referrer=emailarticle (accessed March 7, 2011).

467 Adam Thomson, "WikiLeaks spat leads to US diplomat resigning," *Financial Times*, March 20, 2011. *http://www.ft.com/cms/s/0/00911f6e-530b-11e0-86e6-00144feab49a.html#axzz1HF2PtLkD* (accessed March 21, 2011).

468 Simon Romero, "Ecuador Expels U.S. Ambassador over WikiLeaks Cable," *New York Times*, April 5, 2011. *http://www.nytimes.com/2011/04/06/world/americas/06ecuador.html* (accessed April 9, 2011).

469 "Secretary Clinton's remarks on WikiLeaks documents," *The Hill*, November 29, 2010. *http://thehill.com/blogs/congress-blog/lawmaker-news/130973-secretary-clintons-remarks-on-wikileak-documents* (accessed April 9, 2011).

470 Michael Gordon, "Bush Aide's Memo Doubts Iraqi Leaker," *New York Times*, November 29, 2006, *http://www.nytimes.com/2006/11/29/world/middleeast/29cnd-military.html?ex=1322456400&en=688e0331df987eec&ei=5088&partner=rssnyt&emc=rss* (accessed June 6, 2008).

471 Michael Gordon, "Bush Aide's Memo Doubts Iraqi Leaker."

472 Elie Abel, *Leaking: Who Does It? Who Benefits At What Cost?*

473 Laurence Zuckerman, "Washington's Master Leakers," *Time*, May 23, 1988. *http://www.time.com/time/magazine/article/0,9171,967475,00.html* (accessed June 6, 2008).

474 Stephen Hess, *The Government/Press Connection: Press Officers and Their Offices.*

475 Lid on Leaks, *Time*.

476 Stephen Hess, *The Government/Press Connection: Press Officers and Their Offices.*

477 Peter Hoekstra, "Secrets and Leaks: The Costs and Consequences for National Security."

478 Snepp v. United States, 444 U.S. 507 (1980).

479 Michael Hayden, "Remarks of Central Intelligence Agency Director at the Council on Foreign Relations."

480 Commission on the Intelligence Capabilities of the United States Regarding Weapons of Mass Destruction, Report of the Commission on the Intelligence Capabilities of the United States Regarding Weapons of Mass Destruction.

481 Peter Hoekstra, "Secrets and Leaks: The Costs and Consequences for National Security."

482 Peter Hoekstra, "Secrets and Leaks: The Costs and Consequences for National Security."

483 Gabriel Schoenfeld, "Statement Before the Senate Judiciary Committee," June 6, 2006, *http://www.fas.org/irp/congress/2006_hr/060606schoenfeld.pdf* (accessed June 3, 2008).

484 "Faulty Intel Source 'Curveball' Revealed," CBS News, November 4, 2007, *http://www.cbsnews.com/stories/2007/11/01/60minutes/main3440577.shtml* (accessed June 3, 2008).

485 Dana Priest, "CIA Holds Terror Suspects in Secret Prisons."

486 David Morgan, "House Panel to Probe Post Story," *Washington Post*, November 10, 2005, *http://www.washingtonpost.com/wp-dyn/content/article/2005/11/10/AR2005111001628_pf.html* (accessed June 6, 2005).

487 CIA Fires Source of Leaks for Prize Winning Journalist, *Seattle Times*, April 22, 2006, *http://seattletimes.nwsource.com/html/nationworld/2002946196_cia22.html* (accessed June 6, 2008).

488 Jed Babbin, "Don't Shield the Media: Prosecute the Leakers," Human Events, *http://www.humanevents.com/article.php?id=26414* (accessed June 6, 2008).

489 Mark Mazzetti, "Pakistan Aids Insurgency in Afghanistan, Reports Assert," *New York Times*, July 25, 2010, *http://www.nytimes.com/2010/07/26/world/asia/26isi.html* (accessed July 27, 2010).

490 Joshua Partlow and Karin Brulliard, "Pakistan decries WikiLeaks release of U.S. military documents on Afghan war," *Washington Post*, July 27, 2010, *http://www.washingtonpost.com/wp-dyn/content/article/2010/07/26/AR2010072602393_pf.html* (accessed July 27, 2010).

491 House Permanent Select Committee on Intelligence, Espionage Laws and Leaks, 96th Cong., 1st sess., January 24, 25, and 31, 1979.

492 William Casey, "Remarks Before the Society of Professional Journalists," September 24, 1986.

493 Robert Gates, "Unauthorized Disclosures: Risks, Costs, and Responsibilities," in "Intelligence Leaks."

494 Murray Waas, "Is There a Double Standard on Leak Probes?" *National Journal*, April 25, 2006, *http://news.nationaljournal.com/articles/0425nj1.htm* (accessed June 6, 2008).

495 Commission on the Intelligence Capabilities of the United States Regarding Weapons of Mass Destruction, Report of the Commission on the Intelligence Capabilities of the United States Regarding Weapons of Mass Destruction.

496 Murray Waas, "Is There a Double Standard on Leak Probes?" *National Journal*, April 25, 2006, *http://news.nationaljournal.com/articles/0425nj1.htm* (accessed June 6, 2008).

497 Commission on the Intelligence Capabilities of the United States Regarding Weapons of Mass Destruction, Report of the Commission on the Intelligence Capabilities of the United States Regarding Weapons of Mass Destruction.

498 Tim Hackler, "The Press and National Security Secrets."

499 William Casey, "Remarks Before the Society of Professional Journalists," September 24, 1986.

500 "Project Jennifer: Hughes Glomar Explorer," *Global Security*, *http://www.globalsecurity.org/intell/systems/jennifer.htm* (accessed June 8, 2008).

501 "Hughes Glomar Explorer," *Dante's Page*, *http://w3.the-kgb.com/dante/military/explpic2.html* (accessed June 8, 2008).

502 Behind the Great Submarine Snatch, *Time*, December 6, 1976.

503 James Bruce, "The Consequences of Permissive Neglect: Laws and Leaks of Classified Intelligence."

504 Behind the Great Submarine Snatch, *Time*, December 6, 1976.

505 "Submarines," Haze Gray and Underway, *http://www.hazegray.org/faq/smn7.htm#G12* (accessed June 8, 2008).

506 "Notice of Availability for Donation of Test Craft Ex SEA SHADOW," Federal Register 71, no. 178 (September 14, 2006), *http://edocket.access.gpo.gov/2006/pdf/E6-15266.pdf* (accessed June 8, 2008).

507 Ted Gup, "The Ultimate Congressional Hideaway," Washington Post, May 31, 1992, *http://www.washingtonpost.com/wp-srv/local/daily/july/25/brier1.htm* (accessed June 6, 2008).

508 Thomas Mallon, "Mr. Smith Goes Underground," American Heritage Magazine, Volume 51, Issue 5, September 2000, *http://www.americanheritage.com/articles/magazine/ah/2000/5/2000_5_60.shtml* (accessed March 10, 2010).

509 James Bruce, "The Consequences of Permissive Neglect: Laws and Leaks of Classified Intelligence."

510 James Bruce, "The Consequences of Permissive Neglect: Laws and Leaks of Classified Intelligence."

511 Robert Gates, "Unauthorized Disclosures: Risks, Costs, and Responsibilities," in "Intelligence Leaks."

512 Porter Goss, "Loose Lips Sink Spies."

513 "Thomas Jefferson on Politics and Government: Freedom of the Press."

514 "Frontline: Newswar - Interview, Seymour Hersh," PBS, *http://www. pbs.org/wgbh/pages/frontline/newswar/interviews/hersh.html* (accessed June 8, 2008).

515 "Hersh: U.S. mulls nuclear option for Iran," CNN, *http://www.cnn. com/2006/POLITICS/04/10/hersh.access/index.html* (accessed June 8, 2008).

516 Judith Miller, "A Personal Account; My Four Hours Testifying in the Federal Grand Jury Room," *New York Times*, October 16, 2005, *http://query. nytimes.com/gst/fullpage.html?res=9F05E1D7143FF935A25753C1A9639C 8B63* (accessed June 8, 2008).

517 "CBS Ousts 4 for Bush Guard Story," CBS, *http://www.cbsnews.com/ stories/2005/01/10/national/main665727.shtml* (accessed June 8, 2008).

518 Dave Moniz, Jim Drinkard, and Kevin Johnson, "Texan has made allegations for years," *USA Today*, September 21, 2004, *http://www.usatoday. com/news/politicselections/nation/president/2004-09-21-burkett-side_x.htm* (accessed June 8, 2008).

519 Daniel Schorr, "Standing Up for News Leaks," *Christian Science Monitor*, May 27, 2005, *http://www.csmonitor.com/2005/0527/p09s02-cods. html* (accessed June 8, 2008).

520 Marcus Baram, "Baghdad Diarist Writes Fiction," ABC News, *http:// abcnews.go.com/US/story?id=3455826&page=1* (accessed June 8, 2008).

521 Marcus Baram, "Baghdad Diarist Writes Fiction."

522 Marcus Baram, "Baghdad Diarist Writes Fiction."

523 ASNE to Senate Majority Leader Harry Reid, July 21, 2008, *http://asne. org/portals/0/Publications/Public/CoalitionLetter.pdf* (accessed November 30, 2009).

524 John Ashcroft, "Statement Before the United States Senate Select Committee on Intelligence Concerning Unauthorized Disclosure of Classified Information."

525 Peter Hoekstra, "Secrets and Leaks: The Costs and Consequences for National Security," July 25, 2005, *http://www.heritage.org/Research/ HomelandSecurity/wm809.cfm* (accessed June 4, 2008).

526 James Bruce, "The Consequences of Permissive Neglect: Laws and Leaks of Classified Intelligence."

527 Congress, Senator Richard Shelby of Alabama speaking for the Intelligence Authorization Act for Fiscal Year 2001, S.2507, 106th Cong., 2nd sess., Congressional Record (6 December 2000): 11649-51, *http://www. fas.org/irp/congress/2000_cr/s120600.html* (accessed June 8, 2008).

528 United States v. Samuel Loring Morison, 604 F. Supp. 655 (1985).

529 CIA v. Sims, 471 U.S. 159 (1985).

530 "Confirmation Bias," *Science Daily*, *http://www.sciencedaily.com/ articles/c/confirmation_bias.htm* (accessed June 11, 2008).

531 Rachel Smolkin, "Judgment Calls: How top editors decide whether to publish national security stories based on classified information."

532 "Quotes: Leaking Classified Information," CI Centre, *http://cicentre. com/Documents/DOC_Quotes_Leaks.htm* (accessed June 11, 2008).

533 Bob Woodward, *Veil: The Secret Wars of the CIA 1981-1987* (New York, NY: Simon and Schuster, 1987).

534 Bob Woodward, *Veil: The Secret Wars of the CIA 1981-1987*, Chapter 23, pp. 447-463.

535 The information contained in this chapter is derived from Chapter 23, pp. 447-463, of Woodward's book. The accuracy of this information is not being confirmed. The purpose for including the details surrounding this disclosure of classified information is to examine the internal cost-benefit anal-

ysis performed by members of the media. Readers should remain cognizant that the information provided is written from a journalist's point of view.

536 Elie Abel, Leaking: *Who Does It? Who Benefits At What Cost?*

537 Cass Sunstein, "Government Control of Information."

538 Geoffrey Stone, "Government Secrecy vs. Freedom of the Press."

539 Cass Sunstein, "Government Control of Information."

540 Elie Abel, Leaking: *Who Does It? Who Benefits At What Cost?*

541 "Q & A - Gen. Michael Hayden," C-SPAN.

542 Josh Gerstein, "Spies Prep Reporters on Protecting Secrets," *New York Sun*, September 27, 2007. *http://www.nysun.com/national/spies-prep-reporters-on-protecting-secrets/63465/* (accessed June 11, 2008).

543 Jack Nelson, "What Leaks Are Good Leaks?" *Los Angeles Times*, January 5, 2003. *http://articles.latimes.com/2003/jan/05/opinion/op-nelson5* (accessed June 11, 2008).

544 Jack Nelson, "What Leaks Are Good Leaks?"

545 Jennifer LaFleur, "Federal officials and media have Dialogue over secrecy," *The News Media and the Law*, Vol. 27, No. 1, Winter 2003. *http://www.rcfp.org/news/mag/27-1/cov-federalo.html* (accessed June 11, 2008).

546 Jack Nelson, "What Leaks Are Good Leaks?"

547 LaFleur, "Federal officials and media have Dialogue over secrecy."

548 Newspaper Association of America and National Newspaper Association to HPSCI, May 23, 2006.

549 The six specific categories of information prohibited from being disclosed without official authorization include security and intelligence, defence, international relations, foreign confidences, information which might lead to the commission of crime, and the special investigation powers

under the Interception of Communications Act of 1985 or the Security Service Act of 1989. In addition to the requirement that information disclosed relates to one of these six categories, it must also be shown that the unauthorized disclosure is damaging to the national interest.

550 Richard Norton-Taylor, "Will Wikileaks kill the Official Secrets Act?" *Guardian Online*, November 29, 2010. *http://www.guardian.co.uk/law/2010/nov/29/will-wikileaks-kill-official-secrets-act* (accessed February 8, 2011).

551 "The DA-Notice System, Summary of Questions," Defence Press and Broadcasting Advisory Committee. *http://www.dnotice.org.uk/faqs.htm* (accessed February 9, 2011).

552 Pauline Sadler, "The D-Notice System," Australian Press Council, May 2000. *http://www.presscouncil.org.au/pcsite/apcnews/may00/dnote.html* (accessed February 8, 2011).

553 Cameron Stewart, "Attorney General Robert McClelland urges media to accept security curbs," *The Australian*, November 26, 2010. *http://www.theaustralian.com.au/national-affairs/attorney-general-robert-mcclelland-urges-media-to-accept-security-curbs/story-fn59niix-1225961188070* (accessed February 8, 2011).

554 Robert Gates, "Unauthorized Disclosures: Risks, Costs, and Responsibilities."

555 Report of the Interdepartmental Group on Unauthorized Disclosures of Classified Information.

556 "Michael Hayden Remarks," First Amendment Center, October 29, 2010. *http://www.c-spanvideo.org/program/HaydenR* (accessed April 26, 2011).

557 28 CFR 50.10, "Policy with regard to the issuance of subpoenas to member of the news media" (1980). *http://edocket.access.gpo.gov/cfr_2003/julqtr/pdf/28cfr50.10.pdf* (accessed June 4, 2008).

558 Department of the Navy v. Egan, 484 U.S. 518 (1988).

559 New York Times v. United States, 403 U.S. 713 (1971).

560 National Security Act of 1947, 50 U.S.C. 403 (1947). *http://www. intelligence.gov/0-natsecact_1947.shtml* (accessed June 4, 2008).

561 Intelligence Reform and Terrorism Prevention Act of 2004, 50 U.S.C. 401 (2004). *http://frwebgate.access.gpo.gov/cgi-bin/getdoc.cgi?dbname=108_ cong_public_laws&docid=f:publ458.108.pdf* (accessed June 4, 2008).

562 Executive Order no. 13,526 (2009).

563 Executive Order no. 13,526 (2009). *http://www.whitehouse.gov/the-press-office/executive-order-classified-national-security-information* (accessed January 12, 2010).

564 Executive Order no. 13,526 (2009).

565 Executive Order no. 12,065, Code of Federal Regulations, title 3, volume 43 (1978). *http://www.fas.org/irp/offdocs/eo/eo-12065.htm* (accessed June 4, 2008).

566 Executive Order no. 13,526 (2009).

567 Executive Order no. 13,526 (2009).

568 5 U.S.C. 7532 (1966).

569 Office of Personnel Management, Standard Form 312, "Classified Information Nondisclosure Agreement" (2000). *http://contacts.gsa.gov/ webforms.nsf/0/03A78F16A522716785256A69004E23F6/$file/SF312.pdf* (accessed June 4, 2008).

570 Executive Order no. 13,526 (2009).

571 28 CFR 50.10, "Policy with regard to the issuance of subpoenas to member of the news media" (1980).

572 28 CFR 50.10, "Policy with regard to the issuance of subpoenas to member of the news media" (1980).

573 18 U.S.C. 793 (1982).

574 18 U.S.C. 794 (1982).

575 52118 U.S.C. 798 (1982).

576 5 U.S.C. 8312 (1994).

577 Geoffrey Stone, "Freedom of the Press v. National Security," *The Huffington Post*, May 21, 2006. *http://www.huffingtonpost.com/geoffrey-r-stone/freedom-of-the-press-v-n_b_21382.html* (accessed June 4, 2008).

578 Geoffrey Stone, "Freedom of the Press v. National Security."

579 Geoffrey Stone, "Freedom of the Press v. National Security."

580 Atomic Energy Act, Pub. L. 83-703 (1954).

581 Report of the Subcommittee on Secrecy and Disclosure to the Senate Select Committee on Intelligence, 1978. *http://intelligence.senate.gov/pdfs/95national_security_secrets.pdf* (accessed April 15, 2011).

582 New York Times v. United States, 403 U.S. 713 (1971).

583 Report of the Subcommittee on Secrecy and Disclosure to the Senate Select Committee on Intelligence, 1978.

584 House Permanent Select Committee on Intelligence, Espionage Laws and Leaks, 96th Cong., 1st sess., January 24, 25, and 31, 1979.

585 Report to the National Security Council on Unauthorized Media Leak Disclosures, March 1996.

586 Bill Clinton, "Statement by the President to the House of Representatives," November 4, 2000. *http://www.fas.org/sjp/news/2000/11/wh110400.html* (accessed June 4, 2008).

587 Federal Agency Data Mining Reporting Act of 2007, S.236, 110th Cong., 1st sess., (June 2007). *http://www.govtrack.us/data/us/bills.text/110/s/ s236.pdf* (accessed June 4, 2008).

588 Improving America's Security Act of 2007, S.4, 110th Cong., 1st sess., (March 2007), *http://www.govtrack.us/data/us/bills.text/110/s/s4.pdf* (accessed June 4, 2008).

589 U.S. Bill of Rights.

590 U.S. Constitution, amend. 1.

591 George Mason, "Virginia Declaration of Rights," June 12, 1776. *http:// www.constitution.org/bcp/virg_dor.htm* (accessed June 4, 2008).

592 John Adams and Samuel Adams, "Constitution for the Commonwealth of Massachusetts," June 15, 1780. *http://www.lexrex.com/enlightened/laws/ mass1780/mass_main.html* (accessed June 4, 2008).

593 Robert Kaiser, "Public Secrets," *Washington Post*, June 11, 2006. *http://www.washingtonpost.com/wp-dyn/content/article/2006/06/09/ AR2006060901976.html* (accessed June 4, 2008).

594 Library of Congress, Congressional Research Service, CRS Report for Congress: The Whistleblower Protection Act: An Overview (Washington, DC: Government Printing Office, March 12, 2007). *http://www.fas.org/sgp/ crs/natsec/RL33918.pdf* (accessed June 8, 2008).

595 Library of Congress, Congressional Research Service, CRS Report for Congress: National Security Whistleblowers (Washington, DC: Government Printing Office, December 30, 2005). *http://www.nswbc.org/ Reports%20-%20Documents/NationalSecurityWhistleblowers(CRSReport).pdf* (accessed June 8, 2008).

596 Library of Congress, Bill Text 105th Congress (1997-1998) H.R.3694.ENR. *http://thomas.loc.gov/cgi-bin/query/F?c105:6:./ temp/~c105KzoGY0:e55303:* (accessed July 28, 2010).

GARY ROSS

597 Free Flow of Information Act of 2007, H.R.2102, 110th Cong., 1st sess., (October 2007). *http://www.govtrack.us/data/us/bills.text/110/h/h2102.pdf* (accessed June 4, 2008).

598 MaryAnn Spoto, "N.J. court rules blogger is not protected under shield law in porn company defamation case," *The Star-Ledger*, April 22, 2010, http://www.nj.com/news/index.ssf/2010/04/nj_court_rules_blogger_not_pro.html (accessed May 9, 2010).

599 Pickering v. Board of Education, 391 U.S. 563 (1968).

600 National Federation of Federal Employees v. United States, 695 F. Supp. 1196 (1988).

601 Snepp v. United States, 444 U.S. 507 (1980).

602 Haig v. Agee, 453 U.S. 380 (1981).

603 Department of Navy v. Egan, 484 U.S. 518 (1988).

604 Geoffrey Stone, "Government Secrecy vs. Freedom of the Press."

605 Geoffrey Stone, "Government Secrecy vs. Freedom of the Press."

606 Saxbe v. Washington Post Co., 417 U.S. 843 (1974).

607 Pell v. Procunier, 417 U.S. 817 (1974).

608 Rachel Brand, "Statement Before the House Committee on the Judiciary Concerning H.R. 2102," June 14, 2007, *http://www.usdoj.gov/opa/mediashield/rlb-testimony061407.pdf* (accessed June 4, 2008).

609 David Kravets, "Journalist Free After 226 Days in Prison," *San Diego Union Tribune*, April 4, 2007, *http://www.signonsandiego.com/uniontrib/20070404/news_1n4jailed.html* (accessed June 4, 2008).

610 Times Reporter Testifies On Leak, *CBS News Online*, September 30, 2005, *http://www.cbsnews.com/stories/2005/09/30/national/main892127.shtml* (accessed January 2, 2010).

611 David Kravets, "Journalist Free After 226 Days in Prison," *San Diego Union Tribune*, April 4, 2007.

612 Pentagon Papers Case Dismissed, *Time*, May 21, 1973.

613 United States v. Samuel Loring Morison, 604 F. Supp. 655 (1985).

614 Vernon Loeb, "Clinton Ignored CIA in Pardoning Intelligence Analyst," *Washington Post*, February 17, 2001, *http://www.fas.org/sgp/news/2001/02/wp021701.html* (accessed June 4, 2008).

615 Spencer Hsu, "State Dept. contractor charged in leak to news organizations," *Washington Post*, August 28, 2010, *http://www.washingtonpost.com/wp-dyn/content/article/2010/08/27/AR2010082704602.html* (accessed October 21, 2010).

616 Charlie Savage, "Ex-C.I.A. Officer Named in Disclosure Indictment," *New York Times*, January 6, 2011. *http://www.nytimes.com/2011/01/07/us/07indict.html* (accessed March 30, 2011).

617 U.S. District Court for the District of Maryland, Northern Division, "United States of America v. Thomas Andrews Drake," April 14, 2010, *http://www.fas.org/sgp/news/2010/04/drake-indict.pdf* (accessed May 9, 2010).

618 U.S. Department of Justice, Eastern District of Virginia, "News Release," January 20, 2006, *http://www.usdoj.gov/usao/vae/Pressreleases/01-JanuaryPDFArchive/06/20060120franklinnr.pdf* (accessed June 4, 2008).

619 United States v. Lawrence Anthony Franklin, Eastern District of Virginia, Criminal No. 1:05CR225, May 26, 2005.

620 "Former FBI Contract Linguist Pleads Guilty to Leaking Classified Information to Blogger," FBI, Baltimore Division, December 17, 2009, *http://baltimore.fbi.gov/dojpressrel/pressrel09/ba121709.htm* (accessed December 18, 2009).

621 Virginia: Navy Lawyer Is Guilty of Communicating Secret Information, *New York Times*, May 18, 2007, *http://www.nytimes.com/2007/05/18/washington/18brfs-navy.html* (accessed June 4, 2008).

622 David S. Cloud, "U.S. Soldier charged with leaking Iraq war video," *Los Angeles Times*, July 7, 2010, *http://articles.latimes.com/2010/jul/07/nation/la-na-iraq-WikiLeaks-20100707* (accessed July 26, 2010).

623 New York Times v. United States, 403 U.S. 713 (1971).

624 New York Times v. United States, 403 U.S. 713 (1971).

625 New York Times v. United States, 403 U.S. 713 (1971).

626 Near v. Minnesota, 283 U.S. 697 (1931).

627 United States v. Progressive Inc., 467 F. Supp. 990 (1979).

628 "The Progressive H-Bomb Cover," *Wikipedia, http://en.wikipedia.org/wiki/File:The_Progressive_H-bomb_cover.jpg* (accessed November 20, 2009).

629 Cable News Network, Inc. v. Noriega, 498 U.S. 976 (1990).

630 CNN Found in Contempt for Use of Noriega Tapes, *New York Times*, November 2, 1994, *http://www.nytimes.com/1994/11/02/us/cnn-found-in-contempt-for-use-of-noriega-tapes.html* (accessed January 2, 2010).

631 Cable News Network, Inc. v. Noriega, 498 U.S. 976 (1990).

632 CNN Is Sentenced for Tapes And Makes Public Apology, *New York Times*, December 20, 1994, *http://query.nytimes.com/gst/fullpage.html?res=9C0CE4DA1338F933A15751C1A962958260* (accessed June 4, 2008).

633 Bartnicki v. Vopper, 532 U.S. 514 (2001).

634 Gabriel Schoenfeld, "Has the 'New York Times' Violated the Espionage Act?"

635 Tim Hackler, "The Press and National Security Secrets: When Is It Right to Withhold the News?" *Periscope*, Summer 2006, *http://www.timhackler.com/press_national_security_secrets.html* (accessed June 4, 2008).

636 Seymour Hersh, "Submarines of U.S. Stage Spy Missions Inside Soviet Waters," *New York Times*, May 25, 1975, *http://graphics.nytimes.com/packages/pdf/weekinreview/19750525_HershNYT_Holystone.pdf* (accessed June 4, 2008).

637 Edward Levi, "Memorandum for the President," March 29, 1975, *http://www.pbs.org/wgbh/pages/frontline/newswar/preview/levi.html* (accessed June 4, 2008).

638 Adam Liptak, "Cheney's To-Do Lists, Then and Now," *New York Times*, February 11, 2007.

639 Stephen Engelberg, "C.I.A. Director Requests Inquiry on NBC Report," *New York Times*, May 20, 1986, *http://select.nytimes.com/gst/abstract.html?res=F50710FE385F0C738EDDAC0894DE484D81* (accessed June 4, 2008).

640 Potter Stewart, "Or of the Pres," *Hastings Law Journal* 26, no. 631 (1975).

641 Potter Stewart, "Or of the Pres," *Hastings Law Journal* 26, no. 631 (1975).

642 "Thomas Jefferson Second Inaugural Address," The Avalon Project at Yale Law School.

643 Alexander Hamilton, "The Federalist No. 84," Constitution Society, http://www.constitution.org/fed/federa84.htm (accessed June 4, 2008)

BIBLIOGRAPHY

"1983 Beirut Barracks Bombing," *Wikipedia. http://en.wikipedia.org/ wiki/1983_Beirut_ barracks_bombing* (accessed June 5, 2008).

Abel, Elie. *Leaking: Who Does It? Who Benefits At What Cost?* New York, NY: Priority Press Publications, 1987.

Adams, John, and Adams, Samuel. "Constitution for the Commonwealth of Massachsetts," June 15, 1780. *http://www.lexrex.com/enlightened/ laws/mass1780/mass_main.html* (accessed June 4, 2008).

Aftergood, Steven. "Secrecy and Accountability in U.S. Intelligence." Federation of AmericanScientists. *http://www.fas.org/sgp/cipsecr. html* (accessed June 8, 2008).

Altman, Daniel P. Special Agent in Charge, U.S. Agency for International Development, Office of Inspector General, interview by author, Betheny Beach, DE, July 3, 2010.

Ashcroft, John. "Statement Before the United States Senate Select Committee on Intelligence Concerning Unauthorized Disclosure of Classified Information, September 5, 2001. *http://www.fas.org/sgp/ othergov/ashcroftleaks.pdf* (accessed June 3, 2008).

Ashcroft, John, to Hastert, Dennis. October 15, 2002. *http://www.fas.org/ sgp/othergov/ dojleaks.html* (accessed June 4, 2008).

ASNE to Senate Majority Leader Harry Reid. July 21, 2008. *http://asne. org/portals/0/Publications/Public/CoalitionLetter.pdf* (accessed November 30, 2009).

Babbin, Jed. "Don't Shield the Media: Prosecute the Leakers." *Human Events. http://www.humanevents.com/article.php?id=26414* (accessed June 6, 2008).

Baker, Brent. "Cokie and Steve Roberts Hail Pulitzer Prize Winning Stories on Bush's 'Abuse of Power.'" *Newsbusters. http://newsbusters. org/node/5071* (accessed June 10, 2008).

Baquet, Dean, and Keller, Bill. "When Do We Publish a Secret," *New York Times*, July 1, 2006. *http://www.nytimes.com/2006/07/01/opinion/01keller.html* (accessed January 2, 2010).

Baquet, Dean. "Why we exposed the bank secret," *Los Angeles Times*, June 27, 2006. *http://articles.latimes.com/2006/jun/27/opinion/oe-baquet27* (accessed January 2, 2010).

Baram, Marcus. "Baghdad Diarist Writes Fiction." *ABC News. http://abcnews.go.com/US/story?id=3455826&page=1* (accessed June 8, 2008).

Benczkowski, Brian, to Rockefeller, John D. February 4, 2008. *http://www.fas.org/irp/congress/2007_hr/threat.pdf* (accessed July 30, 2009).

Blair, Dennis. "Unauthorized Disclosures of Classified Information," July 1, 2009.

Bradlee, Ben. *A Good Life: Newspapering and Other Adventures*. New York, NY: Simon and Schuster, 1996.

Brand, Rachel. "Statement Before the House Committee on the Judiciary Concerning H.R. 2102," June 14, 2007. *http://www.usdoj.gov/opa/mediashield/rlb-testimony061407.pdf* (accessed June 4, 2008).

Brokaw, Tom, Cronkite, Walter and Koppel, Ted, to SSCI. May 25, 2006. *http://www.naa.org/~/media/3570430F97464C018CA4177BD022DBDD.ashx* (accessed June 4, 2008).

"Broken Arrow Nuclear Weapons Accidents," *Aerospace Weekly. http://www.aerospaceweb.org/question/weapons/q0268.shtml* (accessed June 5, 2008).

Bruce, James. "The Consequences of Permissive Neglect: Laws and Leaks of Classified Intelligence." *Studies in Intelligence* 47, no. 1 (2003). *https://www.cia.gov/library/center-for-the-study-of-intelligence/csi-publications/csi-studies/studies/vol47no1/article04.html* (accessed June 4, 2008).

Bumiller, Elisabeth, and Landler, Mark. "U.S. Envoy Urges Caution on Forces for Afghanistan," *New York Times*, November 11, 2009. *http://www.nytimes.com/2009/11/ 12/us/politics/12policy.html* (accessed January 29, 2010).

Bush, George H.W. "Remarks by George Bush at the Dedication Ceremony for the George Bush Center for Intelligence," April 26, 1999. *https://www.cia.gov/news-information/speeches-testimony/1999/bush_speech_042699.html* (accessed June 4, 2008).

Calame, Byron. "Behind the Eavesdropping Story, a Loud Silence," *New York Times*, January 1, 2006. *http://www.nytimes.com/2006/01/01/opinion/01publiceditor.html* (accessed January 2, 2010).

Casey, William. "Remarks Before the Society of Professional Journalists," September 24, 1986.

Casper, Gerhard. "Comment - Government Secrecy and the Constitution." *California Law Review* 74, no. 3 (1986).

"CBS Ousts 4 for Bush Guard Story," CBS. *http://www.cbsnews.com/stories/2005/01/10/national/main665727.shtml* (accessed June 8, 2008).

Central Intelligence Agency. "Family Jewels Memorandum," May 16, 1973. *http://www.gwu.edu/...nsarchiv/NSAEBB/NSAEBB222/index.htm* (accessed June 3, 2008).

Church, George. "Chronicle of a Security Leak," *Time*, September 29, 1980. http://www.time.com/time/magazine/article/0,9171,952775-2,00.html (accessed June 9, 2008).

"The CIA's Family Jewels," George Washington University, The National Security Archive. *http://www.gwu.edu/...nsarchiv/NSAEBB/NSAEBB222/* (accessed June 8, 2008).

"Classified information in the United States," *Wikipedia. http:// en.wikipedia.org/wiki/ Classified_information_in_the_United_States* (accessed June 4, 2008).

Clinton, Bill. "Statement by the President to the House of Representatives," November 4, 2000. *http://www.fas.org/sjp/ news/2000/11/wh110400.html* (accessed June 4, 2008).

"CNN Found in Contempt for Use of Noriega Tapes," *New York Times*, November 2, 1994. *http://www.nytimes.com/1994/11/02/us/cnn-found-in-contempt-for-use-of-noriega-tapes.html* (accessed January 2, 2010).

"Code of Ethics," Society of Professional Journalists. *http://www.spj.org/ ethicscode.asp* (accessed June 8, 2008).

Cohen, William. "National Secrets, Too Frequently Told," *New York Times*, September 5, 2001.http://www.nytimes.com/2001/09/05/ opinion/national-secrets-too-frequently-told.html (accessed June 11, 2008).

Committee on Classified Information, Report to the Secretary of Defense by the Committee on Classified Information. November 8, 1956. *http://www.thememoryhole.org /foi/coolidge.html* (accessed June 3, 2008).

Commission on the Intelligence Capabilities of the United States Regarding Weapons of Mass Destruction. Report of the Commission on the Intelligence Capabilities of the United States Regarding Weapons of Mass Destruction. Washington DC: Government Printing Office, 2005. *http://www.gpoaccess.gov/wmd/ index.html* (accessed June 4, 2008).

"Confirmation Bias," *Science Daily. http://www.sciencedaily.com/articles/c/ confirmation_bias.htm* (accessed June 11, 2008).

Conway, Moncure Daniel. *The Life of Thomas Paine*. New York, NY: Knickerbocker Press, 1893. *http://www.thomaspaine.org/bio/ ConwayLife.html* (accessed June 4, 2008).

Cunningham, Jim. "Cracks in the Black Dike: Secrecy, the Media and the F-117A." *Airpower Journal* (Fall 1991). *http://www.airpower. maxwell.af.mil/airchronicles/apj/ apj91/fal91/cunn.htm* (accessed June 9, 2008).

Denniston, Lyle. "The Constitution That Delicate Balance: National Security and Freedom of the Press" (panel interview conducted at Columbia University Seminar on Media and Society, New York, NY, 1984). *http://www.learner.org/resources/series72.html* (accessed June 4, 2008).

Downie, Len. "Making Tough Calls on National Security" (panel interview at 2007 American Society of Newspaper Editors, First Amendment Summit, Washington, DC, January 18, 2007). *http:// www.asne.org/index.cfm?id=6420* (accessed June 5, 2008).

"Eli Cohen," *Wikipedia. http://en.wikipedia.org/wiki/Eli_Cohen* (accessed June 5, 2008).

Espionage Act, Pub. L. No. 65-24, 40 Stat. 217 (1917).

Executive Order no. 12,065, Code of Federal Regulations, title 3, volume 43 (1978). *http://www.fas.org/irp/offdocs/eo/eo-12065.htm* (accessed June 4, 2008).

Executive Order no. 13,526 (2009). *http://www.whitehouse.gov/the- press-office/executive-order-classified-national-security-information* (accessed January 12, 2010).

Executive Order no. 13,328, Code of Federal Regulations, title 3, volume 1 (2005). *http://www.fas.org/irp/offdocs/eo/eo-13328.htm* (accessed June 4, 2008).

"Faulty Intel Source 'Curveball' Revealed," *CBS News*, November 4, 2007. *http://www.cbsnews.com/stories/2007/11/01/60minutes/main3440577.shtml* (accessed June 3, 2008).

Federal Agency Data Mining Reporting Act of 2007, S.236, 110th Cong., 1st sess. (June 2007). *http://www.govtrack.us/data/us/bills.text/110/s/s236.pdf* (accessed June 4, 2008).

"Former FBI Contract Linguist Pleads Guilty to Leaking Classified Information to Blogger," FBI, Baltimore Division, December 17, 2009. *http://baltimore.fbi.gov/dojpressrel/pressrel09/ba121709.htm* (accessed December 18, 2009).

"Fox News/Opinion Dynamics Poll," *Fox News*, June 29, 2006. *http://www.foxnews.com/projects/pdf/FOX228_release_web.pdf* (accessed June 4, 2008).

Francis, Samuel. "The Intelligence Identities Protection Act." The Heritage Foundation. *http://www.heritage.org/Research/NationalSecurity/IB70.cfm* (accessed June 5, 2008).

Free Flow of Information Act of 2007, H.R.2102, 110th Cong., 1st sess. (October 2007). *http://www.govtrack.us/data/us/bills.text/110/h/h2102.pdf* (accessed June 4, 2008).

"Free Speech, Reporting on National Security," *PBS Online News Hour*. *http://www.pbs.org/newshour/bradlee/transcript_security.html* (accessed June 10, 2008).

"Frontline: Newswar - Interview, Seymour Hersh," PBS. *http://www.pbs.org/wgbh/pages/frontline/newswar/interviews/hersh.html* (accessed June 8, 2008).

Gates, Robert. "Unauthorized Disclosures: Risks, Costs, and Responsibilities." In "Intelligence 'Leaks,'" Special issue, *American Intelligence Journal* (1988).

Gates, Robert, to Levin, Carl, August 16, 2010. *http://www.fas.org/sgp/ othergov/dod/gates-wikileaks.pdf* (accessed October 29, 2010).

Geraghty, Tim. "A Brief History of Classified Leaks." *National Review Online*, October 1, 2003. h*ttp://www.nationalreview.com/geraghty/ geraghty200310010843.asp* (accessed June 9, 2008).

Goodale, James. "The First Amendment and Freedom of the Press." U.S. Department of State, Bureau of International Information Programs. *http://usinfo.state.gov/journals/ itdhr/0297/ijde/goodale. htm* (accessed June 10, 2008).

Gordon, Michael. "Bush Aide's Memo Doubts Iraqi Leaker," *New York Times*, November 29, 2006. *http://www.nytimes.com/2006/11/29/ world/middleeast/29cnd-military.html* (accessed January 2, 2010).

Goss, Porter. "Loose Lips Sink Spies," *New York Times*, February 10, 2006. *http://www.nytimes.com/2006/02/10/opinion/10goss.html* (accessed June 5, 2008).

Graham, Katharine. *Personal History*. New York, NY: Random House, 1997.

Grier, Peter. "Soldier arrested in Wikileaks classified Iraq video case," *Christian Science Monitor*, June 7, 2010. *http://www.csmonitor.com/ USA/Military/2010/0607/Soldier-arrested-in-Wikileaks-classified-Iraq-video-case* (accessed June 7, 2010).

Gup, Ted. "The Ultimate Congressional Hideaway," *Washington Post*, May 31, 1992. *http://www.washingtonpost.com/wp-srv/local/daily/ july/25/brier1.htm* (accessed June 6, 2008).

Hackler, Tim. "The Press and National Security Secrets," Association of Former Intelligence Officers, *The Intelligence Professional Series,* no. 8 (1992).

_____. "The Press and National Security Secrets: When Is It Right to Withhold the News?" *Periscope*, Summer 2006. *http://www.*

timhackler.com/ press_national_security_secrets.html (accessed June 4, 2008).

Hamilton, Alexander. "The Federalist No. 84." Constitution Society *http:// www.constitution.org/fed/federa84.htm* (accessed June 4, 2008).

Hamilton, Lee. "Being a Partner and Critic to the Congress." *CongressLink. http://www.congresslink.org/print_expert_hamilton. htm* (accessed June 10, 2008).

Hansen, James. "Soviet Deception in the Cuban Missile Crisis." CIA, Center for the Study of Intelligence. *https://www.cia.gov/library/ center-for-the-study-of-intelligence/csi-publications/csi-studies/ studies/vol46no1/article06.html* (accessed June 10, 2008).

Harman, Jane. "Opening Statement Before the House Permanent Select Committee on Intelligence: Hearing on the Role and Responsibilities of the Media in National Security," May 26, 2006. *http://www.fas.org/irp/congress/2006_hr/052606harman.pdf* (accessed June 8, 2008).

Hayden, Michael. "Advising the Office of the Director of National Intelligence of Possible Violations of Law, Regulation or Policy," March 29, 2006.

_____. "Remarks of Central Intelligence Agency Director at the Council on Foreign Relations," September 7, 2007. *http://www.fas. org/irp/cia/product/dcia090707.html* (accessed December 9, 2009).

"Hersh: U.S. mulls nuclear option for Iran," CNN. *http://www.cnn. com/2006/POLITICS/04/10/hersh.access/index.html* (accessed June 8, 2008).

Hertling, Richard, to Leahy, Patrick. March 1, 2007. *http://www.scribd. com/doc/334133/Letter-from-Hertling-to-Senator-Leahy?ga_related_ doc=1* (accessed June 3, 2008).

Hess, Stephen. *The Government/Press Connection: Press Officers and Their Offices.* Washington, DC: The Brookings Institution, 1984.

Hoekstra, Peter. "Opening Statement Before the House Permanent Select Committee on Intelligence: Hearing on the Role and Responsibilities of the Media in National Security," May 26, 2006. *http://www.globalsecurity.org/intell/library/congress/ 2006_ hr/060526-hoekstra.pdf* (accessed June 8, 2008).

_____. "Secrets and Leaks: The Costs and Consequences for National Security," July 25, 2005. *http://www.heritage.org/Research/ HomelandSecurity/wm809.cfm* (accessed June 4, 2008).

Hoekstra, Peter, to Keller, Bill. August 7, 2007. *http://www.humanevents. com/article.php?id=21855* (accessed June 11, 2008).

Holt, Pat. *Secret Intelligence and Public Policy: A Dilemma of Democracy.* Washington, DC: Congressional Quarterly, 1994.

"House committee weighs press' role in intelligence leaks," Reporters Committee for Freedom of the Press. *http://www.rcfp.org/ news/2006/0530-prr-housec.html* (accessed June 10, 2008).

Hsu, Spencer. "State Dept. contractor charged in leak to news organizations," *Washington Post*, August 28, 2010. *http:// www.washingtonpost.com/wp-dyn/content/article/2010/08/27/ AR2010082704602.html* (accessed October 21, 2010).

Improving America's Security Act of 2007, S.4, 110th Cong., 1st sess. (March 2007). *http://www.govtrack.us/data/us/bills.text/110/s/s4.pdf* (accessed June 4, 2008).

Information Security Oversight Office, Report to the President, May 31, 2007. *http://www.fas.org/sgp/isoo/2006rpt.pdf* (accessed June 8, 2008).

"Informed Comment." *http://www.juancole.com/2007_03_01_juancole_ archive.html* (accessed June 9, 2008).

Intelligence Reform and Terrorism Prevention Act of 2004, 50 U.S.C. 401 (2004). *http://frwebgate.access.gpo.gov/cgi-bin/getdoc.*

cgi?dbname=108_cong_public_laws &docid=f:publ458.108.pdf (accessed June 4, 2008).

Interagency Task Force Concerning Protections Against Unauthorized Disclosures of Classified Information, Report to the Attorney General of the United States, Washington, DC: Government Printing Office, 2002.

"Internet Security Advisory Group Publications." Internet Security Advisory Group. *http://www.isag.com/library/index.html* (accessed June 5, 2008).

"The Iraq Archive: The Strands of War," *New York Times*, October 22, 2010. *http://www.nytimes.com/2010/10/23/world/ middleeast/23intro.html* (accessed October 29, 2010).

"The James Madison Center: Quotes on Various Issues." James Madison University. *http://www.jmu.edu/madison/center/main_pages/ madison_archives/quotes/great/issues.htm* (accessed June 4, 2008).

Joscelyn, Thomas. "Source Code." *The Daily Standard. http://www. weeklystandard.com/ Content/Public/Articles/000/000/006/541acool. asp* (accessed June 10, 2008).

"Justification," *Dictionary.com. http://dictionary.reference.com/browse/ justification* (accessed June 9, 2008).

Kaplan, Fred. "The Goods on Saddam." *Slate Magazine* (January 31, 2003). http://www.slate.com/toolbar.aspx?action-print&id=2077961 (accessed June 5, 2008).

Keller, Bill. "Letter From Bill Keller on The Times's Banking Records Report," *New York Times*, June 25, 2006. *http://www.nytimes. com/2006/06/25/business/media/25keller-letter.html* (accessed June 10, 2008).

_____. "Making Tough Calls on National Security" (panel interview at 2007 American Society of Newspaper Editors, First

Amendment Summit, Washington, DC, January 18, 2007). *http://www.asne.org/index.cfm?id=6420* (accessed June 5, 2008).

Kurtz, Howard. "President Wants a Plumber," *Washington Post*, November 19, 2009. *http://www.washingtonpost.com/wp-dyn/content/article/2009/11/19/ AR2009111901008.html* (accessed November 20, 2009).

_____. "After reporter's subpoena, critics call Obama's leak-plugging efforts Bush-like," *Washington Post*, April 30, 2010. *http://www.washingtonpost.com/wp- dyn/content/article/2010/04/29/ AR2010042904656.html* (accessed May 5, 2010).

Kissinger, Henry. "The China Connection." *Time*, October 1, 1979. *http://www.time.com/time/magazine/article/0,9171,947490,00.html* (accessed June 6, 2008).

LaFleur, Jennifer. "Federal officials and media have dialogue over secrecy." *The News Media and the Law*, Vol. 27, No. 1, Winter 2003. http://www.rcfp.org/news/mag/27-1/cov-federalo.html (accessed June 11, 2008).

"Leaks Seen as Motivated More by Personal than Political Reasons," The Pew Research Center, April 5, 2007. http://pewresearch.org/pubs/446/news-leaks-remain-divisive-but-libby-case-has-little-impact (accessed June 4, 2008).

Leonard, J. William. "Managing Secrets in a Changing World," First Amendment Center, March 16, 2004. http://www.firstamendmentcenter.org/commentary.aspx?id=12878 &printer-friendly=y (accessed June 4, 2008).

Levi, Edward. "Memorandum for the President," March 29, 1975. http://www.pbs.org/wgbh/ pages/frontline/newswar/preview/levi.html (accessed June 4, 2008).

Levine, Adam. "Top U.S. military official: WikiLeaks founder may have 'blood' on his hands," CNN, July 30, 2010. http://edition.cnn.com/2010/US/07/29/wikileaks.mullen.gates/ index.html#fbid=1wi0HJ6QJqN (accessed July 31, 2010).

Library of Congress, Bill Text 105th Congress (1997-1998) H.R.3694. ENR. http://thomas.loc.gov/cgi-bin/query/F?c105:6:./ temp/~c105KzoGY0:e55303: (accessed July 28, 2010).

Library of Congress, Congressional Research Service, CRS Report for Congress: Assassination Ban and E.O. 12333: A Brief Summary (Washington, DC: Government Printing Office, January 4, 2002). http://www.fas.org/irp/crs/RS21037.pdf (accessed June 8, 2008).

Library of Congress, Congressional Research Service, *CRS Report for Congress: National Security Whistleblowers* (Washington, DC: Government Printing Office, December 30, 2005). *http://www.nswbc.org/Reports%20-%20Documents/ NationalSecurityWhistleblowers (CRSReport).pdf* (accessed June 8, 2008).

Library of Congress, Congressional Research Service, *CRS Report for Congress: The Whistleblower Protection Act: An Overview* (Washington, DC: Government Printing Office, March 12, 2007). *http://www.fas.org/sgp/crs/natsec/RL33918.pdf* (accessed June 8, 2008).

Lichtblau, Eric, and Risen, James. "Bank Data is Sifted by U.S. in Secret to Block Terror," *New York Times*, January 23, 2006. *http://www. nytimes.com/2006/06/23/washington/ 23intel.html* (accessed June 3, 2008).

Liptak, Adam. "Cheney's To-Do Lists, Then and Now," *New York Times*, February 11, 2007. *http://www.nytimes.com/2007/02/11/ weekinreview/11liptak.html* (accessed January 2, 2010).

"The Long Arm of the Law," Federal Bureau of Investigation. *http://www. fbi.gov/page2/jan06/longarm010506.htm* (accessed June 5, 2008).

Mackey, Robert. "Taliban Study WikiLeaks to Hunt Informants," *New York Times*, July 30, 2010. *http://thelede.blogs.nytimes. com/2010/07/30/taliban-study-wikileaks-to-hunt-informants/* (accessed July 30, 2010).

Mallon, Thomas. "Mr. Smith Goes Underground," *American Heritage Magazine*, Volume 51, Issue 5, September 2000. *http://www. americanheritage.com/articles/magazine/ah/2000/5/2000_5_60. shtml* (accessed March 10, 2010).

Marty, Dick. *Secret detentions and illegal transfers of detainees involving Council of Europe member states: second report*, Council of Europe, Committee on Legal Affairs and Human Rights, June 7, 2007. *http://www.cfr.org/publication/13570/ secret_detentions_and_illegal_ transfers_of_detainees_involving_council_of_europe_member_states. html* (accessed June 4, 2008).

Mason, George. "Virginia Declaration of Rights," June 12, 1776. *http:// www.constitution.org/bcp/virg_dor.htm* (accessed June 4, 2008).

Maxwell, Alison. "CIA Chief: Leakers Abound," *Government Executive. http://www.govexec.com/story_page.cfm?filepath=/ dailyfed/0198/012998a2.htm* (accessed June 5, 2008).

Mazzetti, Mark. "Pakistan Aids Insurgency in Afghanistan, Reports Assert," *New York Times*, July 25, 2010. *http://www.nytimes. com/2010/07/26/world/asia/26isi.html* (accessed July 27, 2010).

McConnell, Michael. "Guidance on the Declassification of National Intelligence Estimate Key Judgments," October 24, 2007. *http:// www.fas.org/irp/dni/nie-declass.pdf* (accessed June 4, 2008).

"Motivation," *Word Reference. http://www.wordreference.com/definition/ motivation* (accessed June 8, 2008).

Muir, Chris. "NSA Surveillance Leak Case Watch: Eavesdropping and the 2004 Presidential Election." FullosseousFlap's Dental Blog. Entry posted December 8, 2006. *http://flapsblog.com/category/politics/nsa-leak-case/* (accessed June 10, 2008).

Myers, Steven, Sanger, David, and Schmitt, Eric. "U.S. Considers New Covert Push Within Pakistan," *New York Times*, January 6, 2008.

http://www.nytimes.com/2008/01/06/ washington/06terror.html
(accessed January 2, 2010).

Nakashima, Ellen. "Former NSA executive Thomas A. Drake may pay high price for media leak," *Washington Post*, July 14, 2010. *http://www.washingtonpost.com/wp-dyn/content/article/2010/07/13/AR2010071305992_pf.html* (accessed July 23, 2010).

National Security Act of 1947, 50 U.S.C. 403 (1947). *http://www.intelligence.gov/0-natsecact_1947.shtml* (accessed June 4, 2008).

Nelson, Jack. "U.S. Government Secrecy and the Current Crackdown on Leaks," *The Joan Shorenstein Center on the Press, Politics and Public Policy* (Fall 2002). *http://www.hks.harvard.edu/presspol/research_publications/papers/working_papers/2003_1.pdf* (accessed June 4, 2008).

_____. "What Leaks Are Good Leaks?" *Los Angeles Times*, January 5, 2003. *http://articles.latimes.com/2003/jan/05/opinion/op-nelson5* (accessed June 11, 2008).

Newspaper Association of America and National Newspaper Association to HPSCI, May 23, 2006. *http://www.naa.org/~/media/0CB9272ED CA64213A4991CD8DA066D3A.ashx* (accessed June 4, 2008).

"News War, Part 2: Secrets, Sources and Spin," Frontline: Newswar. *http://www.pbs.org/wgbh/ pages/frontline/newswar/etc/script2.html* (accessed June 10, 2008).

"'New York Times Stirs Controversy in Exposing Government Secrets," National Public Radio. *http://www.npr.org/templates/story/story.php?storyId=5515699* (accessed June 10, 2008).

Nixon, Richard. "Address to the Nation About the Watergate Investigations," August 15, 1973. *http://www.pbs.org/wgbh/amex/presidents/37_nixon/psources/ps_water2.html* (accessed June 3, 2008).

"A Note from the Editors," *New York Times*, October 22, 2010. *http://www. nytimes.com/2010/10/23/world/middleeast/23box.html* (accessed October 29, 2010).

"Notice of Availability for Donation of Test Craft Ex SEA SHADOW," *Federal Register* 71, no. 178 (September 14, 2006). *http://edocket. access.gpo.gov/2006/pdf/E6-15266.pdf* (accessed June 8, 2008).

Novak, Robert. "Mission to Niger," *Washington Post*, July 14, 2003. *http:// www.washingtonpost.com/wp-dyn/content/article/2005/10/20/ AR2005102000874.html* (accessed March 14, 2010).

"ODNI Announces Establishment of Open Source Center." Office of the Director of National Intelligence. *http://www.dni.gov/press_ releases/20051108_release.htm* (accessed June 3, 2008).

Office of the Director of National Intelligence, Intelligence Community Directive 701, "Security Policy Directive for Unauthorized Disclosures of Classified Information," March 14, 2007.

Office of Personnel Management, Standard Form 312, "Classified Information Nondisclosure Agreement," (2000). *http://contacts.gsa. gov/webforms.nsf/0/ 03A78F16A522716785256A69004E23F6/$file/ SF312.pdf* (accessed June 4, 2008).

Olmsted, Kathryn. *Challenging the Secret Government: The post-Watergate investigations of the CIA and FBI.* Chapel Hill, NC: University of North Carolina Press, 1996.

Partlow, Joshua, and Jaffe, Greg. "Karzai calls WikiLeaks disclosures 'shocking' and dangerous to Afghan informants," *Washington Post*, July 29, 2010. *http://www.washingtonpost.com/wp-dyn/content/ article/2010/07/29/ AR2010072901762.html* (accessed October 29, 2010).

Patron, Rachel. "Does the media have freedom of speech," *Florida Sun-Sentinel*, March 28, 2008. *http://articles.sun-sentinel.com/2008-03-*

28/news/0803270121_1_printing-press-free-press-new-york-times (accessed January 2, 2010).

"The Pentagon Papers: Secrets, Lies and Audiotapes," The National Security Archive, George Washington University. *http://www.gwu. edu/~nsarchiv/NSAEBB/NSAEBB48/* (accessed July 27, 2010).

Perry, William. "Unauthorized Disclosures of Intelligence," July 31, 1996. *http://www.fas.org/sgp/clinton/perry.html* (accessed June 5, 2008).

"Piecing Together the Reports, and Deciding What to Publish," *New York Times*, July 25, 2010. *http://www.nytimes.com/2010/07/26/ world/26editors-note.html?pagewanted=all* (accessed July 26, 2010).

Plato. *The Republic.* Translated by R.E. Allen. New Haven, CT: Yale University Press, 2006.

"Plugging Media Leaks," *News Hour with Jim Lehrer. http://www.pbs.org/ newshour/bb/media/jan-june00/leaks_6-29.html* (accessed June 9, 2008).

"Plugging the Leak: The case for a Legislative Resolution of the Conflict Between the Demands of Secrecy and the Need for an Open Government," *Virginia Law Review* 71, no. 5 (June 1985).

"Policy with regard to the issuance of subpoenas to member of the news media," 28 CFR 50.l0 (1980). *http://edocket.access.gpo.gov/cfr_2003/ julqtr/pdf/28cfr50.10.pdf* (accessed June 4, 2008).

Poulson, Kevin, and Zetter, Kim. "'I Can't Believe What I'm Confessing to You': The Wikileaks Chats," *Wired.com*, June 10, 2010. *http://www. wired.com/threatlevel/2010/06/wikileaks-chat/* (accessed October 29, 2010).

Powell, Colin. "A Policy of Evasion and Deception," *Washington Post*, February 5, 2003. *http://www.washingtonpost.com/wp-srv/nation/ transcripts/powelltext_020503.html* (accessed June 9, 2008).

Priest, Dana. "CIA Holds Terror Suspects in Secret Prisons," *Washington Post*, November 2, 2005. *http://www.washingtonpost.com/wp-dyn/content/article/2005/11/01/ AR2005110101644.html* (accessed June 3, 2008).

_____. "National Security Secrets and Democracy: Leaks, Whistleblowers and the Press" (panel interview at 2006 American Bar Association 16th Annual Review of the Field of National Security Law, Washington, DC, December 1, 2006). *http://38.105.88.161/ Search/basic.asp?BasicQueryText=security+wh istleblowers&SortBy=bestmatch* (accessed June 10, 2008).

_____. "Reporting National Security under Threat of Indictment" (panel interview at 2006 Media Law Resource Center Annual Dinner, Washington, DC, November 9, 2006). *http://www. medialaw.org/Template.cfm?Section=Archive_by_Date1&Template=/ ContentManagement/ContentDisplay.cfm&ContentID=4730* (accessed June 8, 2008).

Priest, Dana, and Arkin, William. "A hidden world, growing beyond control," *Washington Post*, July 19, 2010. *http://projects. washingtonpost.com/top-secret-america/articles/a-hidden-world-growing-beyond-control/* (accessed July 23, 2010).

"The Progressive H-Bomb Cover," *Wikipedia, http://en.wikipedia.org/wiki/ File:The_Progressive _H-bomb_cover.jpg* (accessed November 20, 2009).

"Project Jennifer: Hughes Glomar Explorer," *Global Security. http://www. globalsecurity.org/ intell/systems/jennifer.htm* (accessed June 8, 2008).

"Protection of Classified National Security Council and Intelligence Information (NSDD 19), January 12, 1982. *http://www.fas.org/irp/ offdocs/nsdd019.htm* (accessed June 5, 2008).

"Purposeful Leaks," *National Review* (September 11, 1987). *http://www. thefreelibrary.com/* Purposeful+leaks.+(Congressional+leaks+to+pr ess)-a05169250 (accessed June 4, 2008).

"Q & A - Gen. Michael Hayden," C-SPAN. *http://www.q-and-a.org/ Transcript/ ?ProgramID=1123* (accessed June 10, 2008).

"Quotes: Leaking Classified Information," CI Centre. *http://cicentre.com/ Documents/ DOC_Quotes_Leaks.htm* (accessed June 11, 2008).

Reno, Janet. "Statement Before the Senate Select Committee on Intelligence Concerning Unauthorized Disclosures of Classified Information," Federation of American Scientists. *http://www.fas. org/sgp.othergov/renoleaks.html* (accessed June 3, 2008).

"Reporting in the Time of Conflict: Secrecy vs. the Story," Newseum. *http://www.newseum.org/warstories/essay/secrecy.htm* (accessed June 5, 2008).

Report of the Interdepartmental Group on Unauthorized Disclosures of Classified Information, March 31, 1982. *http://www.fas.org/sgp/ library/willard.pdf* (accessed June 3, 2008).

Richelson, Jeffrey. *The U.S. Intelligence Community.* Boulder, CO: Westview Press, 1999.

Risen, James. "Reporting National Security under Threat of Indictment" (panel interview at 2006 Media Law Resource Center Annual Dinner, Washington, DC, November 9, 2006). *http://www. medialaw.org/Template.cfm?Section=Archive_by_Date1&Template=/ ContentManagement/ContentDisplay.cfm&ContentID=4730* (accessed June 8, 2008).

Risen, James, and Lichtblau, Eric. "Bush Lets U.S. Spy on Callers Without Courts," *New York Times*, December 16, 2005. *http://www.nytimes. com/2005/12/16/politics/16program.html* (accessed June 3, 2008).

"Robert McCormick," *New World Encyclopedia. http://www. newworldencyclopedia.org/entry/Robert_McCormick* (accessed June 5, 2008).

Ruddy, Christopher. "Russia Defector: Large Number of Spies Act as Journalists." *Newsmax. http://archive.newsmax.com/ articles/?a=2000/5/14/143832* (accessed June 10, 2008).

Rumsfeld, Donald. "The Impact of Leaking Classified Information," July 12, 2002. *http://www.fas.org/sgp/bush/dod071202.pdf* (accessed June 5, 2008).

_____. "U.S. Department of Defense News Briefing," September 12, 2001. *http://www.fas.org/sgp/news/2001/09/dod091201.html* (accessed June 5, 2008).

"Samuel Loring Morison." *Answers.com. http://www.answers.com/ samuel%20loring%20morison* (accessed June 4, 2008).

Sanger, David, and Barstow, David. "Iraq Findings Leaked by Cheney's Aide Were Disputed," *New York Times*, April 9, 2006. *http://www. nytimes.com/2006/04/09/washington/ 09leak.html* (accessed January 2, 2010).

Sanger, David, and Broad, William. "U.S. Secretly Aids Pakistan in Guarding Nuclear Arms," *New York Times*, November 18, 2007. *http://www.nytimes.com/2007/11/18/washington/ 18nuke.html* (accessed January 2, 2010).

Schlesinger, James. "The Constitution That Delicate Balance: National Security and Freedom of the Press" (panel interview conducted at Columbia University Seminar on Media and Society, New York, NY, 1984). *http://www.learner.org/resources/series72.html* (accessed June 4, 2008).

Schmitt, Eric. "U.S. Envoy's Cables Show Worries on Afghan Plans," *New York Times*, January 25, 2010. *http://www.nytimes.com/2010/01/26/ world/asia/26strategy.html* (accessed January 29, 2010).

Schmitt, Eric, and Savage, Charlie. "U.S. Military Scrutinizes Leaks for Risks to Afghans," *New York Times*, July 28, 2010. *http://*

www.nytimes.com/2010/07/29/world/asia/ 29wikileaks.html?_
r=1&pagewanted=all (accessed July 30, 2010).

Schoenfeld, Gabriel. "Has the 'New York Times' Violated the
Espionage Act?" *Commentary* (March 2006). *http://www.*
commentarymagazine.com/viewarticle.cfm/has-the-new-york-
times—violated-the-espionage-act—10036 (accessed June 4, 2008).

_____. "The Leak Wars." *Commentary* magazine, September 12,
2007. *http://www.commentarymagazine.com/blogs/index.php/*
schoenfeld/916 (accessed June 11, 2008).

_____. "Statement Before the Senate Judiciary Committee," June 6,
2006. *http://www.fas.org/irp/congress/2006_hr/060606schoenfeld.pdf*
(accessed June 3, 2008).

_____. "The Price of One Leak." *Commentary*, June 11, 2007. *http://*
www.commentarymagazine.com/blogs/index.php/schoenfeld/523
(accessed June 5, 2008).

Schorr, Daniel. "Standing Up for News Leaks." *Christian Science Monitor*,
May 27, 2005. *http://www.csmonitor.com/2005/0527/p09s02-cods.*
html (accessed June 8, 2008).

Shane, Scott. "Increase in the Number of Documents Classified by the
Government," *New York Times*, July 3, 2005. *http://www.nytimes.*
com/2005/07/03/politics/03secrecy.html (accessed January 2, 2010).

_____ . "There are Leaks. And Then There are Leaks," *New York
Times*, April 30, 2006. *http://www.nytimes.com/2006/04/30/*
weekinreview/30shane.html (accessed January 2, 2010).

Sheehan, Neil. "Vietnam Archive: Pentagon Study Traces 3 Decades of
Growing U.S. Involvement," *New York Times*, June 13, 1971. *http://*
select.nytimes.com/gst/ abstract.html?res=F10B1FFD3D5813748DD
DAA0994DE405B818BF1D3 (accessed June 8, 2008).

Shenon, Philip. "Times Reporter Subpoenaed Over Source for Book," *New York Times*, February 1, 2008. *http://www.nytimes.com/2008/02/01/washington/01inquire.html* (accessed January 2, 2010).

Shover, Neal, and Hochstetler, Andy. *Choosing White-Collar Crime*. New York, NY: Cambridge University Press, 2006.

Smolkin, Rachel. "Judgment Calls: How top editors decide whether to publish national security stories based on classified information." *American Journalism Review* (October/November 2006). *http://www.ajr.org/Article.asp?id=4185* (accessed June 5, 2008).

Snider, L. Britt. "Recollections from the Church Commission." *Studies in Intelligence* (Winter 1999-2000). *https://www.cia.gov/library/center-for-the-study-of-intelligence/csi-publications/csi-studies/studies/winter99-00/art4.html* (accessed June 8, 2008).

Spencer, Richard. "Wikileaks: Nick Clegg backs calls for investigation," *Telegraph*, October 24, 2010. *http://www.telegraph.co.uk/news/worldnews/middleeast/iraq/8084116/Wikileaks-Nick-Clegg-backs-calls-for-investigation.html* (accessed October 29, 2010).

Spoto, MaryAnn. "N.J. court rules blogger is not protected under shield law in porn company defamation case," *The Star-Ledger*, April 22, 2010. *http://www.nj.com/news /index.ssf/2010/04/nj_court_rules_blogger_not _pro.html* (accessed May 9, 2010).

"State of the First Amendment 2006," First Amendment Center. *http://www.firstamendmentcenter.org/about.aspx?item=state_first_amendment_2006* (accessed June 4, 2008).

Stewart, Potter. "Or of the Pres." *Hastings Law Journal* 26, no. 631 (1975).

Stone, Geoffrey. "Freedom of the Press v. National Security." *Huffington Post*, May 21, 2006. *http://www.huffingtonpost.com/geoffrey-r-stone/freedom-of-the-press-v-n_b_21382.html* (accessed June 4, 2008).

_____. "Government Secrecy vs. Freedom of the Press." *Harvard Law and Policy Review* 1, no. 1 (Winter 2007).

"Submarines," Haze Gray and Underway. *http://www.hazegray.org/faq/smn7.htm#G12* (accessed June 8, 2008).

Sunstein, Cass. "Government Control of Information." *California Law Review* 74, no. 889 (1986).

Supporting Intelligence and Law Enforcement Programs to Track Terrorists and Terrorist Finances, H.Res.895, 109th Cong, 1st sess, (June 2006). *http://www.govtrack.us/ data/us/bills.text/109/hr/hr895.pdf* (accessed June 5, 2008).

"Supreme Court Denies Freedom in Spy Case," *New York Times*, June 12, 1988. h*ttp://www.nytimes.com/1988/06/12/us/supreme-court-denies-freedom-in-spy-case.html* (accessed January 2, 2010).

"Thomas Jefferson on Politics and Government: Freedom of the Press." University of Virginia Online Library. *http://etext.virginia.edu/jefferson/quotations/jeff1600.htm* (accessed June 3, 2008).

"Thomas Jefferson Second Inaugural Address." The Avalon Project at Yale Law School. *http://avalon.law.yale.edu/19th_century/jefinau2.asp* (accessed June 3, 2008).

"Times Reporter Testifies On Leak," *CBS News Online*, September 30, 2005. *http://www.cbsnews.com/stories/2005/09/30/national/main892127.shtml* (accessed January 2, 2010).

"Top Secret The Battle for the Pentagon Papers." USC Center on Communication Leadership. *http://www.topsecretplay.org/index.php/content/courts* (accessed June 4, 2008).

"Transcript of General Hayden's Interview with WTOP's J.J. Green," Central Intelligence Agency. *https://www.cia.gov/news-information/press-releases-statements/press-release-archive-2007/transcript-of-general-haydens-interview-with-wtop.html* (accessed June 5, 2008).

U.S. Air Force. January 11, 2005. Air Force Doctrine Document 2-5, *Information Operations. http://www.dtic.mil/doctrine/jel/service_ pubs/afdd2_5.pdf* (accessed June 4, 2008).

U.S. Congress. House. Permanent Select Committee on Intelligence: *Espionage Laws and Leaks*. 96th Cong., 1st sess., January 24, 25, and 31, 1979.

U.S. Congress. House. Rep. Dennie Oxley of Indiana speaking for the Resolution Supporting Intelligence and Law Enforcement Programs to Track Terrorists and Terrorist Financing, H.Res. 895, 109th Cong., 2nd sess.. *http://www.fas.org/irp/congress/ 2006_cr/h062906. html* (accessed June 8, 2008).

U.S. Congress. House. Rep. Louis Slaughter of New York speaking for the Resolution Supporting Intelligence and Law Enforcement Programs to Track Terrorists and Terrorist Financing, H.Res. 895, 109th Cong., 2nd sess. *http://www.fas.org/irp/congress/ 2006_cr/h062906. html* (accessed June 8, 2008).

U.S. Congress. House. Rep. Peter Hoekstra of Michigan speaking for the Resolution Supporting Intelligence and Law Enforcement Programs to Track Terrorists and Terrorist Financing, H.Res. 895, 109th Cong., 2nd sess. *http://www.fas.org/irp/congress/ 2006_cr/h062906. html* (accessed June 8, 2008).

U.S. Congress, Senate. Federal Agency Data Mining Reporting Act of 2007, S.236, 110th Cong., 1st sess., *Congressional Record* 153 (March 2007).

U.S. Congress, Senate. Committee on the Judiciary, Examining DOJ's Investigation of Journalists Who Publish Classified Information: Lessons from the Jack Anderson Case, 109th Congress, 2nd sess., June 6, 2006. *http://www.fas.org/irp/congress/ 2006_hr/journalists. html* (accessed June 8, 2008).

U.S. Congress, Senate. Report of the Commission on Protecting and Reducing Government Secrecy, 103rd Cong., 1997, S. Doc. 105-

2: Government Printing Office, 1997. *http://www.access.gpo.gov/ congress/commissions/secrecy/index.html* (accessed June 3, 2008).

U.S. Congress, Senate. Select Committee on Intelligence, Hearing of the Committee on the Nomination of General Michael Hayden to be the Director of the Central Intelligence Agency, 110th Congress, 1st sess., May 18, 2006. *http://www.fas.org/irp/congress/ 2006_ hr/051806transcript.pdf* (accessed June 5, 2008).

U.S. Congress. Senate. Senator Richard Shelby of Alabama speaking for the Intelligence Authorization Act for Fiscal Year 2001, S.2507, 106th Cong., 2nd sess., *Congressional Record* (6 December 2000): 11649-51. *http://www.fas.org/irp/congress/ 2000_cr/s120600.html* (accessed June 8, 2008).

U.S. Department of Justice, Eastern District of Virginia, "News Release," January 20, 2006. *http://www.usdoj.gov/usao/vae/Pressreleases/01-JanuaryPDFArchive/ 06/20060120franklinnr.pdf* (accessed June 4, 2008).

U.S. District Court for the District of Maryland, Northern Division, "United States of America v. Thomas Andrews Drake," April 14, 2010. *http://www.fas.org/sgp/news/2010/04/drake-indict.pdf* (accessed May 9, 2010).

U.S. Intelligence Community Information Sharing Strategy, February 22, 2008. *http://www.dni.gov/reports/IC_Information_Sharing_Strategy. pdf* (accessed June 3, 2008).

U.S. National Archives and Records Administration, 2005 Report on Cost Estimates for Security Classification Activities. *http://www.archives. gov/isoo/reports/2005-cost-report.html* (accessed June 8, 2008).

U.S. National Security Council, National Security Council Meeting Minutes, October 7, 1974. *http://fordlibrarymuseum.gov/library/ document/nscmin/mscmin.html* (accessed June 3, 2008).

Waas, Murray. "Is There a Double Standard On Leak Probes?" *National Journal*, April 25, 2006. *http://news.nationaljournal.com/ articles/0425nj1.htm* (accessed June 6, 2008).

Weiner, Tim. "CIA Severs Ties to 100 Foreign Agents," *New York Times*, March 3, 1997. *http://www.nytimes.com/1997/03/03/us/cia-severs-ties-to-100-foreign-agents.html* (accessed January 2, 2010).

Whatley, Frederick W. "Reagan, National Security, and the First Amendment: Plugging Leaks by Shutting Off the Main." The CATO Institute. *http://www.cato.org/pubs/pas/pa037.html* (accessed June 5, 2008).

Whistleblower Protection Enhancement Act of 2007, H.R.985, 110th Cong., 1st sess. (March 2007). *http://www.govtrack.us/data/us/bills.text/110/h/h985.pdf* (accessed June 4, 2008).

Woodward, Bob. "A Journalist's Perspective on Public Disclosures," in "Intelligence 'Leaks,'" Special issue, *American Intelligence Journal* (1988).

_____. "McChrystal: More Forces or 'Mission Failure.'" *Washington Post*, September 21, 2009. *http://www.washingtonpost.com/wp-dyn/content/article/2009/09/20/ AR2009092002920.html* (accessed January 29, 2010).

_____. *Veil: The Secret Wars of the CIA 1981-1987*. New York, NY: Simon and Schuster, 1987.

Woolsey, R. James. "National Security and Freedom of the Press" (panel interview at 2006 American Enterprise Institute Conference, Washington, DC, September 7, 2006). *http://www.aei.org/events/filter.,eventID.1383/transcript.asp* (accessed June 5, 2008).

Xanders, Edward. "A Handyman's Guide to Fixing National Security Leaks: An Analytical Framework for Evaluating Proposals to Curb Unauthorized Publication of Classified Information." Virginia Law School, *Journal of Law and Politics* 5, no. 759 (1989). *http://www.gmsr.com/article/A%20Handyman's%20Guide%20to%20Fixing%20National%20Security%20Leaks.pdf* (accessed June 5, 2008).

Zuckerman, Laurence. "Washington's Master Leakers." *Time,* May 23, 1988. *http://www.time.com/time/magazine/article/0,9171,967475,00. html* (accessed June 6, 2008).

INDEX

ABOUT THE AUTHOR

Gary Ross is a Special Agent with the U.S. Department of Homeland Security. His academic background includes a Master of Science of Strategic Intelligence (MSSI) degree from the National Intelligence University and a Bachelor of Arts (BA) degree from Michigan State University, with a dual major in Criminal Justice and Psychology. He has completed advanced training at the National Foreign Affairs Training Center, the Joint Counterintelligence Training Academy, and the Federal Law Enforcement Training Center.

During his 20-year career in federal law enforcement, Mr. Ross has conducted and supervised criminal, counterintelligence, and counterterrorism investigations and operations with the Department of Homeland Security, the Office of the Director of National Intelligence, the Naval Criminal Investigative Service, and the Department of Labor. He was a recipient of the Department of Defense Team Award for National Security Investigations in 2007 and the Director of Central Intelligence Team Award for Countering Foreign Denial and Deception in 2003.

Among the places Gary has called home are Chicago, IL; Poulsbo, WA; Yokosuka, Japan; and Springboro, OH. He currently resides in Montclair, VA, with his wife and three daughters. Looking at the stamps in his passport, work has taken him to Japan, South Korea, Thailand, Sri Lanka, Singapore, Indonesia, Bahrain, England, Italy, and Mexico. He has been afloat on an aircraft carrier in the Pacific Ocean and submersed in a Trident submarine in the Hood Canal.

The author can be contacted by e-mail at *gary.ross@ymail.com*. He welcomes comments about his research from readers interested in the vital topic of national security and the media.